Scientific Thinking in Speech and Language Therapy

SCIENTIFIC THINKING IN SPEECH AND LANGUAGE THERAPY

Carmel Lum
University of Cambridge

2002 LAWRENCE ERLBAUM ASSOCIATES, PUBLISHERS
Mahwah, New Jersey   London

EMERSON COLLEGE LIBRARY

Acquisitions Editor:	Emily Wilkinson
Executive Assistant to Editorial:	Bonita D'Amil
Cover Design:	Kathryn Houghtaling Lacey
Textbook Production Manager:	Paul Smolenski
Full-Service & Composition:	UG / GGS Information Services, Inc.
Text and Cover Printer:	Sheridan Books, Inc.

This book was typeset in 10/12 pt. Times Roman, Bold, and Italic.
The heads were typeset in Americana, Americana Bold, and Americana Bold Italic.

Lawrence Erlbaum Associates, Inc., Publishers
10 Industrial Avenue
Mahwah, New Jersey 07430

Library of Congress Cataloging-in-Publication Data

Lum, Carmel.
    Scientific thinking in speech and language therapy / Carmel Lum.
        p. cm.
    Includes bibliographical references and index.
    ISBN 0-8058-4029-X (alk. paper)
    1. Speech therapy–Research–Methodology.   2. Science–Methodology. I. Title.

RC428. L86 2001
616.85'506'072–dc21

                                                                    2001040471

DEDICATION

To Richard

Contents

List of Tables

List of Figures

A Note to the Reader
and the Lecturer

This is not a book about statistics or research design. It is a book written for students and practitioners in speech and language therapy who are interested in finding out what it means to *know* and how one can recognize *valid knowledge*. This book is intended to be primer, a basic introduction to many major topics, leading to some understanding of the fundamentals in scientific thinking. It is hoped that readers will follow up on this text with more detailed sources that are more focused on specific topics and offer more detail than this text.

Although the terms *scientific* and *nonscientific* thinking are used throughout the text, the reader needs to be aware that scientific thinking is only just one instance of valid thinking (Kuhn, Amsel, & O'Loughlin, 1988). The terms *scientific* and *nonscientific* thinking imply an unfortunate distinction, as they sugggest that valid thinking is specific to scientific endeavors, but that is not true. The ideas in this book are situated in clinical contexts throughout the book for those who need to see these ideas translated into the realm of clinical practice. Many examples are also contextualized in everyday situations to assist those who find it easier to relate to subjects unconstrained by the indoctrination of professional knowledge and bias.

It is known in many courses, I am sure, that undergraduate students in clinical courses tend to demand high levels of transparency between the content of a course and practice. The question of when is an ideal time to introduce the ideas encompassed in this book is subject to debate. Some educators, such as Giere (1997), hold the view that the right time is in the first year of an undergraduate course. In speech and language therapy courses, this is also the time when students still know too little about the domain to appreciate the value of using clinical examples. Consequently, common sense dictates that it is important to use examples that refer to situations that students understand. A good selection of examples situated in everyday life situations attempt to satisfy this requirement.

An attempt was made to select further reading material that is commensurate with the knowledge level and requirements of readers (the undergraduate, postgraduate and practitioner). To help postgraduate and practitioners identify suitable reading, the term 'graduate reading' is used in the recommended reading lists.

This book also accompanies a collection of tutorial exercises, all of which have been tried and tested with all levels of undergraduate speech and language therapy students. A majority of these exercises are designed around key topics or chapters in the text. Readers may obtain a copy of the companion workbook from www.scithink.co.uk.

Note that in the book, the term *speech and language therapy* is used synonymously with the U.S. term speech and language pathology.

Preface

Scientific and critical thinking do not come naturally. It takes training, experience and effort. . . . We must always work to suppress our need to be absolutely certain and in total control and our tendency to seek the simple and effortless solution to a problem. Now and then the solutions are simple but usually they are not.
—M. Shermer, *Why People Believe Weird Things*, 1997, p. 59

This book was originally motivated by events that influenced me almost 2 decades ago. It started during my first 4 years of clinical practice, when I realized that patients receiving rehabilitation therapy were not *cured* by therapy. Such naïvete belonged appropriately to a period in the history of the health professions when it was simply unthinkable for clinicians to question the efficacy of clinical practice. More years passed before I recognized and understood the factors that induced and maintained this type of thinking in clinical education and later, in professional practice. When what I knew failed to resolve my patients' problems, I could rationalize, for a while, a case for why the patient was not a suitable candidate for therapy. But when it became apparent that the practice of therapy in the field appeared to be guided mainly by intuition or personal preferences of clinicians, I felt unsettled for quite a time. It appeared to me that my education in a health science degree course did not equip me with knowledge or a framework by which it was possible to know or recognize a truth, if such a thing existed.

It has taken a couple decades that included learning and thinking outside the realm of speech and language therapy to understand this experience. During the same period, there has been an enormous change in the awareness and attitudes of the health professions. It has become increasingly acceptable to question the efficacy of interventions, and this is a truly liberating development in the field of speech and language therapy. Health professionals of all disciplines today speak more comfortably about whether interventions are effective, and students are slowly recognizing that it is becoming acceptable to question and challenge the status of the knowledge they are given during their training. However, the motivation of this new awareness appears driven more by changes in the political and economic climate of health care than by the need to simply understand the scientific basis of what we offer patients. Consequently, in speech and language therapy, we see the emergence of an awareness of therapy that is tied to pragmatic issues (e.g., notions of time, efficiency), functional outcomes (e.g., transparency of treatment effects), and clinical programs promising instant and cost-effective results.

In the current economic climate, the search for cost-effective treatment sits high on the agendas of clinical managers. Yet it makes little sense if these very same treatments are found to be clinically ineffective. In this environment, theoretical questions can appear insignificant and possibly even irrelevant. Discovering whether an intervention works is interesting, but this needs to be appreciated within a wider context of understanding what defines valid knowledge in a scientific profession. What are the principles, or rules, that define what constitutes evidence forming the knowledge base of a scientific profession? How will we recognize it?

Being a clinician can be an uncomfortable experience for someone who is navigating between blind conviction and scientific skepticism. Not having an answer does not seem to be an option for students facing their educators and for experienced clinicians facing their patients. Part of this appears to be attributable to the ethos in clinical courses, where vocation and training are usually encouraged and promoted over education and debate. Unfortunately, education and training experiences that are impoverished in scientific skepticism do not equip the graduate with thinking skills to deal with new situations. The result is a professional who embraces every novel therapy idea that comes along or one who holds rigidly to what has been done for the past 20 years. As educators, we fail our students when we do not give them a scientific basis from which to reason about what they do. Graduates and clinicians are also not assisted when they emerge from their courses not knowing that in many, many cases, it is acceptable not to know the solutions to patients' problems. Understanding scientific thinking can be a liberating discovery for the practitioner. I hope the reader finds this an illuminating read.

—Carmel Lum
University of Cambridge, UK
2001

Acknowledgments

Many people have contributed to the ideas and thoughts that have shaped this book. I thank Tom Matyas, who was an inspirational lecturer in communicating his research methods course during my early student years. This course introduced me to ideas I later understood were within the realm of the subject history and philosophy of science. I thank my lecturers in the History and Philosophy Department at the University of Melbourne, who made their subjects very accessible and allowed me to see how the history of other fields paralleled aspects of the development and experiences of the speech and language profession. I am grateful to these lecturers, who accepted doubt and the absence of answers as legitimate aspects of knowing.

I wish to also acknowledge an enormous debt to my students at Queen Margaret University College, who, being hard taskmasters, have presented me with the greatest challenge of all as I have attempted to foster in them an enthusiasm for this subject. They have been very patient, provided useful feedback, and at least rewarded me by not failing on mass in the subject. Specifically, I must thank ex-students Mele Taumoepeau and Anne Rowe, who undertook the daunting task of reading a very unpolished manuscript and offered useful (polite) feedback. I also thank Maggie Snowling of the Department of Psychology, University of York for allowing herself to be subjected to the same arduous task, relieved only slightly (I believe) by the accompaniment of mince pies and Christmas wine.

Over the past 2 decades, I have received ideas from many people, making it difficult for me to recall my sources at times. There are, however, significant contributors whom I recall as major inspirational points in my thinking and who have since contributed to my formulation of this book. They include Anderson (1971), for his simple conceptualization of a scientific method that has allowed me to communicate some sense of the generic principles of a scientific method; Halpern (1996), whose text is an excellent read and helpful in illustrating the commonsensibility of sound reasoning and how to communicate complex ideas simply; Campbell and Stanley (1963), whose classic work on experimental design has always helped structure my own thinking about experiments with both group and single-case studies; Pannbacker & Middleton (1994), whose work is a constant reminder to me that the challenge before educators is about teaching students to think rather than teaching them to design experiments; and Palys (1997) and Denzin and Lincoln (1998), for ideas in qualitative research. In addition, I wish to acknowledge the contributions from clinicians of various health trusts in Britain (Edinburgh, Harrogate, Salisbury, Sunderland, and Livingston), and Julie Morris, who, with me, co-conducted the workshops evaluating interventions and critical appraisal of intervention literature. Thanks to Emily Wilkinson (commissioning editor for Lawrence Erlbaum Associates), who has waited patiently for this text to materialize. Kitty Jarrett for her helpful copy-editing of the manuscript. And most important of all, I owe a huge debt to Richard, who has been an excellent sounding board, unflagging in his support, who must be as relieved as I am to see this manuscript leave my desk.

Scientific Thinking in Speech and Language Therapy

1

Introduction

Science is nothing but trained and organised common sense.
— T. H. Huxley, 1825–1895

Mere awareness of research is not sufficient for a profession that seeks truth and knowledge. Research is an activity concerned with systematic gathering of information about matters in which one is interested. It does not in itself lead one to the truth or to explanations for events.

Historically, the search for truth has taken many forms. Our ancient ancestors searched for truth among the elements, the gods represented by the sun, wind, earth, fire, animals, rocks, and trees—all vividly captured in mythologies of the Australian aborigines, the First Nation tribes in North America, the stone tablets of the Middle Eastern kingdoms, and so one. This represented one approach, or *paradigm*. If one were to not look to external sources such as these in the quest for knowledge or truth, then an alternative approach might be to look within oneself for the answers (i.e., introspect). Two hundred years ago, introspection was taken seriously and considered an important approach to discovering knowledge. The scientist would ponder and reflect on a yet-unsolved question (e.g., What do I do when I read the word *irresistible*? What happens in my mouth when I speak

1

the sentence "Mary has a little lamb"?). The answer to this question (i.e., whatever the person thought he or she did when reading this word or speaking the sentence) would be taken as *knowledge* about the reading or speaking process. Introspection is, of course, wholly inadequate as an approach or paradigm to discovering truthful, factual knowledge because people vary and disagree among themselves. This paradigm also provides no basis for testing the truthfulness of this information because the information is private and really only known to the individual volunteering this information. It is also very difficult to distinguish this type of truth from the truth of dreams, hallucinations, and other private experiences. So, sometime around the beginning of the 20th century, a group of learned philosophers debating the question of truth decided it was crucial that knowledge be observable and measurable. This led to *behaviorism*, a school of thought that dominated research and thinking through the 1970s. Dissatisfaction with simply reporting observable behaviors eventually led to the emergence of new approaches that admitted the role of mental processes and their measurement in the mid-1950s. In psychology, this was called *cognitive psychology*.

Although the quest for truth has taken many paths, two broad groupings encompass the vast array of different beliefs and views on what constitutes truth and how to get at it. Basically, one group adheres to a scientific doctrine and the other consists of several doctrines, many of which accept truth as defined by introspection and the self.

Professions adhering to a scientific doctrine accept that adherence to science means that the search for truthful knowledge must accord with set of agreed principles, guidelines, and criteria for defining knowledge. However, this identification with science as the basis for defining knowledge is clearer in some professions than in others. Whether a discipline or profession attains the status of being a science is a related, but separate, issue. The goal of striving for scientific status by a professional group is, however, not a trivial matter, particularly in the case of the public being encouraged to accept that a profession's knowledge base is dominated and subject to control by scientific standards.

SPEECH AND LANGUAGE THERAPY AS AN APPLIED SCIENCE

The study of speech and language therapy draws heavily for its theoretical bases from the domains of psychology, medicine, linguistics, and, to a lesser extent, sociology. A traditional view of the speech and language therapy discipline is that it acquires its theoretical perspective on a particular condition from one of the other domains and applies this knowledge to the treatment of a communication disorder. Speech and language therapy is an applied science in the sense that the study and practice of speech and language therapy is predicated on adopting relevant theories and methods from other disciplines and applying these to the context of abnormal communication. The nature of the relationship between speech and language therapy and other fields suggests two things:

- Progress in areas of speech and language therapy could be secondary to the developments in these other primary disciplines.
- The definition of the scientific status of speech and language therapy could be contingent on how successfully these other domains have attained scientific status within their own fields.

It is reasonable to posit that the scientific disposition of speech and language therapy reflects the scientific status of the theories and methods it borrows from other disciplines. These disciplines vary among and within themselves as to how they approach investigating problems, which in turn has an effect on whether their ideas are considered to have scientific merit. For example, let's contrast linguistics and psychology. In linguistics, introspection still forms a major approach in situations such as judging the grammatical correctness of sentences, whereas psychology traditionally relies on experiments to inform about the nature of grammatical judgments.

Although speech and language therapy has a codependent relationship with other disciplines, the modern speech and language therapist has a legitimate role as a researcher, someone who is capable of making independent contributions to theory development, whether or not it has a transparent relationship with practice.

WHO WE ARE AND WHAT GUIDES OUR CHOICES IN PRACTICE

At some point, members of the speech and language therapy profession must reflect seriously on what it means to be a discipline with a scientific basis and how this is determined. If the scientific identity of the speech and language therapy profession were uncertain, then it follows that its members could become confused when asked, "Are speech and language therapists clinical scientists? care-givers? teachers? remedial educators? Are they spiritual healers? Are they simply heart-on-sleeve do-gooders? Do they work within the same realm as those in alternative therapies? Who decides whether they do or not? How do we differentiate what we do from the group of caregivers and healers who are perhaps not counted among the group of orthodox (i.e., scientific) professions? In what way is the practice of speech and language therapy scientific? What are the markers of scientific practice?

Were science not the guiding hand in speech and language therapy practice, then it is difficult to imagine what could take its place as the guiding doctrine. All that would be available to clinicians would amount to nothing more than a set of arbitrary rules to define good practice. The image of speech clinicians guided by intuition rather than more principled and tested methods would persist. Ignorance and confusion would prevail among clinicians; they would not know why certain therapy ideas do or do not qualify as valid methods of speech therapy practice (e.g., dysphagia, group therapy, computer-based therapy, reflexology). Why are some therapeutic solutions accepted more readily than others? For example, compare the Lee Silverman Voice program designed to remediate the soft-spoken voices of Parkinson's disease patients (Ramig, Countryman, Thompson, & Horii, 1995) and the Tomatis method (Tomatis, 1963). Both treatment methods claim to ameliorate patients' vocal conditions (and more—in the case of the Tomatis treatment). At the time of this writing, there were only two efficacy studies on the Lee Silverman method, one of which was published by the group advocating this new treatment and the other study, though by a different group of researchers, was equivocal. The Tomatis method is presented in many more publications (admittedly in nonprofessional journals), and yet it remains the more obscure treatment of the two methods. Why? What is informing this preference?

Clinicians debate the value of qualitative versus quantitative approaches and real-life intervention approaches versus formal decontextualized clinic-based intervention approaches. Issues like these can divide communities of clinicians

FIG. 1.1. Lost in the therapy wilderness.

because of closely held beliefs that one approach is vastly superior to another. These are complementary perspectives of a patient, and yet there are clear differences in the core values and preferences expressed by different clinicians about how best to approach patient management. Situations like this make it important that clinicians grasp the meaning of their professional actions beyond simply what they are doing and what appears congenial for their patients. The focus has to be on *how* we think about our patients. Besides thinking, it is also essential for clinicians to have a language for expressing why some treatment methods are more valid than others (see Fig. 1.1).

RESEARCH AND SCIENCE EDUCATION OF SPEECH AND LANGUAGE THERAPISTS

Clinicians' engagement in and appreciation of the importance of research is relatively recent. The value of research does, however, appear to exist in a vacuum when it exists without reference to any greater guiding meta-principle or philosophy. This state of affairs may go some way toward explaining why disagreements about therapy approaches tend to focus on superficial aspects of treatments or procedures rather than on their intrinsic scientific value. Some of the confusion appears to be due to a failure to discriminate between research as an activity and research as a part of a greater scientific endeavour. Confusion over research and methods of scientific inquiry is also evident in understanding the difference between outcome and efficacy studies. The ready adoption of new therapy approaches based on face validity (i.e., the approach appears to be useful to the patient on the surface rather than on the basis of any scientific explanation for its efficacy) is also an indication of a certain scientific naïveté.

In countries such as the United Kingdom and Australia, most clinicians encounter research when they take undergraduate courses in statistics and research methods. A smaller number have the opportunity to conduct research projects, usually to fulfill the requirements of an honors degree. A typical therapy course introduces statistics and research methods quite independently of other subjects in the curriculum. The motivation for teaching these subjects is often described in course handbooks in terms of equipping the student with skills to complete a research project to fulfill course requirements.

The present approach to educating clinicians presents certain inherent difficulties starting with selection interviews through the nature of instruction. Speech and language therapy courses that still conduct interviews as a part of the process of selecting students for a course are undoubtedly applying criteria that the assessors believe will produce the "right" type of clinician. This belief means we do not know, for example, whether the characteristics favored by these selection committees predict student success in the course or success as a professional.

In regard to the nature of instruction, many courses offer students courses in statistics and research methods. These are very important courses, and, if taught effectively, they have a major positive and enduring impact on the student clinician's thinking. A problem for students entering an introductory statistics course in speech therapy, however, is that they often have to confront new material in several domains simultaneously, such as statistics, research methods, and speech therapy subjects. In addition, students bring to the subject the usual collection of well-known misconceptions and reasoning fallacies. Not surprisingly, students typically express a loathing for statistics, confusing it with mathematics, and fail to see the relevance of both research methods and statistics to the professional work. In consequence, some students' academic self-esteem, although generally good in other subjects, is low in statistics and research methods.

Courses vary in how much time they give to covering topics related to the philosophy of science and its methods. It appears to me the greatest failure in many conventional courses is the failure to help students make a connection between the concepts expressed in statistics and research methods courses with other clinical courses. Students rarely make this connection for themselves, and ultimately students go on to become clinicians who regard these subjects as being largely irrelevant to clinical practice. Statistics and research methods are regarded as tools solely for the researcher's use. How many lecturers incorporate statistics in teaching clinical problems, such as how to perform a McNemar test on client data to assess whether the client has improved in therapy? The concepts that the clinician and the researcher are both clinical scientists and that both are players in the larger scientific arena are rarely fostered in therapy education. One consequence of this conduct of teaching is the perception by students (and later clinicians) that there is a schism between research and speech and language therapy practice.

Some educators may feel that the dichotomization of clinicians into clinicians and scientists or clinicians and researchers is justified. It then becomes difficult to ignore the rather truncated situation of educators speaking keenly to speech and language therapy students in terms of hypotheses, models, and theories when minimal attention is given to developing the student's understanding of these terms. Mathews (1994) brought these points to the fore when he argued for an improvement in science teaching through the teaching of the history and philosophy of science:

> Knowledge of science entails knowledge of scientific facts, laws and theories—the products of science—it also entails knowledge of the processes of science—the technical and intellectual ways in which science develops and tests the knowledge it claims. (p. 3)

Although Matthews made these points when deploring the fact that students who are engaged in basic science courses graduate with little understanding of science, much of what he says also applies to health science courses. In other words, most health education programs offer students the small picture (e.g., the opportunity to undertake a research project) and rarely the big picture (e.g., the philosophical and historical context that embraces and defines the meaning of research activity).

One solution to this situation is to provide a broad prestatistics (e.g., a critical thinking skills course) course that introduces general principles of inquiry in a way that is decoupled from pure statistics. Such a course would teach valid thinking and address scientific thinking as one instance of valid thinking. Student clinicians and would-be researchers would both benefit from a course in scientific thinking as preparation for follow-on courses in statistics, research design, and research projects.

This type of learning, however, would have a much better chance of influencing thinking if the concepts explained in a scientific thinking and/or research methods course were considered with other subjects taken by the student. It would therefore be desirable for speech and language therapy educators and clinical tutors to repeatedly illustrate and express these concepts within various speech and language therapy contexts. This means that the presentation of a clinical disorder topic in a therapy course should include an evaluation of the arguments, identify theoretical predictions, and assess the evidence and question the claims made. This would be in addition to providing students with factual information about the disorder under consideration. Making this link between scientific thinking and other clinical subjects in speech therapy is important because research in thinking suggests that the transfer of thinking skills to other contexts rarely occurs spontaneously (Nickerson, 1987). Giere (1997) also asserted that scientific reasoning, like any other skill, can be acquired only through repeated practice.

Application of thinking skills in a variety of contexts (academic and practical) is also thought to be necessary for promoting the transfer of knowledge between subjects or contexts (Baron & Sternberg, 1987) . Helping students make this link with science would ideally be among the main education goals of educators delivering a speech and language therapy course. It would also require educators to view their role as being facilitators in changing student's thinking. This task cannot, however, be left solely to the one lecturer who takes the research methods course. Mathews (1994) identified three competencies that he believed would assist educators in their teaching of science to students: a knowledge and appreciation of science, some understanding of the history and philosophy of science, and some educational theory or pedagogical view that informs their choice of classroom activities.

In speech and language therapy courses, the primary emphasis is traditionally on students receiving an account of a particular speech disorder, its diagnostics, and treatment, usually, less emphasis is given to discussions about the methodological issues, the standard of evidence, or an evaluation of the scientific merit of information. If students were able to observe more often how a scientific framework is used by their educators to evaluate information they are given about a disorder routinely and how arguments are constructed and tested, more students might graduate with a clearer understanding of where science and argument fit in the scheme of therapy practice. More importantly, they would observe, understand, and learn how to deal with uncertainty (i.e., when there are no answers). This is all predicated on the profession and its members recognizing that its pursuit of knowledge lies in the pursuit of understanding science. The remainder of this book speaks to those who seek this understanding.

AIMS OF THIS BOOK

Any profession, such as speech and language therapy, that lays claim to being scientific undertakes a public commitment to derive its knowledge base according to scientific principles. As science appears to define the knowledge base of speech and language therapy, it then becomes imperative that speech and language therapists have an understanding of what scientific principles mean and how they apply in the research and clinical practice.

This book attempts to explain the conventional view of science and knowledge and to illustrate how scientific principles and their related concepts are applied. Toward the end of the book, the reader is given the opportunity to see the "blurring of the boundaries", when what constitutes knowledge is debated. It is important to proceed in this order since this book is intended for the novice reader who has little knowledge of science. The book is planned to give some basic understanding of the subject, and it is deliberately written without regard for controversy. This staging is necessary so that the reader is able to focus on understanding the principles without distraction. Many believe that in order to understand how we arrived at our position today, we need to understand where our ideas originated. The reader will hopefully emerge with new perspectives regarding the role of science in speech and language therapy. It is also hoped that the reader will gain a new appreciation that science is about a *mode of thinking* that has wide application in many spheres of life. This book should give the reader a sense that all this information rightly belongs in speech and language therapy practice. Experienced clinicians should also find some of the perspectives in this book enticing and find a productive way to think and speak about many of the issues confronting them in clinical work and in the profession.

Both the scientific clinician and researcher can be likened to detectives on a case. They need to understand some basic principles about how one investigates, understand some basic concepts associated with investigations, know how to get information to help solve the case, know how to verify information, and know how to use resource tools to obtain or clarify the information obtained. *Concepts* in this case refers to topics like arguments, types of reasoning, falsification, concepts of validity/reliability, subjectivity/objectivity, chance/probability, and research design/methods knowledge. And in this case *resource tools* refers to library skills, CD-ROM database access skills, and statistics and information technology skills.

NOTE TO THE READER

An attempt was made to select further reading material that is commensurate with the knowledge and requirements of readers (the undergraduate, post graduate and practitioner). To help postgraduate and practitioners identify suitable references, the term "Graduate Reading" is used in the recommended reading lists.

GRADUATE READING

Mathews (1994) offers a brief but comprehensive overview of science education and its demise and the role of history and philosophy of science.

2

Science and Pseudoscience

That is the essence of science: Ask an impertinent question and you are on your way to the pertinent answer.

—J. Bronowski, 1908–1974

Many students begin a speech and language therapy course with certain aspirations and beliefs. During a selection interview, a very common response to the question "Why have you applied for this course?" usually evokes this type of reply from prospective students: "I am interested in working with people and in speech therapy. I like the idea of variety—you never know what will walk through the door each day with the range of speech disorders that exist. I have always wanted to work in a caring profession to help people." Another common answer to this question is the I-knew-someone type of answer: "My neighbor had a stroke and lost her speech. She received a lot of help from a speech clinician at her hospital and recovered her speech. I thought speech therapy offered an interesting and worthwhile career, and that's why I want to be a speech clinician."

Among those selected to attend a selection interview, there might be one person who reports an interest in undertaking research in the field one day, and not surprisingly, candidates never say they aspire to become managers or administrators. The overall impression given, then, is that most undergraduate speech and language therapy students embark on the course understanding that they will become clinicians, treating and helping people with communication disorders. This is also consistent with the image often promoted and marketed by training institutions of speech and language therapy courses. The image conveyed to the public depicts speech and language therapy as a caring profession that helps people with their communication difficulties. For many people associated with the speech and language therapy profession, this is the beginning and the end of the story.

Research in the context of speech and language therapy might be mentioned, along with various other activities associated with descriptions of the teaching department, but rarely with reference to clinical practice in the field (i.e., away from the teaching department). It is rather uncommon to see an account of research described as an integral aspect of the clinician's identity or as a necessary endeavor in the profession. Similarly, clinicians are rarely described as clinical scientists, but if they were, the prospective applicant would be more likely to understand the type of knowledge and the standards of performance expected in therapy practice.

BELIEFS

Speech and language therapy students typically begin their programs with a set of beliefs or values that, like all other things, must eventually undergo change. For example, one study, reported that 74% of first-year medical students believed that knowledge of nutrition was important to their profession. By the third year, however, only 13% of the students believed this to be true (Weinsier et al., 1987) and a subsequent national survey of medical practitioners suggested such disinterest in the relevance of nutrition was maintained (Levine et al., 1997). We know, however, very little about the changes in the belief systems of speech and language therapy clinicians from the start of training to when they become established clinicians. Discussions with first-year undergraduate students suggest that many are still unaware of speech and language therapy as an interdisciplinary applied science. They also appear to view remediation in terms of a reeducation model. Students' remarks suggest they believe that therapy will help patients, and none have thought to ask whether therapy is effective in remediating speech disorders. If the question of the efficacy of interventions is raised, the students generally project a naïve view that interventions will be off-the-shelf solutions that must be effective—otherwise, clinicians would not be allowed to practice, would they? Surely, training courses would not be allowed to run if they did not produce clinicians with effective methods.

These beliefs are probably typical of many health professions students. It is, however, reasonable to think that some beliefs will in time be challenged through course learning and encounters with conflicting evidence during practice. We do not know what effect these changes have on the clinician. Needless to say, beliefs and values are very likely to be tied to the personality of the individual, and people vary in their readiness to accept and respond to challenges. Table 2.1

TABLE 2.1

How This Book Aims to Change Thinking and Beliefs

Novices Beliefs	Where Addressed in This Book	Outcome
I believe everything I read.	Student Workbook, Exercise 1	The information in textbooks may not always be subject to review for its factual accuracy. In a democratic society, there is great tolerance for a variety of opinions and views, not all of which can be taken as valid forms of knowledge. Even a "good" publication is often at risk of being out-of-date because information travels slowly between discovery and publication.
I believe I am an idiot because I could not follow the lecturer in statistics classes.	Chapter 1	A failure to understand the concepts explained in a statistics course could be due to one being too worried about the math and everything else that is new in the course.
Speech and language therapy and alternative therapies have much in common. They all help people get better.	Chapter 2	Speech and language and therapy strives to be a scientific discipline, and alternative therapies subscribe to different philosophies.
I believe the expert must be right.	Chapter 3	That an opinion expressed by someone with an impressive reputation in the profession or who is an old hand at therapy is no guarantee of sound knowledge.
I believe research and science are the same thing.	Chapter 4	Research is about information gathering. Scientific research consist of a set of rules that directs the method one uses to collect data to arrive at valid knowledge about an event.
I believe that event A has caused B to happen because B always happens after A has occurred.	Chapter 5	Events A and B are related and may always happen together, but this does not mean that one has caused the other to happen because they can both be caused by C, a factor about which no one was aware.
I believe my theory about a disorder is correct because all the cases I have seen show the same signs.	Chapter 5	All hypotheses must be tested under controlled conditions.

Belief statement	Chapter	Explanation
I believe models, hypotheses, theories, and laws are more relevant in research than in speech and language therapy practice.	Chapters 6 and 12	The practice of speech and language therapy needs to be guided by scientific theory and/or hypotheses for therapy to be scientifically explained. Which tests and therapy procedures one selects is guided by theory. Models are a useful shorthand way to illustrate what we want to say about the way communication works.
I believe I know when I can relate to what I am hearing. There is no need to read journals—it only takes common sense.	Chapters 7 and 9	Scientific knowledge has a standard that says knowledge must meet a criterion of being publicly shared knowledge. This allows us to distinguish between real knowledge and intuition or hallucinations.
I am so experienced I do not need to use formal tests to know what is going on with my patient. I use impressionistic judgments.	Chapters 7 and 9	Formal tests help minimize observe expectancy effects and memory failure in recalling a patient's performance. Uncontrolled subjective measures do not qualify as scientific observations.
I believe that a useful therapy is one that uses materials and a theory relevant to the problem	Chapter 9	A therapy is useful for a disorder when three is scientific evidence demonstrating this claim.
I believe we only need one study to show that a therapy is effective.	Chapters 5, 7 and 8	Scientific knowledge takes time and it evolves thorough a series of studies that ideally replicate the same finding. Even though statistics are used to determine the probability of arriving at a study's result by chance, there is always a remote possibility that chance could have contributed to the one study's result.
I believe the result my patients achieved on a test is an accurate relfection of his ability.	Chapters 8 and 9	Patients, like nonpatients, show normal variation.
My eyes and ears do not lie: So what I see and hear of the patient must be true.	Chapter 9	My eyes and ears will see and hear what they expect to see and hear. I cannot trust these senses.
I believe that if the patient feels better, my treatment must be effective.	Chapter 9	Patients need not be reliable reporters of their own experiences.
I believe qualitative research is not scientific.	Chapter 10	Qualitative research can be scientific if it is a well-controlled study.
I believe researchers and practitioners have different goals in speech and language therapy.	Chapter 11	Researchers and practitioners in this profession share the same goals as clinical scientists.

(Continued)

13

TABLE 2.1
(Continued)

Novices Beliefs	Where Addressed in This Book	Outcome
I believe the best evidence for whether therapy works is whether the patients say it works.	Chapter 12	Patients have various motivations for saying whether a therapy worked. The only way to know with any degree of certainty is by adopting a more systematic and controlled method of conducting and evaluating therapy. If therapy cannot be evaluated, then we will not know whether therapy is effective with a patient. We may have opinions about this, but we will not know.
I believe there is an art to therapy. One has to look at the whole person.	Chapter 14	The patient is a person and not simply a bundle of symptoms. Objective assessments sample from a range of the patient's behaviors and can be used to inform me of my patient's problems as well his areas of ability. If objective tests are absent or inadequate, the solution is to develop better tests rather than to abandon objectivity.

describes the common beliefs held by many students and anyone who still has to learn to reason scientifically. The middle column identifies the topics in this book that are relevant to each transitional stage in thinking. The last column shows possible outcomes in how the reader might start to think about these various issues in speech and language therapy.

IDENTIFYING WITH SCIENCE

Richards (1987) wrote that *science* in Latin means knowledge (i.e., a body of knowledge). *Science* can also mean a set of rules by which to acquire knowledge (i.e., adopting a principled approach to the discovery of knowledge; Grinnell, 1992). Science is a philosophical doctrine that specifies criteria and standards for describing, explaining, and deciding what stands as real knowledge or truth. In essence, it is a quest for knowledge supported by evidence (Curd & Cover, 1998). The aim is to discover and explain regularities in events occurring in the environment. There is ample evidence that the profession of speech and language therapy seeks to be identified as a scientific discipline. For example, many of the names of speech therapy departments contain the word *science* (e.g., Department of Speech and Language Sciences, Human Communication Science Department), and science degrees are awarded for speech and language therapy courses (e.g., bachelor of science, bachelor of applied science). The profession of speech and language therapy also keenly supports activities commonly characterizing scientific communities (e.g., research, conference meetings, journal publications).

In these respects, speech and language therapy differs little from other health care professions groups, such as physiotherapy, occupational therapy, medicine, and psychology, all of which also seek identification with science. We see further evidence of this in terms such as medical science, behavioral science, linguistic science, and even management science. The status of science in society is such that even cosmetics companies appeal to an image of science in their marketing. For example, many department-store cosmetics companies, sales staff are dressed in white uniforms, simulating labcoats. They offer microscope equipment for skin analysis, and the products are often even sold under names that have clear connotations to medicine, clinics, and sterile conditions. So, why are so many professions (and laypersons) attracted to science as the defining basis of knowledge?

Science and the Speech and Language Therapy Profession

Why do health care disciplines appear to want to emulate the precise, methodological laboratory practices associated with physics? A discipline cannot be considered a science simply because *science* is part of the name of its departments or academic degrees. It cannot be considered a scientific discipline simply because its members participate in activities such as conferences, professional meetings, research, and published writings. These activities are *scientistic*, but they do not define speech and language therapy as a scientific discipline. Does it really matter whether speech and language therapy is a truly scientific profession?

Have you ever wondered about the difference between speech and language therapy and other occupations (e.g., elocutionists) and complementary therapies (e.g., iridology, reflexology, aromatherapy) or pseudo-scientific interventions such as neurolinguistic programming (NLP)? They differ from one another in significant ways. A scientific profession seeks to explain phenomena according to scientific principles. This involves developing a hypothesis and then testing the hypothesis by collecting data, analyzing it, and then finding out if the information gathered supports or refutes the hypothesis. It is a dynamic process by which every study and experiment is viewed as being one step closer to discovering the truth of what we want to know about something. Our understanding (i.e., knowledge) is continually, over time, being refined. This understanding is assumed by investigators who study whether the treatments available to patients are effective. Speech and language therapy subscribes to this view of itself.

In other caring practices (e.g., reflexology, iridology, aromatherapy, acupuncture), the public is persuaded to accept the available remedies or solutions because they belong or originate from an age-old tradition. The effectiveness of the remedy is supposed to derive from the fact that these practices have withstood the test of time and are of great age. The mystical qualities of age-old knowledge are probably best captured in the study of astrology, a familiar form of an "ancient science" known to the public. Knowledge here is described as being unchanged or static in time. Figure 2.1 illustrates a typical range of advertisements commonly encountered by the public.

Thus one characteristic of science is that it represents an evolution toward discovering the truth. Reflexology and other complementary therapies are examples of the pseudosciences and are characterized by appeals to tradition. It usually comes as a surprise to the novice clinician to learn that the knowledge base of speech and language therapy is constantly evolving. This has nothing to do with the discipline being fickle or unconfident. It is simply due to the way in which scientific knowledge evolves as a result of methodical and systematic investigations.

The other difference between science and pseudoscience lies in how scientific knowledge is derived. In pseudosciences, knowledge is, as stated previously, based on age-old traditional knowledge or has, through trial and error, been found to be useful. In contrast, science presupposes that there is a principled approach to the discovery of knowledge, known as the *scientific method* (Gower, 1997). According to Bunge (1984), pseudoscience is "a body of beliefs and practices but seldom a field of active inquiry; it is tradition bound and dogmatic rather than forward looking and exploratory" (p. 41). Curd and Cover (1998) stated that among the various criteria argued to distinguish between science and a pseudoscience, a main criterion is to ask whether there is evidence; if evidence

Consultation with ancient sciences has helped determine our future

Astrology is one of the world's most ancient sciences. It began over 2000 B.C. in Babylonia. Then the Egyptians introduced the zodiac, based on the constellations, and this was used extensively by the ancient Greeks and Romans to forecast individual horoscopes.

Throughout history, Kings, Queens, Presidents and Generals have consulted astrologers before making vital decisions that have affected the very history of mankind.

Today, people with psychic gifts help solve crimes and give advice to businessmen on investing on the stockmarket.

The amazing accuracy of their predictions has completely baffled the sceptics.

Athena Starwoman, renowned as one of the world's most accurate psychic astrologers, has carefully selected a group of naturally gifted psychics to share her knowledge and pass on their predictions to those in need.

The pressures of life have never been greater than they are now. The pace of living, the cost of living, make decisions on careers, finance, family and intimate relationships more vital than ever before.

Making these decisions without any consultation is at least foolhardy and at worst disastrous.

Athena's psychic astrologers are there to help you now. Their help and advice is entirely confidential and has proven to be of great benefit to many thousands of people.

Don't leave things till they get any worse, pick up that phone now.

Call Athena's psychics now!

Athena Starwoman's Psychics & Clairvoyants:
1900 100 999   1902 264 064

Psychic Astrologers	Psychic Money Line:	Psychic Soul Mate Love Line	Credit Card Bookings
1900 140 199	**1900 140 135**	**1900 140 166**	**1800 681 655**

ATHENA'S RECORDED MAGIC TAROT: 1902 261 524   Professional readings intended as a guide only.   & Athena Starwoman's Club Enquiries

Astrology, Psychic, Clairvoyant, Love & Money call cost: $4.95/min. Tarot: 95c/min. Higher charges for mobile & public phones. Open 8am to midnight (EST) 7 Days.

FIG. 2.1.   Common form of an advertisement for the ancient sciences
Source: Woman's Day, June 22, 1998, p. 72.

is lacking, then it is a pseudoscience. In contrast, Popper, 1972 (cited in Curd & Cover) proposed that the critical test of a science versus a pseudoscience is to ask "What do I need to do (or show in an experiment) to prove my theory wrong?" Advocates of a pseudoscience are expected to have great difficulty addressing this question, partly due to an unwillingness to consider an alternative view, and partly due to the theory being untestable in the first place (Bunge, 1984). An astute reader might think that the performance of experiments ought to be a distinguishing hallmark of all bodies of scientific knowledge. This understanding would be incorrect, however, since experiments are also well known among advocates of extrasensory perception (ESP).

Do not think, however, that all knowledge comes only from methodical scientific research. There are enough reports of accidental discoveries in science to challenge this view (e.g., the discoveries of penicillin, Velcro, x-rays, smallpox vaccination). This is commonly referred to as *serendipity* in scientific discoveries. It does not, however, undermine the worth of science in defining knowledge, since it can be argued that a researcher is more likely to stumble across such "accidental" discoveries by looking systematically in the first place (Grinnell, 1992). Sometimes this hybrid process of discovery is termed *pseudoserendipity* (Roberts, 1989).

TABLE 2.2
Characteristics of Science and Pseudoscience

Science	Pseudoscience
Objective	*Subjective*
• Based on systematic methods that involve hypothesis testing, systematic observations, and verification	• Often scientistic (i.e. uses terms that make events appear scientific but there is in fact no evidence)
Productive	*Not productive*
• Evolving process.	
• Progress depends on an accumulated growth of knowledge over time, during which useful features are retained and nonuseful features are discarded	• Knowledge does not change
	• Moribund state of knowledge based on age-old traditions
• Based on a system of confirmation or rejection of hypotheses (Shermer, 1997)	
Verifiable	*Not verifiable*
• Knowledge based on empirical evidence	• Knowledge based on anecdotes

We can discriminate between science and pseudoscience in the ways shown in Table 2.2. This dichotomy between science and pseudoscience is deliberately simplified for the purposes of illustration, so that the novice student can appreciate the main distinctions between two major approaches to claiming knowledge and offering care on these bases. Keep in mind that, as in many other areas in life, we are most likely dealing with a continuum between science and pseudoscience rather than a dichotomy. Today's pseudoscience could become or contribute to tomorrow's science. For example, think of the magic of mesmerism and the science of psychology, the magic of alchemy and the science of chemistry, and the magic of astrology and the science of astronomy. (*Magic* here does not refer to the trickery and foolery of a conjurer but rather to phenomena that appear supernatural because the scientist is unwilling or unable to provide a reasonable explanation for these events.)

FURTHER READING

Crombie & Davies (1996) Chapter 1 is useful on the topic of research.
Payton (1994) is an alternative reference on research.
Richards (1987) offers an accessible account on science.
Roberts (1989) is a good source for examples of accidental discoveries in science.
Schon (1991) Chapters 1 and 2 offer a perspective on the role of reason and science though this text deals with meta knowledge issue related to skill and practice.
Shermer (1997) Foreword, Chapters 1 and 2 provide an insightful perspective on science.

GRADUATE READING

Bird (1998) presents a succinct account of the distinction between science and pseudoscience by contrasting creationism and evolutionary theory.

Bunge (1984) offers a useful elaboration of the definition of science and pseudoscience, including a comparison of the attitudes and activities of scientists and pseudoscientists.

Curd & Cover (1998) provide an interesting enunciation of the issues and proposals argued for distinguishing between science and pseudoscience, with examples in astrology and creationism.

Thomas (1971) presents a comprehensive thesis on the relationship between science and earlier forms of pseudoscience and magic.

3

Arguments

It is wonderful that five thousand years have now elapsed since the creation of the world, and still it is undecided whether or not there has ever been an instance of the spirit of any person appearing after death. All argument is against it; but all belief is for it.

—S. Johnson, 1709–1784

OPINIONS, REASONED JUDGMENT, AND FACTS

When people think they have knowledge about something and want to persuade others to their viewpoint, they do one of several things. They might pass an opinion, sometimes even with great emotion, in the hope that others in the group will accept it. They might simply state the facts and let others decide for themselves, or they might express a well-reasoned judgment (particularly when the facts are not available).

The following examples illustrate these various expressions of knowledge:

- The speech and language therapy course at Granger University is the best training course in the country. That's why I am here. *(Opinion)*

- The speech and language therapy course at Granger University is the best training course in the country because the small student numbers allow ample opportunities for clinical training and so produce more confident graduates. *(Reasoned judgment)*
- The speech and language therapy course at Granger University is the best training course in the country because, unlike in other speech therapy courses, 99% of its graduates attain full-employment within 4 months after graduation. *(Fact)*

An opinion is a statement based on personal preference and taste. A reasoned judgment is still a preference, but it is supported by reasons, and reasons are often included in the structure of an argument. A fact is a statement whose truth can be verified.

ARGUMENTS

Another form of communicating knowledge is by argument. A common interpretation of the term *argument* among the general public is that it is a verbal dispute, an unpleasant event often associated with hostility and unpleasantness. An alternative meaning of *argument*—the one that is intended here—is a set of reasons offered to support a conclusion (LeBlanc, 1998; Weston, 1992). The reasons are usually termed *premises*. In formulating arguments, it is necessary to consider the positive as well as the negative aspects of an issue (i.e., to critically evaluate an issue). *Critical* is another term that can be used several ways; it is often interpreted to mean negative commenting about something raised in a discussion, a debate, or an essay. For this book's purposes, however, *critical* means that one needs to weigh the positive and negative factors of an issue. Arguments are so much a part of daily life that unless the individual is associated with education, there is little reason to become conscious of the structure of arguments.

Why We Use Arguments

Arguments are used to explain and defend conclusions. We confront arguments in many areas of living, such as the following:

- In education, when required to write an argumentative essay
- In legal disputes
- In persuading a friend to do a favour
- In public debate
- In research
- In clinical case conferences

A good argument is one that offers reasons and evidence and that does not merely repeat the conclusions.

Johnson and Blair (1994) likened a good argument to a good map, where there is a rational route that starts with certain premises; if one is consistent, one will be led directly to a very specific conclusion. A bad argument involves many dead-end and detour paths, called *fallacies*. Johnson and Blair pointed out that it is rare for an argument to be so good or so bad that it cannot benefit from criticism. Johnson and Blair suggested that when an argument is held to be airtight, it could also be due to a lack a familiarity with the subject or the issues. They suggested that when someone regards an argument as worthless, it also could be due to the person being blinkered. In analyzing an argument, the aim is to assess the positive and negative aspects of an argument as they stand, without involving any preexisting views on the subject. So one should be able to ask, "Irrespective of what I believe, is the argument presented a good one?" The following text provides a set of simple guidelines for evaluating arguments.

General Rules for Identifying and Constructing Good Arguments

1. *Distinguish premises and conclusions*—premises is a statement that states your reasons. A conclusion is a statement for which you are giving reasons. Ask what you are trying to conclude or assert and what your reasons are.

Clinical Example

John has dysarthric speech because his words are slurred. (*The premise is that his words are slurred and the conclusion is that he is dysarthric.*)

---

2. *Present your ideas in a natural order*—You can do this in two ways: (a) Put your conclusion first, followed by your reasons; or (b) set your premises first and then draw your conclusion at the end.

Example

Joining the Registration Board for Health Clinicians is necessary for the speech therapy profession to survive in the current litigious climate. (*Conclusion*)

The number of complaints about individual clinicians is increasing each year as the public become more educated about the complaint procedures within the health system. (*Reason*)

Each complaint lodged with the Speech and Language Therapy Association (SLTA) consumes a considerable amount of administrative staff time and membership money due to legal fees. This cannot be continued indefinitely. (*Reason*)

Because the SLTA also cannot afford to seek independent state registration of its members, it is necessary that it join other health professions in securing state registration for all its speech and language therapy members. (*Reason*)

3. *Start from reliable premises*—No matter how well you argue for your conclusion, the argument is not good if your reasons (or premises) are incorrect in the first place.

Example

Nobody in the world is really happy. Therefore, it seems that human beings are just not made for happiness. Why should we expect what we can never find? (Weston [1992] *pointed out the untruth of the premise* everybody in the world is unhappy. *Since the premise is untrue, the conclusion* human beings are made for unhappiness *must also be wrong.*)

4. *Use definite, specific, concrete language*—Write without using ambiguous terms.

Example

John produced /t/ incorrectly on 3/10 trials, /k/ incorrectly on 5/10 trials, and /l/ incorrectly on 8/10 trials. (*Definite, specific, concrete language*)

John produced several different kinds of errors in the test. (*Vague, unclear language*)

5. *Avoid loaded language*—Avoid using language that sways the emotions of the audience either for or against the view you present.

Example

The clinician who impatiently pulled the book out of his tiny hands intimidated the poor boy. (*Loaded language*)

The boy looked at the clinician when she removed the book from him. (*Neutralized language*)

Emotive language can also be used, for example, to provoke a class of students into developing argument and debating skills.

Example

Members of the working class are promiscuous because they have more children per family unit than those of other classes. (*Emotive language*)

Members of the working class tend to have more children per family unit than do those of other social classes. (*Neutralized language*)

6. *Use consistent terms*—Using consistent terms in an argument is important in helping the audience stay focused on the key elements of the argument. So avoid using synonyms or other descriptors to refer to a term. If you use the term *stuttering*, then stick to it rather than switch between a variety of other terms, like *stammering*, *dysfluency*, and *cluttering*. Different terms may convey differences in meaning to others, even when you might see no appreciable difference between various terms.

7. *Use one meaning for each term*—It is important not to use the same term to refer to different meanings. For example, if the term *a phonological disorder*, refers to a spoken speech disorder, then it is important that this term not also be used to refer to a spoken comprehension problem if that is not its intended meaning.

Types of Arguments

There are various types of arguments, such as the following:

- Arguments by example
- Arguments from authority
- Arguments by analogy
- Arguments by cause
- Arguments by deduction
- Arguments by induction

These types of arguments are described in the following sections.

Arguments by Example.   Clinicians, like laypeople, use all forms of arguments in ordinary living situations. The first type of argument, argument by example, is very common. It is very important to remember that an example of something does not constitute evidence or proof because there might be other reasons involved.

Clinical Example

Joan has a memory problem. For example, I saw her wandering in the ward. (*There might be other reasons for Joan wandering, for example, she might have looking for someone, she simply wanted a walk to stretch her legs, or she was simply bored.*)

Arguments by Authority.   This type of argument is common in clinical circles and happens possibly because it is the quickest way to deal with uncertainty. A person may feel that going to the journals will take up time and that the journals may not contain the information sought anyway. When we do not have sufficient factual or reliable evidence, it is very easy to be persuaded by someone who claims to know based on his or her experience. This type of argument often requires that the person be perceived as credible and be an authority in some way. A clinician who relies on this form of argument will be vulnerable to the persuasive power of anyone who has a convincing persona. The argument structure goes like this:

Dr. X (a popular or respected individual) claims procedure X works or Factor Y causes Z.

Popularity and respect are qualities that represent endorsement of this person by the community.

Dr. X is valued in the community and therefore Dr. X's ideas must be valued.

Dr. X's ideas must be credible or right.

Clinical Example

Mrs. Carson claims that perseveration is a poor prognostic factor in the recovery of speech loss caused by brain damage. Because Mrs. Carson has worked with this patient group for 20 years, the assertion must be true. *The argument breaks down because the premise that the length of personal experience equates with how much valid knowledge is possessed is incorrect. Hence, if the premise is incorrect, then the conclusion must also be wrong.*

Advertisements sometimes appeal to an authority by associating the novel intervention or therapy with a "qualified" clinician who also happens to be a registered nurse or a social worker. The purpose of this association is to make the novel approach appear more credible than perhaps is justified.

Unfortunately, relying on figures of authority for knowledge about clinical practice poses a number of problems. Individuals may have their own motives and unconscious biases for claiming what they do. If we were to accept an argument from authority, then we need to ensure that the certain criteria are met. Some of the criteria given by Weston (1992) included the following:

1. *Sources should be cited.* Some factual statements need not be defended and so do not need citations (e.g., "*John is a boy*," "*The capital of Britain is London*"). Citations help establish the reliability of the statement by disclosing the source and allow the reader to locate the source of the information for himself or herself.

2. *Determine whether the sources are impartial.* Does the person stand to gain anything (e.g., money, competition, desirable professional alliances) by expressing this view? Figure 3.1 illustrates that even the most prestigious research institutions may have funding alliances that can bring their results into question. The article shown in Fig. 3.1 was published in *The Age* newspaper,

---

Focus on fluid urged in diet

By Shaun Viljoen

Australians should pay more attention to what they drink as part of their diet, according to a CSIRO report released yesterday.

The study, by the organisation's Health Sciences and Nutrition division, found that many people were unaware of the nutritional importance of beverages.

Senior researcher Dr Katrine Baghurst said people had a tendency to concentrate on what they ate, and not on what they drank.

"Beverages almost seem to be forgotten when people discuss diet", she said.

The organisation's research, based on the results of a national nutrition survey held in 1995-96, indicates that liquids contribute significantly to the average Australian's daily consumption of sugar, calories and vitamins.

The study found that in the average adult diet, more than three-quarters of antioxidant intake-which may help prevent cancer and heart disease-comes from beverages, particularly tea.

Drinks also contribute to 15 percent of folate intake- which may help to stop birth defects- and 40 per cent of sugar intake, according to the report.

The study was commissioned by tea producer Liptons.

Dr Baghurst said that the company's involvement had no effect on the integrity of the research.

She said that at least 30 per cent of CSIRO's funding came from work with outside corporations.

FIG. 3.1. Corporate biases in research findings.

a national Australian newspaper, on August 26, 1999. It is a good example of the potential influence that corporate interests can exert in research.

3. *Cross-check sources.* How do other informed figures regard this information? When agreement is sought on something very factual and tangible (e.g., whether to admit children with speech disorders to a clinic), consensus among people is likely to be high. But when the issue is vague and complex, consensus is likely to be lower and wider consultation necessary. When relying on an "expert," it is important to obtain a second opinion from another expert in the field.

Arguments by Analogy.   Arguments by analogy are constructed with reference to another, usually well-known relationship. The premise here is based on the assumption that two independent situations are in principle, the same. If this not true, then the conclusion must be false.

Example

As Woody Allen said, "A marriage is like a shark; you have to keep moving forward to stay alive." (*Is the premise marriage is like a shark really true? If the differences between a marriage and a shark are relevant and matter to the argument, then the conclusion might be valid.*)

Arguments by Causes.   Arguments by causes, which are discussed further in Chapter 5, are arguments about cause and effect.

Example

I notice that when parents read to their children a lot, these children have higher reading vocabularies than children who are not read to by their parents. So, I think it is very important for parents to read to their children if their children are to become proficient readers. (*This is a simple inference, and it may be that the two events are correlated rather than one event causing another. Perhaps children who are read to often also happen to be middle-class children who have good diets and stimulating home lives, and they are naturally interested in reading.*)

Arguments by Deduction.   All the arguments presented so far are in a form where the conclusions do not necessarily follow from the premises or the premises may be incorrect. For example, in the case of reading to children, another conclusion could also be drawn from the same premises. It may be that parents who read to their children a lot also happen to be parents who stimulate their children in other ways (e.g., outings, storytelling). To avoid the problems presented by the types of arguments discussed previously, deductive arguments are often preferred as a way of presenting well-formed arguments. Deductive arguments are highly valued in science because the form or structure of the argument is inherently represented by logic (Garnham & Oakhill, 1994; Robertson, 1999). The logical form of the argument ensures that when the premises are true, the conclusion that follows must also be true. There are different types of deductive arguments. The main point to note with deductive arguments is that the conclusion is the only one that can be drawn, given the premises. One form of a deductive argument is as follows:

The pharmacy, the butcher shop, and the supermarket are the only stores in Lillydale. (*True premise*)
At least one store shuts by 5 p.m. (*True premise*)
The pharmacy and the supermarket are open 24 hours per day. (*True premise*)
Therefore, the butcher shop must shut by 5 p.m. (*True conclusion*)

Clinical Example

Mr. Jones is unable to comprehend spoken speech. (*True premise*)

A theory of normal auditory comprehension states that the skill requires normal abilities in hearing, discrimination skills, auditory short-term memory, auditory recognition of words, and links between auditory processing and meaning. (*True premise*)

Tests show that Mr. Jones has normal hearing, discrimination skills, auditory short-term memory, and auditory recognition of words. (*True premise*)

Therefore, Mr. Jones must have difficulties in linking auditory processes to meaning. (*True conclusion*)

Here is another expression of a deductive argument:

> All women are human. *(True premise)*
> Janet is a woman. *(True premise)*
> Therefore, Janet is human. *(True conclusion)*

Clinical Example

All aphasics have some form of brain damage. *(True premise)*
Janet is aphasic. *(True premise)*
Therefore, Janet has brain damage. *(True conclusion)*

The result of a deductive argument is known as a *syllogism*. Deductive arguments can be considered valid only if the premises are true and lead to a true conclusion. If the premises do not lead to a true conclusion, the argument is invalid. We can represent the form of the argument in the preceding example like this:

> *All As are Bs.*
> *C is an A.*
> *Therefore, C is a B.*

This is another form of a deductive argument:

> *All As are Cs.*
> *All Bs are As.*
> *Therefore, all Bs are Cs.*

This argument can also be expressed as follows:

> All teachers are educators. *(True premise)*
> All lecturers are teachers. *(True premise)*
> Therefore, all lecturers are educators. *(True conclusion)*

It is easy to think that if the premises were false, we would automatically derive a false conclusion. This belief should be dispelled by the following example. It is possible to have an argument where the premises are false but the conclusion is correct, as shown here:

> All speech-impaired people are brain damaged. *(False premise)*
> All individuals with cerebral palsy are speech-impaired people. *(False premise)*

Therefore, all individuals with cerebral palsy are brain damaged. *(True conclusion)*

It is also possible to have an argument where the premises are false and the conclusion is false:

All beefeaters are bovine spongiform encephalitis (BSE) victims. *(False premise)*
All men are beefeaters. *(False premise)*
Therefore, all men are BSE victims. *(False conclusion)*

The main point to take away from these examples is that although we can derive a true conclusion on the basis of false premises, an argument with true premises will always lead to a true conclusion. So, in evaluating whether an argument is valid, it is important to question whether the premises are true and examine the form of the argument since both of these will decide whether the conclusion is true.

Another type of deductive argument is referred to as *hypothetical argument*. This is sometimes referred to as the "if-then" rule and is common in clinical reasoning. It has this form:

If A, then B.
A exists.
Then, B must exist.

Example

If it rains, then the game must stop.
It is raining.
Then, the game must stop.

Clinical Example

If a child scores below the norm for his age group on a memory test, then he has memory deficits.
John scores below the norm.
Then, John must have memory problems.

We can deduce the consequence of an event just by knowing what precedes it (i.e., the antecedent conditions). This makes this quite a productive form of an argument. There is, however, one fallacy that should be avoided: affirming the consequent. For example, it could be true that failing a memory test is associated with a memory impairment (If A, then B). However, we cannot then say that a below-normal score on a memory-span task (B) *necessarily* means this is caused by John having a memory problem (then B must exist). There may be other reasons contributing to John's failure on the memory test (e.g., he may have an attention or a hearing problem).

Deductive arguments start with a general statement, a law, and a hypothesis that then guides one to look at events to see if there is evidence to support or disconfirm the hypothesis or law. This is sometimes described as *going from the general to the specific*. In science, deductive arguments are often used because the observed outcome is bound to be the logical outcome of certain preexisting conditions. The possibility of discovering new knowledge by deducing it from known premises (laws or hypothesis) is also more probable with deductive arguments than with other types of arguments. It is the closest approximation to an explanation of the cause of an event (Lambert & Brittan, 1992; Robertson, 1999). Deductive arguments tend to be represented in the physical sciences (i.e., physics, maths, chemistry), where laws or axioms specify clear rules for the conduct of events.

Arguments by Induction.   An inductive argument[*] arises when one attempts to generalize a conclusion to the universe based on a restricted set of observations (Bird, 1998). In contrast to deductive arguments, this type of argument is sometimes described as *going from the specific to the general*. In our day-to-day encounters, we build up experiences (sometimes only one event is experienced) that eventually lead us to form particular conclusions about things, people, and so on. This type of reasoning often forms the basis of people's beliefs concerning racial prejudice, superstition, food-avoidance behaviors, lucky tokens, and the like. The positive side to inductive reasoning is that humans may be able to avoid unpleasant or life-threatening situations after experiencing a small number of such events. For example, if you become ill after eating curry for the first time, then the next time you encounter curry, you are likely to avoid it on the basis that you think all curries make you ill (i.e., a generalization based on one particular instance). In fact, you may start proclaiming to others that curries make you ill. There are problems with this type of argument in terms of its power to explain events. Inductive arguments are also more likely than other types of arguments to draw on intuition, analogy, and metaphor as ways of attempting to explain events.

Example

Every red-haired person I've met has a fiery temper.
Therefore, red-hairedness and temper appear to be genetically linked.

---

*Inductive arguments should not be confused with inductive methods.

> *Clinical Example*
>
> All speechless patients we have observed have had their brain lesions is the anterior parts of the brain.
>
> Therefore, I conclude that the anterior part of the brain is responsible for speech.

Unverifiable terms such as *all* and *every* present problems in arguments. In the example of the relationship between red hair and temper, it would be necessary to see every human in the universe before one could verify the truth of the argument. So, one feature of inductive arguments is that they are difficult to prove or test. The other problem associated with inductive arguments is that although the conclusions of these arguments appear reasonable and accord with common sense, their conclusions are not deductively valid. In other words, the conclusions in inductive arguments still leave open the possibility for other reasonable conclusions. In the example, the relationship between red-hairedness and temper may be purely coincidental and have nothing to do with a genetic relationship. If such arguments are not deductively valid, then on what basis can we justify an argument. Common sense is not a valid basis for justifying arguments; this is known as the justification problem (Lipton, 1998). Since other conclusions may be entertained, such arguments are usually regarded as invalid. Philosophers doubt that this type of argument leads to knowledge (Hume, 1739; Flew, 1997). Conclusions in inductive arguments are justified on the basis of *past experience*, and this is not a sufficient justification for being confident about a conclusion that includes reference to future events. The strength of inductive arguments also tend to rest on the number of observations one has made. For example, if *every* means 6 people, then this argument is less convincing than one that is based on 10,000 people.

Although deductive arguments are typically proposed as representing the desired form of scientific argument, in reality, people engaged in scientific research often reason and work inductively. For example, inferences born out of observation might be used to formulate hypotheses (induction) which are later tested deductively. In *generalization*, a scientist argues that the results from one experiment or study can be generalized to others not studied, and in inferences, a scientist infers from the data a theory or hypothesis (Lipton, 1998).

There are various ways to test arguments, and indeed there is much to the discussion of arguments that goes well beyond the scope of this text. LeBlanc (1998), Richards (1987), and Weston (1992) provide further information and examples.

THE PRINCIPLE OF FALSIFIABILITY

Popper (1972) proposed a principle known as the *principle of falsifiability*. The common example given to illustrate his point relates to a story about swans. Once, everyone believed all swans are white because that was all anyone ever saw—until black swans were observed in Australia. Thereafter, people's understanding of swans was irrevocably altered based on this new observation. Therefore, Popper argues that it is, logically impossible to prove a general proposition is true because one will always be limited by one's observations. In other words, any number of observations cannot show a proposition to be true, but just one observation can show a proposition to be false.

The main thrust of Popper's argument is that it is easier to disprove a claim than to prove it.* This principle captured in Popper's argument was particularly directed at inductive research.

In the earlier example, we have to find only one red-haired person with a placid disposition to successfully present evidence against the claim made in the argument concerning red-hair and tempers.

FURTHER READING

Halpern (1996) offers a clear introduction on arguments with real-life examples.

LeBlanc (1998) provides a reader-friendly text entirely devoted to the topic of arguments, with exercises and real-life examples.

Robertson (1999) offers an easy-to-read account of deductive and inductive thinking, with useful, illustrative examples in the context of logical and scientific reasoning.

Weston (1992) is a brief pocket text that provides a comprehensive overview on the main types of arguments.

GRADUATE READING

Bird (1998) presents an account of the different nuances of induction.

Garnham & Oakhill (1994) cover deductive reasoning inductive reasoning, and logical arguments in detail.

Johnson & Blair (1994) offer an in-depth examination of the structure of arguments.

O'Hear (1984) explains falsifiability with a good selection of examples.

---

*Although falsifiability is an important feature of a scientific theory/hypothesis, Popper's position gives rise to the *problem of the empirical basis* (Bird, 1998).

4

Discovering Knowledge

Irrationally held truths may be more harmful than reasoned errors.
— T. H. Huxley, 1825–1895

THE IMPORTANCE OF UNDERSTANDING SCIENCE

Chapter 3 describes the different ways in which we can communicate what we know in an effort to persuade others to accept what we know. But, what about knowledge itself—can we trust it? As scientific clinicians, we are concerned with the quality of knowledge we possess and apply in practice. Are we biased or selective? Untrained thinkers are often inclined to seek evidence that confirms what they believe to be true, known as *confirmation bias* (Halpern, 1996). It seems more natural to seek information that supports rather than disproves what one believes to be true.

To think critically about what we know, it helps to think *scientifically*. A scientific thinker can be characterized as possessing the qualities of skepticism, but also being open minded to new ideas, having a willingness to communicate new findings to peers, and being reluctant to accept any new idea without evidence of its scientific worth (Bunge, 1984). The term *scientific thinking* encompasses all these qualities of a scientist. Scientific thinking is only one facet of critical thinking (i.e., valid thinking; Kuhn, Ansel & O'Louglin, 1988). There are other facets to critical thinking that are beyond the scope of this book. Examples include decision making, problem-solving, creative thinking and reasoning.

It is also worth remembering that some of the concepts presented here are often taught in statistics and research methods courses. Speech and language therapists need to understand scientific reasoning and how it contributes to knowledge in the profession for several reasons. If the speech and language therapy profession were a truly scientific profession,

- The knowledge base of the profession of speech and language therapy would be based on scientific principles
- Clinicians would understand how to satisfy scientific standards in clinical practice
- Answers to issues concerned with the efficacy of intervention would result from principled and systematic investigations
- Clinicians and researchers in speech and language therapy and other scientific researchers would have a common language by which to communicate evidence and evaluate knowledge incorporated into speech and language therapy practice.

Science and Research

Most people are familiar with the terms *science* and *research*, though few stop to ponder their meaning. Laypersons and professionals alike seem to share a common understanding that *science* and *research* are in some way good—that research is a valid social activity and that science is a desirable characteristic of every civilized, modern society. However, few people can explain why they have this intuitive sense that science is desirable or why anything that looks scientific is well regarded and better respected or more valued than other alternatives.

Have you ever wondered what is so special about science that new and developing professions publicly self-proclaim their field to be a "science"? It is as if by doing so, they are claiming for the profession or field the qualities that characterize the traditional science subjects of physics or chemistry. So, today, many fields are labeled "scientific," such as social science, health science, political science, computer science, domestic science, linguistic science, and speech science. In essence, these relatively new areas of study are claiming that the information that defines the knowledge base of their field or profession is derived by the same *empirical method* used by traditional scientific fields. This empirical method involves observation, experimentation, and the derivation of laws or theories based on these facts through logical argument. One approach in scientific research is known as the *scientific method* (Carey, 1998; Chalmers, 1994; Gower, 1997). The scientific method guides and constrains the conduct of research in a way that optimizes the result's likelihood of being a scientific account of the phenomena under study (Grinnell, 1992). Carey stated that the scientific method is "a rigorous process by which new ideas about how some part of the natural world works are put to the test" (p. 5).

Science, Statistics, and Technology

It is not common for the scientifically naïve person (e.g., students, non-science-educated members of the public) to equate technology with science. Perhaps this is related to stereotypical images of people in white lab coats working around machines with lots of dials. Instruments and technology used in research are merely tools used often to support scientific inquiry. Sometimes, advances in science remain at a standstill until new technology emerges that allows previously difficult measurement problems to be solved or allows previously hidden objects to be seen (e.g., the microscope, brain imaging machines; Clarke & Fujimara, 1992; Kuhn, 1996). Technology does not ensure that a result has scientific merit, but evidence and argument do. Sometimes, there is a tendency to overrate the value of instruments and to consider them as being more reliable than people. It is worth remembering that the instrument is the product of the scientist's efforts, and the scientist makes a discovery, not the instrument. There can be debate over whether technology is put to a valid purpose or questions over whether conditions of scientific rigor are met. To reiterate, technology is, after all, the product of engineering effort. Its scientific value is determined by how it is put to use. For example, the development of phrenological machines and their modern-day equivalent, functional magnetic resonance imaging measure something of the head, but the scientific contribution of this information remains to be discovered. The polygraph (i.e., lie detector) is another example of an instrument that is not always used scientifically. It is designed to detect physiological changes (e.g., perspiration, heart rate) that occur when a person is lying. The problem, however, is that these changes can occur independently of lying.

Another common misconception is that *statistics* is synonymous with *science*. The use of statistics does not make a discipline scientific. The scientific basis of a discipline depends on evidence derived through practice of the scientific method. Statistics is research tool—a mathematical procedure for calculating the probability of the evidence being true against the probability being due to chance, or for inferring whether there might be a relationship between events. There have been significant contributions to our scientific understanding of human behavior, however, by great scientists who have not used statistics (e.g., Piaget, Skinner).

What Is Science?

When did science begin? And what is it? *Science* is a term that refers to several different aspects, such as a philosophical doctrine, an individual's reasoning, a subject of study (e.g., physics), and a methodology of investigation. It is difficult to have a fixed view of science since today's science could have been yesterday's hocus-pocus or gibberish. Rather than attempt a specific definition of the term *science*, it may be more useful to take a historical view of how science and belief evolved, with particular reference to Western science (see Table 4.1). The account given here is intended to be a simple sketch of how events have shaped science, magic, and the beliefs we have about the world around us.

History tells us that the first signs of science were present around 2500 BC, when humans could predict solar eclipses and the early Egyptian and Babylonian civilizations had fixed units of measurement for volume, length, and weight. These civilizations therefore possessed an understanding of the principles of geometry and arithmetic, which means they were capable engineers and land surveyors. Also, astrology and astronomy were practiced. Knowledge from these ancient civilizations traveled to Greece, where it integrated into local Greek mythology and philosophy. The present form of science is attributed to the Greek sages of Asia minor (the Ionian philosophers), such as Thales (580 BC), who moved away from animism and held the view that water and rain were natural and not divine processes.

Between 300 BC and 75 BC, Greek philosophers were actively engaged in thinking about the disciplines of mathematics, astronomy, biology, and physics. Experimental science as we know it today was not practiced. Instead, philosophers engaged in speculation and used language to build elaborate theories that were rarely if ever confirmed by experiment. They were rationalists, trying to argue from reason.

The Dark Ages in western Europe lasted for about the next 500 years. During this time, nothing of significance happened culturally, intellectually, or scientifically, and Greek science was forgotten. This was a period of idolatry, and reason was abandoned in favor of dogma. Western intellectual life was moribund, and there was a preoccupation with petty warfare, European-Britannic wars, and political and religious tensions. However, in Persia and Arabia learning continued to flourish.

Meanwhile, there were major political and religious upheavals in Egypt, Syria, Israel, and neighboring countries. These upheavals involved the spread of Christianity, culminating ultimately in the splitting of the Roman Church. Eventually, during the Middle Ages (i.e., around the 12th century, the Dark Ages began receding, but for some time thinking in Western Europe was still strongly influenced by what the church sanctioned as being ecclesiastically correct ideas. In this climate, reason was discouraged, and experiments were forbidden. The main prevailing and accepted sources of knowledge at this time were the works of Aristotle and Plato and the Holy Scriptures. Science, being little more than a branch of philosophy, was declining.

TABLE 4.1

Brief Review of the History of Western Science and Explanation

Approximate Datelines and Scientific Fields	Significant Scientific Developments	Beliefs and Scientific Quests	Method of Inquiry and Explanation	Other Events
The Ancient World	Early Egyptian and Babylonian civilizations had fixed units of weight, volume and length.	Greek mythology established	Superstition, animism, and pagan idolatory	Pyramids built at least 500 years earlier. Hieroglypics of Egypt
3000 BC *Mathematics* *Geometry* *Astronomy*	Created calender via observations.	*Astrology* Egyptians believed urea, blood, sperm, tears traveled in body's circulatory system. Babylonians believed Gods inextricably intertwined man's condition and fate within the design of the cosmos. To understand the cosmos would lead to understanding events of earth. Believed disease caused by divine disfavor. *Quest of science:* To predict and or ward of natural disasters and divine disfavor.	Cosmic divination—Sun, moon and stars are deities	Cuneiform writing in Babylonia
7th Century BC *Medicine* *Physics* *Mathematics*	Thales—founded Ionian philosophy (c. 625–547 BC). Moved away from animism. Saw water as a natural and not as a divine process. Hippocratic treatises—Ionian written medical texts in which methods of	Believed the whole earth floated on the basic element, water. Earthquakes caused by movement. *Quest of science:* To understand the divine maker's design of the		Hippocrates lived (c.460–c.370 BC)

(Continued)

TABLE 4.1
(Continued)

Approximate Datelines and Scientific Fields	Significant Scientific Developments	Beliefs and Scientific Quests	Method of Inquiry and Explanation	Other Events
	healing relate to a theory of disease and body malfunction rather than to magic or divine action. Pythagoras—aimed to discover nature's order and harmony though mathematics	universe. Nature had order and form. Man's goal was to discover this order through the hidden languages of mathematics and geometry to understand his universe and his place in it.	Mathematics-geometry	Asclepius –Greek god of healing (6th C BC). Symbolized by snake-entwined staff
4th Century BC Geometry Astronomy Biology Mathematics Ethics, logic, political science and political philosophy Medicine	Alexandrian school of Greek philosophy flourished: Archimedes, Euclid, etc (300–75 BC) Euclid wrote *Elements*. Derived a mathematical language applicable to astronomy, optics, mechanics, and engineering. Plato (427–347 BC) concerned with distinguishing reality and knowledge of it. and dissecting nature into geometric forms, (Theory of forms). Wrote *Timaeus*.	*Alchemy* Believed omnipresence of design present in nature. Mathematics will discover God's design of the universe and mankind. Conceived of the universe in an ideal state where the *earth at the center* is surrounded by water and above it are air and fire. These elements are mixed up on earth and each tries to return to its natural place in the universe (teleology).	Speculation, manipulation of verbal, logical arguments, syllogistic reasoning, later identified as hallmark of Aristotelian philosophy	King Solomon's reign Socrates drank the hemlock (399 BC) Alexander the Great reigns (336 BC) and carries knowledge from Egypt and Mesopotamia to Greece.

Aristotle (384–322 BC) held that natural order of things was due not to divinity but to the individual nature the animate or inanimate thing (Theory of four elements—water, fire, air and earth—as building blocks of nature). Believed heart is the seat of the soul.	Believed motion of the celestial spheres and solid objects moved because they were supported by a translucent material which when exhausted caused them to fall.	Greek knowledge flows into Rome from c. 130 BC as Rome becomes major power in the Mediterranean through likes of Posidonious (135–51 BC). Cicero was his pupil.
Archimedes (c. 287–212 BC) made a significant contribution to mechanical engineering. Built mechanical models of the celestial spheres with an earth-centered universe.	Believed the sun, moon and stars moved by prime mover (i.e., some inherent force within the celestial body). This seeded the idea that the prime mover was God, an idea developed by the church.	
Aristarchus of Samos (280 BC). Hints that the sun and not the earth is the center of the universe.	Believed stars fixed and moved as an outer shell around the earth. No concept of empty space. Universe is finite.	
Herophilus (c. 270 BC) recognized the brain and not the heart was the source of intellect and sensation. Pulse was known as index of heart–beat. Heart's function was to distribute breath or	Believed disease caused by overeating and excess blood, so cures were blood-letting and dieting.	

(Continued)

TABLE 4.1
(Continued)

Approximate Datelines and Scientific Fields	Significant Scientific Developments	Beliefs and Scientific Quests	Method of Inquiry and Explanation	Other Events
	spirit throughout the body via arteries. Nerves carried psychic pneuma.			
1st Century BC —Birth of Christ	Lucretius (c. 95–55 BC) proposed universe is composed of minute atoms that move in a void. That there is more than one cosmic system, ours being just one. No deity or design responsible. Everything built of atomic substances.			Caesar slain (44BC) Cleopatra suicides (31BC)
1st Century	Dioscorides (50–70 AD) wrote	Mohammed commenced preaching (610 AD).		Romans conquer Briton (AD 43–57).
Pharmacology	De Materia Medica, influential text on curative properties of plants, animals and minerals.			New testament written (AD 52–96)
Astronomy	Ptolemy (130–170 AD)- Created the Ptolemaic system—that the sun, moon and stars revolved around the earth. Wrote the Almagest-most complete catalogue of stars of ancient world.		Observation and measurement	
Medicine	Galen (150 AD) believed brain is seat of the soul. Theory of humors.		Believed illness caused by an imbalance of four humors; blood, phlegm, yellow and black biles.	

The Medieval World	Few significant intellectual developments—*The Dark Ages*.	Christianity emerges as a major religion.	Dogma	Romans leave Britain (426 AD)–Celts, Saxons invade Briton. Roman empire politically unstable and depleted by warfare.
5th Century	Intellectual life in the West mostly focused on ecclesiastical matters, theology and divinity. Rome closes "pagan" schools. Lingua franca in science—Greek dies.	Intellectual life is monastic, focusing on literary and theological matters.		Stonehenge (Druid Temple) restored (600 AD) Religious warring between jews and christians. Crusades (1096–1270) sent by Rome to recapture Jerusalem
	Intellectual life in the East continued to flourish. Greek works translated into Syriac. Lingua franca in science—Arabic.			
11th Century	Forgotten Aristotle's works rediscovered in the West through translations. Notion of prime mover sat well with church. But his notion of the universe having no beginning or end did not.			Crusades capture Toledo in Spain (1085). Vast philosophical and scientific library there gradually translated into Latin. Knowledge taken to Europe.
12th Century				Many small country European wars Battle of Hastings (1066) Tower of Pisa built (1154) Marco Polo visits China (c.1272)
13th Century *Optics*	*Early Renaissance* Petrach, (1304–1374). Italian philosopher broke with Aristotelian tradition. Held that animate and inanimate things had their own inherent nature that was not due to divinity.	Religious and philosophic dogma (Aristotle/Plato). Experiments taboo. *Quest of science:* To reconcile genesis with classical science to create a coherent philosophy of	Dogma	The Black Death (1347–53)–20 million died

(Continued)

TABLE 4.1
(Continued)

Approximate Datelines and Scientific Fields	Significant Scientific Developments	Beliefs and Scientific Quests	Method of Inquiry and Explanation	Other Events
		nature that could coexist with Christian revelations.		
15th Century *Astronomy*	Spectacles and magnifying glass invented (1280). *The Renaissance* Copernicus (1473–1543) questioned the established view that the sun revolved around the earth. Presented idea of a sun-centered universe. Withheld publication for many years to avoid problems with church. Paracelsus (1493–1541) was prominent in seeking chemical methods to fight disease. Rejected theory of humors. Theory of magnetism.		Built models and argued with reason Experiments tolerated—tested many inventions	First printing by Gutenberg (1440) Columbus discovers new world (1492) Leonardo da Vinci (1452–1591) surveyor, engineer, architect was also prominent example of artist as scientist.
The Middle Ages 16th Century *Astronomy* *Philosophy,* *mathematics* *Anatomy* *Optics*	Tycho Brahe (1546–1601) made very detailed observations but unable to accept a sun-centered universe retained an earth centered cosmology with the other planets orbiting the sun. Kepler (1571–1630) discovered the elliptical movement of the planets and the controlling cosmic force of the sun after detailed mathematical analysis of Tyco's data	*Alchemy* Common—Science and magic often bed-fellows. University-educated physicians still educated in humoral physiology of Galen, Aristotle, and Hippocrates. Aim to restore balance of the humors. Treatments were emetic, purgative, blood-letting (by leeches, scarification, and venesection). Focus on symptoms, not on the disease. Medicine did not cure much.	Many new instruments made for measurement for modelling cosmology Accuracy of predictions were important for testing truth of hypotheses Observations (empiricism) and reasoning (rationalism) linked	Royal College of Physicians set up in 1518 to license and supervise physicians in City of London and 7 mile radius. Rich and poor alike in Britain suffered from waves of typhoid, influenza, dysentry, small pox, plagues-all victims of ignorance about sanitation, antiseptics and hygiene. Physicians mostly

Francis Bacon (1561–1626) linked practical and theoretical knowledge by advocating observation and inductive reasoning.	Surgery without anaesthetic; mainly amputations, incising abscesses, cutting to reset bone, and trepanning.		tended to rich who could afford fees. Most used home remedies produced by women at home. Poor consumed much alchohol. Nourishing food was very scarce for the poor.
Descartes (1596–1650) introduces skepticism and dualism.	Medieval paganism, superstition, magic, and charms became intertwined and transposed onto ecclesiastical objects, relics, saints tolerated as long as these were in the name of devotion to God.		Political reformation, Church splits. King Henry VIII- Head of Protestant Church (1534)
Versalius produced *De humani corporis fabrica* (1543), a detailed description of human anatomy based on personal observation. Galenic medicine regarded anatomy as irrelevant and claims were not empirically supported.			
Microscope invented (1590).	Protestantism challenged the rituals of the Roman Church and their efficacy.		Slave trade in progress (fr.1520 to mid 19th C- to Americas).
17th Century *Astronomy* *Medicine* *Physics* *Medicine*	Prayers believed to effect patient recovery.		
Galileo improved the telescope and discovers satellites of Jupiter and phases of Venus (1610).		Experiments permitted, subject to ecclesiastical approval	
William Harvey (1610) discovered dual function of heart.	Aristotelian philosophers and clergy condemned Galileo's observations of moon's blemishes as satanic.		Thomas (1650–1715) built first steam pump.
Isaac Newton (1642–1727) discovered Law of Gravitation, using mathethematical proofs to calculate force and ellipses.	Magic, occult sciences. Witchcraft and sorcery common.		AD 1634 Apothecaries (often grocers) administered curatives based on plants and food products.
Giovanni Borelli (1680) analysed human movement in terms of mechanics, leading to Cartesian view of man as a machine.	Empirical knowledge growing in importance and moving away from philosophy. Major debate about whether mathematics could be a real science when it gave quantitative		Medicine focused solely on body and not mental dysfunction. Mental disorders ignored or confined.

(Continued)

TABLE 4.1
(Continued)

Approximate Datelines and Scientific Fields	Significant Scientific Developments	Beliefs and Scientific Quests	Method of Inquiry and Explanation	Other Events
	Boyle (1627–1691) experimented in physics and chemistry. Rejected anecdotal accounts.	descriptions rather than causal explanations—the latter reliant on Aristotelian syllogistic reasoning. Quest of science: To explain human misfortune and to bring relief. To understand nature would mean being able to control it's effects. Knowledge was power.		Fire was a constant threat as most buildings were thatched and wooden. Infant mortality rate very high and average male adult died at 29 years. First settlement in Virginia, USA (1607) Religious and political unrest in Europe
18th Century Medicine	Buffon (1749–1804) conceived of the non-fixity of species. Laid foundation for Darwin.	Quest of science: To observe, test, and understand how things worked	Liberalism and experiments tolerated	Cook lands in Botany Bay in Australia (1770) American revolution (1774–83)
Physics	John Hunter (1728–1793) evaluated progress of disease and effects of treatment through postmortems.		Observation and deduction	George Washington 1st president (1789)
Biology	Benjamin Franklin (1752) discovered identity of lightening.		Taxonomic classifications	
Medicine	Linnaeus developed his classification system for plants.		Mass data collection in	

Period / Discipline	Key developments	Intellectual context	Methods	Historical events
19th Century *Physics*	Edward Jenner (1798) found cure for small pox with vaccine. Wilhem Rongten (1896) discovered x-ray	Science was fashionable among the intellectual elite.	biology, including new worlds	First steam train (1830) *The Rocket* marked the start of the Industrial revolution
Nursing	Florence Nightingale establishes rudiments of modern hospital practise—improved hygiene.	The term *scientist* coined by William Whewell in 1837, now replaced the term *natural philosophy*.	Experiments	Mechanisation on farms and growth of cotton-texture industries in towns meant mass migration of people to cities.
Microbiology	Louis Pasteur (1822–1895) demonstrated the existence of microbes.	Universities traditionally studying natural philosophy, reluctantly permitted the study of experimental science—1870 for Oxbridge universities.	Naturalistic and deductive observations	Science changed lives through new technology. Train network expanded in Britain.
Biology	Darwin's *Origin of Species* (1859) provided evidence of evolution.			Crimean war (1853–56)
Current times			Mathematical proofs	American Civil war (1861–65) First world war (1914–1918)
Early 20th Century *Physics*	Albert Einstein formulated the Theory of relativity.		Experiments	Second world war (1939–45)–many veterans needing rehabilitation and retraining- Allied health professions born
Physics *Aphasiology*	Marie and Pierre Curie discovered radioactivity of uranium and radium—early understanding of nonchemical energy (1896).			
Mid 20th Century	Wisenberg and McBride—1st psychometric Aphasia test (1935).			Voyager finds Jupiter's rings (1979)

Sources: Seale & Pattisen, 1994; Whitfield, 1999.

Great change rose during the Renaissance period, when the Italian Petrach (1304–1374) broke with the scholastic traditions of the Middle Ages. He moved away from the Aristotelian view by proposing that inanimate and animate things had their own individual natures, not some form of a divine nature. However, a revival of interest in science came later, through Copernicus (1473–1543), who questioned the view that the earth was the center of the universe. Whitfield (1999) suggested that the political and religious dissension within the church itself, between Protestants and the Roman Church probably, provided the impetus for individuals to question established ideas. Then followed a series of astronomers, Tyco Brahe, Keplar, and Galileo. Galileo improved the microscope and discovered the satellites of Jupiter, the mountains on the moon, and the phases of Venus. Descartes (1592–1650) and Newton (1642–1727) were significant contributors to an understanding of reason and experimentation. All these people are examples of individuals who made significant contributions to the development of science in the Western world. Instead of scorning experiments and reasoning according to the approved philosophical traditions (e.g., of Aristotle, Plato), they observed events to determine the facts and they experimented to confirm the conclusions they derived from reason. For some, like Galileo and Descartes, it was a formidable task because their investigations ran counter to the views of the church. In those days, to criticize views accepted by the Church was equivalent to criticizing the church, and this was a criminal offence worthy of imprisonment.

When the intellectual life of a community is concerned with questioning and investigating the prevailing status of things, then being in possession of facts and reason become important. Those who only wanted facts (i.e., observations without reason) were thought of as true *empiricists*. Those who thought reasoning was more important than fact were known as *rationalists*. There were long debates among philosophers about what constituted knowledge and how it was best derived. Most philosophers held that reason was just as important as facts and that the business of science is not about belief but about investigating phenomena. Consequently, what an individual believes is held to be less important than what he knows.

So, we're back to the original question: What is science? As stated previously, this is not an easy term to define, though today the many different wordings of definitions converge, as described by Chalmers (1994). Chalmers described a science as *proven knowledge*. Scientific theories are derived in a rigorous (i.e., systematically controlled) way from facts or experience acquired by observation and experimentation. Theories become old (i.e., disbanded) when they can no longer account for the data. In contrast, a new theory is exciting because it remains to be seen how much data it can explain. Science is based on what we can see, hear, and touch, and consequently is referred to as *empirical*. Personal opinion, preferences, or speculative imaginings are not characteristic of what lies within the realm of science.

Objectivity refers to knowledge that is gained through measurable and impartial procedures that can be experienced by all individuals in the community in the same way. Alternatively, Shermer (1997) described science as "a set of methods designed to describe and interpret observed or inferred phenomena, past or present, and aimed at building a testable body of knowledge open to rejection or reconfirmation" (p. 18).

In other words, science today is thought of as a way of thinking that is reflected in the procedures, we use when trying to derive objective knowledge to solve a problem. This was not always the case; during the 18th century, around the time of Newton, science was thought of mainly in terms of its content (i.e., it referred to questions about the nature of matter, the nature of life, and the structure of the cosmos), and science was thought of in terms of *natural philosophy*. Only in recent history has science become more concerned with *method* as we know it today (Whitfield, 1999).

Nonscientific Ways of Knowing

If we do not adopt science and its procedures for acquiring knowledge about the behaviors and disorders of patients, then we have to rely on other ways of knowing. The brief account of how belief evolved and contributed to explanations of things we do not understand is amazing. Table 4.1 shows how civilization began with a belief system that saw divine powers in all the elements and then in other forms of paganism (e.g., worshipping idols), and then how the major religions and scientific reasoning emerged. Many of these different forms of belief systems persist. A great variety of belief systems operate in the world, affecting how people explain events in their lives and how they respond to them. Some of the belief systems described here involve weak arguments that are prone to many forms of error in reasoning or fallacies, and they do not yield good knowledge on which patients and clinicians can depend.

Faith or Belief.   Not everyone has faith, and for those who do, faith is a private experience. It may provide a foundation for generating hypotheses and for dealing with metaphysical issues that are not answerable by science. However, knowledge based on faith (i.e., "I believe what I am doing is right") cannot be shared or understood by the public.

Authority.   The truth value of information communicated by a respectable or leading member of a community (e.g., doctor, high-profile member affiliated with the professional association) is rarely challenged because the source of the information is perceived to be credible. Knowledge based on the opinion of an expert may be confounded with all sorts of personal biases and prejudices (often unconscious) that compromise the factual basis of the information.

Intuition or Introspection.   Having a sense or feeling about something does not make it true, even if the event does happen. The basis of one's intuition or introspection is often unknown, implicit, and frequently not communicable to the public.

Experience.   Benjamin Franklin wrote, "Experience keeps a dear school, but fools will learn from no other." Experience is an expensive teacher. People are imperfect and often have unreliable memories and fall victim to self-fulfilling prophecies (i.e., a person may see and hear what he or she wants to believe). Personal testimonials are also highly unreliable sources of knowledge (Halpern, 1996).

Popularity.   Very often popular figures (e.g., Adolf Hitler, Jim Jones) have a higher-than-normal ability to persuade others to accept what they think or claim as being true. Knowledge derived on this basis is also fraught with problems.

Religion.   Some communities in the world hold religion and the god of that religion as being responsible for all events that happen in the world. However, appealing as this is to some, it is a private experience, and it is difficult to articulate how God has played a part in formulating knowledge.

The Goals of Science?

The ultimate goal of science is to understand the world around us. Understanding in this context means being able to describe fully what a thing is like and to explain why it works the way it does. The goals of scientific research in speech and language therapy are to as follows:

- *To describe, understand, predict, and control behavior.* Bird (1998) argued that the aims of science include understanding, prediction, and control over and above the levels achieved by unaided common sense. Unfortunately, the term *control* is often misconstrued and taken to refer to some infringement of a person's liberties.
- *To control.* Control, in scientific research, refers to the conditions the investigator varies to assess the influence of one variable on another (Coolican, 1999). For example, we might want to compare the effectiveness of two methods of teaching reading without having developmental maturation in the children confound the interpretation of the study's results. In this case, we would need to control the confounding influences of maturation, which we could do in different ways. One way would be to include a group of children of the same age range same social class, and same mix of genders as the experimental group, who are tested but do not receive therapy for their reading. This is called a *control group*. The performance of

the control group allows us to observe the effect of maturation on reading skills. If we know how much improvement occurs naturally due to maturation, then we can infer that any improvement over and above levels achieved in the control group must be due to the effects of therapy. In this way we could control for the effects of maturation on learning to read.

Common sense does not equate with truth or the facts and so cannot be relied on in making judgments. For example, common sense tells us "You can't teach an old dog new tricks," but of course old people can learn new things.

The Key Qualities of Science?

Science relies on:

- *Objective empirical evidence.* This means that evidence is observable and measurable. Measurements should be accurate and the needs to be in agreement by different observers on what is being measured.
- *Replication.* In science, evidence from a study needs to be replicated by subsequent studies before an effect can be considered genuine. In practice, studies are not replicated often enough. This is partly because many grant funding bodies tend to want to publish projects with new ideas rather than one that is an old idea.
- *A skeptical attitude.* Scientists must hold a skeptical attitude and accept new ideas only when these ideas are supported by good evidence.
- *A social enterprise.* Scientists need to check and build on each other's work. Communication is essential to this research process, and scientists publish their studies in journals, speak at conferences, research workshops, and so on so that other scientists can critically appraise the work or replicate it. These various communication forums also help researchers avoid unnecessary duplication in their research (Grinnell, 1992; Longino, 1998).

RESEARCH

The *Concise Oxford English Dictionary* (Pearsall, 1997) describes *research* as "the systematic investigation and study of materials and sources in order to establish facts and reach new conclusions (p. 1217)." Most people would probably view research as consisting of an activity where information is collected, analyzed, and interpreted, with the aim of deriving specific conclusions about an event under study. Research is also an activity shared by individuals with a common need to discover new knowledge to better understand the world around them.

Principles of Scientific Research

Many social activities fit the description of research (e.g., medical audits, surveys in popular magazines, market surveys, polls). However, it is important to realize that not all research is considered scientific. Research is scientific when it complies with a set of principles guiding the conduct of investigations (i.e., the scientific method; Anderson, 1971; Gower, 1997; Grinnell, 1992):

1. The event under study must be real, so that it can be publicly shared (i.e., empirical verification). For example, this principle ensures that personal hallucinations or personal experience are not permissible as forming the basis of truthful knowledge.
2. An investigator must define in unambiguous terms the event, that is being measured, such that others are not hindered when replicating the same study (i.e., operational definition).
3. An investigator can claim that one event has caused another event to happen only if he or she can show that systematic controlled changes in one situation produces corresponding changes in the another (i.e., controlled observation).
4. An investigator can generalize the results of a study to other individuals not studied only if it can be shown that the participants in the sample are representative of the characteristics of the people not in the study (i.e., statistical generalisation).
5. It is possible to claim that something is true only if a majority of replication studies produce the same results (i.e., empirical confirmation).

These are the five principles of the scientific method. Scientific research is based on procedures that comply with the principles of the scientific method.

Scientific Research and Speech and Language Therapy

Traditionally, health research has been identified with the medical and social science fields. These disciplines share the ethos that science defines their knowledge bases. The speech and language therapy profession has also inherited this value as it incorporates many of these subjects in its educational programs. The professionalization of health care disciplines and the establishment of university-based education for these courses mean that, increasingly, health professionals are taking a leading role in researching their own fields. Apart from the fact that the culture and ethos of a university-based education encourages and values research as a major professional activity, social and economic factors also promote research activity among the health professions.

Professional Commitment to Scientific Knowledge

A profession that chooses to define its knowledge base according to scientific principles requires its members to understand scientific research methods and to accept only knowledge that meets those rigorous standards. It follows from this that speech and language therapists need to know how to assess the scientific merit of information and new knowledge before incorporating this into professional practice. Clinicians, as consumers of research, also need to be able to critically interpret research before applying this information to patient care. They also need to understand that some intervention methods applied to patients may or may not be effective. A clinician armed with these skills will be able to modify and improve interventions in a logical, defensible, and well-reasoned way. Further, clinicians have to learn how to communicate this information to the patient so that the patient is well placed to make an informed choice regarding whether to be a recipient or consumer of speech and language therapy services.

THE CULTURE OF ACCOUNTABILITY

Is what we do worth the money? Can we be more efficient? Are our interventions effective? Managers of clinical departments with limited budgets will often be preoccupied with the questions, Hospital managers and clinicians are compelled to show how speech and language therapy services, especially those funded by public moneys, can be justified. This is understandable, particularly in an economic climate focused on rationalizing patient services. The natural focus for managers therefore is on the results of research. Managers might say they want to know whether a particular therapy is effective. As a result, managers may be more sympathetic to supporting research that appears to be useful and practically relevant to therapy (i.e., outcome studies) than basic research that is often seen as being too theoretical and esoteric or irrelevant.

Speech and language therapy managers, in particular, need to understand the science of speech and language therapy because they are often on the frontline, justifying speech and language therapy services. Most managers have little time to be active participants in research, but the nature of management work (and doing it well) requires managers to have an excellent understanding of the processes of evaluation and research. Good evaluations abide by the principles of objectivity. Managers need evaluations to tell them whether present processes are producing desired results as well as to determine the value of what Breakwell and Millward (1995) termed "provision, practice, and provision." These authors highlighted the distinction that unlike an audit, which simply describes events, an evaluation requires an analytic approach.

Speech and language therapy managers often do battle with administrative managers who have a poor understanding of the meaning of the figures they work with when making decisions. For example, hospital administrators spend hours discussing possible sources of variation in the average figures on patient length of stay in the hospital. Any student having completed a course in undergraduate statistics can tell you that an average (the mean) is very sensitive to extreme numbers. So it takes only one patient to stay an unusually long time in the hospital to cause an average to rise or fall in value. Similar fallacious reasoning is repeated when administrators interpret an unexpected increase or decrease in student enrollment as being related to the local economic climate or management actions (e.g., changing the institution's name). There is always normal variation; numbers go up and down all the time, for no reason other than just variation. To attribute greater meaning to these changes than is justified constitutes fallacious reasoning. It is very possible that student enrollment increased because the particular organization offers more vocational courses than a traditional university, and because students have to take out loans to pursue higher education, they might be inclined to choose vocational courses that offer an assurance of a job when the degree is obtained. The arithmetical problem caused by calculating the mean when extreme values are present also affects the grading of students, or the degree classifications awarded to students. The problem of the average being influenced by an extreme score can be overcome by using the median.

Sometimes, as has happened recently in Great Britain, managers have to deal with standards specified by the ruling powers. One example is the Table of Evidence (Muir Gray, 1997), which was given to the UK clinical community by a committee that met and decreed that research evidence, to be useful, needed to satisfy particular design criteria (see Table 4.2). Speech and language therapy managers who have the task of finding effective forms of servicing patients have a formidable task of deciding what constitutes an effective service according to the Table of Evidence.

The Table of Evidence speaks all too clearly to the standard drug-control trials common in medical and pharmaceutical research. How many treatment

TABLE 4.2

Hierarchy of the robustness of evidence desired from a traditional research perspective

Evidence Type	Description
I	Strong evidence from at least one systematic review of multiple well-designed randomized, controlled trials
II	Strong evidence of appropriate use from at lease one properly designed randomized, controlled trial
III	Evidence from well-designed trials without randomization, single group pre-post, cohort, time-series, or matched case-controlled studies
IV	Evidence from well-designed nonexperimental studies from more than one center or research group
V	Opinions of respected authorities, based on clinical evidence, descriptive studies, or reports of expert committees

studies in speech and language therapy will rank at I or II? This example serves to illustrate how increasingly speech and language therapy managers are required to think like researchers to be able to justify their services and argue for or against the relevance of the Table of Evidence. In many instances it is simply not possible to evaluate patients in terms of randomized, controlled trials (RCTs). The problems that the medical community encounters in this respect reflects the experiences of the types of patients seen by many health professionals. For example, the numbers of people who have Tourette's syndrome and who undergo neurosurgery is too small to permit the practice of randomization or even group comparison studies.

Speech and language therapy managers have to spot fallacious reasoning and contest inferior evidence. To focus simply on reported research findings without being concerned with the methods that produced the results (even when the results are favorable) would be inadequate. The integrity of research findings is only as good as the reasoning and methods used to get them. Managers are at an advantage at the negotiating table if they are knowledgeable in appraising information or research evidence presented to them when service delivery issues are discussed. Furthermore, it is not enough to know whether an intervention works, it is important to also know *why* and *how* it works. Managers are often compelled to find cost-effective treatments, but the point to keep in mind is that there is no sense to having a cost-effective treatment if the intervention is not effective in the first place.

DISTINGUISHING BETWEEN SCIENTIFICALLY VALID AND INVALID THERAPIES

Since speech and language therapy began, there has been a common practice of trying new things in therapy. As shown in Fig. 4.1, typically the process starts with someone having a bright idea for therapy. The idea is then packaged for sale. Busy clinicians, who often have a keen eye for resources that might make their work more efficient, purchase the new, untested idea. The problem is that these new practices often stick and continue to circulate in clinical practice, eventually becoming established despite a complete lack of scientific validation.

The cycle is perpetuated when students in clinical placements observe the variety of tools and resources supervising clinicians use in therapy. When students graduate and set up their own armories of therapy resources, they usually attempt to re-create and model their own practices on the therapy conditions they found favorable. The process continues, without any reference to any evaluation of these products or procedures. This cycle is particularly common with products that are gadgets, instruments, electronic equipment, therapy programs, assessments, and products for which there is a claim that communication can be facilitated or measured. Such claims need to be scientifically determined and evaluated.

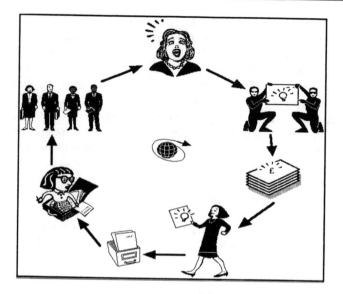

FIG. 4.1. The path of a novel idea to an established therapy routine.

A Consequence of Introducing Untested Therapies

Currently, if someone decides to evaluate the effectiveness of a therapy tool or technique that is already in practice, he or she faces a major problem. Casually introducing untested therapy tools, gadgets or programmes into the established milieu of therapy means it becomes very difficult to evaluate these regimes later. Why? Well, once a novel untested therapy idea is established, it becomes unethical to remove it to evaluate its effectiveness. The irony, of course, is that it was not considered unethical to introduce a therapy resource or procedure of unknown value to the patient in the first place. When the researcher or research funders attempt to redress this situation, they could decide that the optimal research design for controlling unwanted or confounding influences requires a no-treatment control group. The no-treatment control group now poses clinicians or researcher with a major problem. Using a no-treatment control group poses ethical problems, for example some patients are denied a treatment. The assumption made here is that the treatment denied to the patients is an effective treatment.

Consequently, it is important for the profession to distinguish between valid and invalid therapies, by using scientific methods. To do this, there must be a distinction between new therapies at the stage of experimentation and mature therapies that are ready for clinicians to use. *Ready* here means that there is evidence for a therapy's effectiveness, for the types of disorders it should be used with, how it relates to a theory of normal and abnormal function, its shortcomings, and the availability of standardized assessment procedures to identify patients for whom it is suitable.

The Need to Evaluate Patient Response to Therapy

The evolution of scientific practice in speech and language therapy is in an early stage. We are only just beginning to study the effects of specific interventions on patients' communication disorders. It will take some time before a foundation of reliable knowledge is available. Even if the information were available now, there is no guarantee that a particular patient in a clinic would respond to therapy in exactly the same way as patients studied in research. This is because patients with the same disorder can show quite a lot of individual variation. Therefore, it seems that the onus is on each clinician to evaluate the patient's response to therapy in order to find out whether therapy has been effective with that particular patient. To do this, the clinician needs to have an understanding of scientific methods of measurement and observation. It is not desirable to evaluate a patient by cursorily observing the patient or the patient's test results. There are two levels to the issue of efficacy: treatment in general and treatment for a particular patient. The latter relates most to the accountability of care.

Ethics and Research

Clinicians wrestle with the ethics of informed decisions in participating in research, but few consider the ethics of offering unsubstantiated interventions. Unlike the guidelines for invasive treatments, the guidelines and procedures for the application of noninvasive interventions are variable across health care organizations. Formal committee based consent procedures may or may not be required for introducing noninvasive treatment procedures to patients. In some places, it is adequate to simply refer to the service manager. Patients and the parents of treated children rarely ask about the proven value of the therapies applied to them. Even when this issue is brought to the fore—perhaps at a conference or in a passing discussion with colleagues—the matter is usually put aside when all recall how all healthcare professions are sharing similar experiences. It somehow feels better to know that speech and language therapy is not alone, and other health professions experience similar concerns to those expressed here. There is, however, a sense that as health professionals we should be able to provide the patient with better explanations of the treatments they receive.

While there may be a general disdain for no-treatment control groups, it pays to remember that participants often are free to decide whether or not they wish to be involved in research that could mean he or she is denied treatment. As long as participants are fully informed of the conditions, and is given time to reflect on the request for participation, then it is ethical to impose non-treatment control condition. Ethics is a subject often presented to clinicians solely in the context of how patient privacy and liberties might be violated in research and/or how deception has no part in research. It is extremely important to conduct research, nonetheless, but to conduct research ethically. This is the positive message when instructing students about ethics. The negative message is to use the subject of ethics to deter and discourage students and clinicians from engaging in or condoning research on patients. As published intervention studies appear more frequently in journals and other professional literature, it becomes increasingly difficult for clinicians to ignore the literature. New information on efficacious treatments set new professional and ethical standards for defining what treatments are acceptable. It becomes incumbent upon clinicians to be familiar with this growing literature if they are to know what constitutes ethical therapeutic practice.

We accept that there must be high standards for establishing the efficacy of pharmaceutical interventions because of the potential for iatrogenic effects (i.e., patient illness due to the effects of treatment, such as side effects of drugs) and of concerns for public safety. Are there iatrogenic effects in speech and language therapy? This is a reasonable question to ask when the line between effective and ineffective in therapy is ill defined and when the temptation might be to keep a patient on the register for the duration of the patient's problem or until the patient decides to stop attending therapy. An example of iatrogenic effects in therapy may be said to have occurred if a patient loses confidence and becomes dependent on the very system designed to rehabilitate the him or her back to leading a full and independent life. This problem can arise if a patient stays in a rehabilitation hospital for too great a period of time.

The vision of therapy guided by research may be abhorrent to some clinicians, who may feel too constrained by these considerations. Once in a while, such folk present arguments against research-guided therapy by claiming that research reported in journals misrepresents the effectiveness of therapy. In support of this view, they may suggest that journals are biased in that they tend to publish only studies that show statistically significant findings. Although there may be some truth to this claim, the fact remains that research-guided therapy is still a better alternative than therapy guided by intuition. Because intuition-guided therapy has no scientific basis and cannot be verified, and therefore it gives the profession little public accountability. The solution is not to ignore what the journals say; the solution is to remedy the bias in reporting research.

Some clinicians argue that too many studies reported in journals are methodologically flawed and are therefore not useful for guiding therapy. Again, the solution is not to ignore research. The solution is to ensure that there are better research training programs for clinicians and that published research is better reviewed and vetted. The cumulative findings of the best studies for a given disorder may then be collated and communicated to the professional community (e.g., meta-analyses, major publication reviews by expert committees).

KITE-MARKING THERAPY RESOURCES

There is an argument for kite-marking gadgets, tools, and various new therapy resources to assist the busy clinician who wants to be a discerning consumer of therapy aids and resources. New therapy resources constitute a growing market, and there is currently no process for vetting the quality, relevance, and effectiveness of products that find their way into clinics. Publishers usually heavily promote these products because the profit margins are higher on assessment and therapy resources than on textbooks. Clinicians who want to adopt a more scientific approach to their work would find it very useful to know which of these new treatment resources have been evaluated scientifically or have been used in rigorous studies reporting effective treatments. This applies particularly to technological devices marketed as intervention products. Currently anyone can create a product and retail it to clinicians as a therapy resource. For example, what is to discourage someone from creating a rather high-priced product called Sensaforks? The manufacturer may claim that this set of forks assists with better feeding of the patient yet offer nothing better than anecdotal evidence as proof of effectiveness or cite the professional authority of the person who designed the forks. As another example, no controls operate to disallow or discourage someone from claiming that some particular type of technology or approach is useful for treating problems in people with auditory perceptual disorders, stuttering, spoken expression, and so on. Such claims may be backed by "evidence" in published papers—though not necessarily scientific journals.

Clinicians often judge the value of a therapy resource according to whether it looks useful, or has face validity. Although academic discourse and critical reviews of new approaches, texts, and products occurs within the professional literature, critical evaluation of these products is patchy. Clinicians would be better assisted in their task as consumers if there were be a set of public criteria by which clinicians critically appraise new products or practices. This set of criteria could go a long way towards' satisfying scientific standards. The results of such an evaluation could then be communicated in such a way as to denote the scientific merit of the novel product. Examples of this practice can be observed in other fields (e.g., toothbrushes endorsed by the dental associations, literature for families endorsed by the psychological societies, domestic blood pressure machines endorsed by the medical associations).

Few checks exist in the present system against sham therapy products being used in speech and language therapy. This problem occurs not only with therapy gadgets but also with clinicians assuming new areas for intervention. The latter can result in uncontrolled changes in therapy services to patients. Although historically speech and language therapists shared with other health care professionals responsibility for feeding individuals with cerebral palsy, the movement of speech and language therapists into assuming a key role in managing swallowing disorders in acute medical patients is fairly recent. One could speculate on the reasons for this, but there is no doubt that this movement occurred without any prior research aimed at determining whether speech and language therapy intervention was effective (over and above existing services at the time) in resolving swallowing problems in acute medical patients. The common claim that speech and language therapists are better placed to manage swallowing disorders because of their knowledge of oral anatomy has not been challenged. Now that the profession has clearly established swallowing disorders as being within the realm of its responsibility, it will be quite a challenge to evaluate the effects of speech and language therapy intervention with swallowing-disordered patients because a no-treatment or placebo condition can be construed as being unethical.

With any new treatment idea or new approach to therapy, *before* the new idea is incorporated into everyday clinical practice, a clinician should always ask, "What is the evidence that this intervention works? Is this new intervention evaluated by the same people advocating this particular treatment regime? Is the evidence scientific evidence?" A review in a professional publication makes interesting reading, but such a report does not constitute scientific evidence for a new intervention idea or approach.

As the profession's knowledge about methods for evaluation of interventions improves, clinicians will find it increasingly difficult to ignore the requirement to acquire knowledge and master evaluation skills. If the profession wants a more scientific basis for speech and language therapy, then a relatively easy place to start is to demand therapeutic resources that satisfy scientific standards to a greater degree than is currently being observed. This means demanding more rigorously developed tests (e.g., with normed data, with reliability and validity indices). Clinicians should demand that test materials be developed to more rigorous standards, that test materials provide agreement data for test items, and that treatment procedures be accompanied by research evaluation studies.

FURTHER READING

Carey (1998) offers the undergraduate a quick read on the scientific method.
Coolican (1996a) provides a definition of science.
Payton (1994) gives a definition and a description of research.
Seale & Pattison (1994) offer an easy-to-read text with good examples of the history of medical knowledge for different disease.
Whitfield (1999) provides a good, light read on the development and evolution of scientific thinking through the centuries.

GRADUATE READING

Bird (1998) offers an alternative view to the traditional account of the scientific method.
Breakwell & Millward (1995) provide an excellent practical pocket book on evaluation methods for students and clinicians.

Chalmers (1994) offers a few paragraphs on the meaning of science.

Grinnell (1992) provides an easy-to-read introduction to the philosophy of science, though it is written largely for an audience working in the basic sciences.

Gower (1997) traces the development of the scientific method through the ages.

Longino (1998) offers a broad definition of objectivity, including a well-reasoned account of the various meanings of objectivity, as defined by the scientific method, the individual, and a social process.

Thomas (1971) provides an information-packed book that reveals how the boundaries between religion, magic, and science have often been blurred through history.

5

Scientific Description and Explanation

The dodo never had a chance. He seems to have been invented for the sole purpose of becoming extinct and that was all he was good for.

— W. Cuppy, 1884–1949

Chapter 4 says that the ultimate goal of science is to understand the world around us and that understanding in this context means being able to describe fully what a thing is like and to explain why it works the way it does.

Description usually precedes explanation because there is nothing to explain without some facts. Consequently, descriptive research is appropriate when we know very little about the phenomenon under study. In contrast, experimental research is conducted when there are clear propositions about facts or events to be tested.

SCIENTIFIC DESCRIPTION

There are two basic forms of a scientific description: describing the state and describing the process.

FIG. 5.1. A description of the state of things.

Descriptions can be used to describe the fixed state of something. The terms *variable* and *value* are often used in descriptive statements in scientific research (see Fig. 5.1). For example,

- The kettle is green.
- The child repeated the word correctly.

Green locates color as the *variable* of the object kettle. *Correctly* locates the child's performance on the *variable* of response accuracy.

A variable is a set of mutually exclusive properties (Anderson, 1971). For example,

- *Long* and *short* are properties of the variable *length*.
- *Correct* and *incorrect* are properties of the variable *task performance*.
- *Happy, sad*, and *morose* are properties of the variable *mood*.

A value is often a property of a variable. For example,

- *Long* is a value of the variable *length*.
- *55% correct* is a value of the variable *task performance*.

A *state* description usually describes some value of a given variable.

Statements can be used to describe a process, or how something works. For example,

- The kettle boils when the switch is on.
- The child repeated more words correctly as she was given more feedback.

Process descriptions typically describe a causal link between two variables. They usually describe changes in one variable as corresponding to changes in another variable.

SCIENTIFIC EXPLANATION

Science aims to explain all facts parsimoniously. A scientific explanation is generally taken to mean a *causal explanation*. Lambert and Brittan (1992) pointed out that not all "why" questions are necessarily about cause. Take for example, "Why did John scream?" A noncausal explanation might be "John screamed in order to be heard." Compare this to "John screamed because he was in pain." In the latter, the causal explanation presupposes that there has to be an *antecedent condition* of John being in pain before he screams (the *outcome*). This relationship does not hold with the former statement because we do not know why John wanted to be heard.

Another example of an explanation not really being an explanation can be observed in the day-to-day communications between health professionals and between health professionals and caregivers. It is very common for people (professionals and laypeople alike) to confuse a label with an explanation. This is where statements of description are misinterpreted to mean explanatory statements.

Clinical Examples

Consultant:	What is wrong with Mr. Brown's speech?
Clinician:	He has a dyspraxia. (*Explanation*)
Nurse:	What do you think of Mrs. Smith's speech?
Clinician:	Well, she seems much the same, except her ability to find words she wants to say is worse than the previous time I saw her.
Nurse:	I think she's more like a Lewy-Body dementia. (*Explanation*)

Ultimately, science seeks causal explanations for the phenomena we wish to understand (i.e., did X cause Y to happen?). However, *cause* is not an easy term to define. One well-articulated view on cause is the Humean account of cause. The 16th-century Scottish philosopher David Hume presented an argument that says it is not necessary to find a causal connection between two events because this implies an *invariance* (i.e., a fixed relationship) between the two events that cannot always be upheld (Hume, 1739). For example, when a billiard ball rolls toward another ball, the first ball hits the second ball, but several outcomes are possible (e.g., the second ball could go into the pocket, the balls could bounce off the table, the second ball could spin off and miss the pocket). Hume argued that all we can ever observe objectively is a succession of events (i.e., Event A occurs, and then event B follows). The connection between these two events, Hume argued, is subjective because it requires the individual to map an idea (i.e., a mental process, an impression) about what is happening onto the two events (Blake, Ducasse & Madden, 1989).

Hume argued that *causality*, even in its most objective form, means it is only necessary to be able to demonstrate that whenever certain antecedent events are present, other events will follow. It is then important to discover and formulate a law that captures the *regularity* (i.e., the predictability) of this relationship in a general sense. So, in the earlier example, it is more productive to explain the whole sequence of events in terms of a law of motion rather than to say that a ball moved because it was hit by another ball.

It is also important that a scientific explanation be testable. For example, John's speech deficit can be explained in terms of John having been made that way by God, but appealing as this may be to many people, it is not open to scientific investigation and so cannot contribute anything in the way of an explanation. To test the claim about the cause of John's speech, it would be necessary to devise a study that measured the speech of children in places where God was present and in places where God was not present. So we must be able to test a law that claims there is a regularity in the relationship between two or more events (i.e., we can predict one event by knowing another). If the relationship between two events is conjoined in some way, then we should also be able to predict what the outcome will be when certain antecedent conditions are present. This is one reason why predictions are important in research.

The content of the social sciences disciplines—such as psychology, linguistics, and the health sciences—are analyzed at a rather coarse-grained level, where it is quite difficult to isolate events that contribute to the causes of others. Consequently, it is often more accurate to speak of events influencing or predicting other events than to use the term *cause*.

The consequence of accepting a Humean account of cause then is to accept that one can never really *know* in a philosophical sense what the causal relationship is between two events. The closest we will come to understanding cause is when we are able to show that two events are consistently connected (i.e., reliably correlated) in some way and that this relationship is so reliable that we can always predict one event just by knowing that the other event is present. We can infer causation, but in reality we accept that we will never know.

Carl Hempel, another highly influential philosopher, posited the view in the 1940's that scientific explanations need to be deductively valid arguments (i.e., the argument includes a statement of law among the premises and a description of the event to be explained in the conclusion). This became known as the deductive-nomological (D-N) model of explanation. Hempel asserted that laws provide the connection between the event one observes and the conditions leading to the event. In situations where laws do not exist or apply, he proposed a second model of explanation, which is based on an event having high or strong probability of occurring under certain conditions. He termed this model the inductive-statistical (I-S) model of explanation. Many models of explanation are debated, and Curd and Cover (1998) provided an overview of these arguments for different models of scientific explanation.

How would you explain following events:

1. How did the Johnny get a bruise?
2. Why do the seasons change?
3. Why has the man's speech suddenly become muddled?

The following are possible scientific explanations:

1. Johnny acquired the bruise after falling.
2. The gravitational force pulling the earth toward the sun causes the earth to revolve and move in an elliptical path around the sun. The different seasons reflect the angle of the earth in relationship to the sun at different times along this path.
3. The man's speech is muddled because he suffered a stroke.

How We Explained Events in the Past

Prescientific Explanations. Before science, humans saw the world as being full of spirits and gods who ruled the seasons, the day, and human life—and they had to be appeased. This was a time when the prevailing view of events was based on magic and superstition. Prescientific explanations persisted into the Middle Ages and beyond, when it was not uncommon for people to interpret illness as punishment for committing a deed against God or for leading a sinful life (Rawcliffe, 1995).

Animistic Explanations. Primitive societies had communities of people who believed in spirits and that events happened or not depending on whether a spirit or god had been angered or appeased.

Some societies believed that a deity that inhabited volcanoes, if displeased, erupted and claimed lives from surrounding villages. To appease the deity, a young virgin or child would be sacrificed annually. A dormant volcano was interpreted to mean the deity was pleased. People also believed that illness was caused by a patient being possessed by a mischievous spirit and the solution was to call in a witch doctor or shaman to exorcise the evil spirit.

Animism continues today in various forms, particularly among primitive tribal communities in South America, but also in modern communities such as the Philippines, Malaysia, and India, where the traditional cultures of these countries are tolerant of animism and superstitious belief. Animistic explanations for the three cases described earlier would then take this form:

1. John has a bruise because the devil pinched him.
2. The seasons change because the gods deemed it so.
3. The man's speech became muddled because an evil spirit possessed him.

Teleological Explanations.   Teleological explanations were among the first attempts at explaining events scientifically (Losee, 1993). A teleological explanation includes the expression *in order that*. For example, a teleological explanation for the question "Why does a stone fall when dropped from a height?" might be, "In order that it should achieve its natural end (i.e., a resting state as near to the center of earth as possible)." And a teleological explanation for the

One day I will become a big tree. Why will I grow into large tree? I know. The purpose of my being is to grow into a large tree because my purpose is to reach my final state

FIG. 5.2.   Teleology: An acorn grows to realize its final state.

question, "Why does the acorn change and grow as it does?" might be, "In order to realize its final state (i.e., become an oak tree) (see Fig. 5.2).

The Principle, upon which teleological explanations are based, refers to the belief that every object (living and non-living) in the world is compelled to return to a final resting state; this is its purpose.

THE EVOLUTION OF SCIENCE FROM DESCRIPTION TO EXPLANATION

The path from prescientific explanations or descriptions to scientific explanations spans several centuries. Take, for example, the study of astronomy. In the 6th century BC, the Pythagorean view of nature dominated astronomical explanations. Pythagoreans believed the sun revolved around the earth. That was how it appeared to humans, who saw the sunrise on one horizon and the sunset on the other. Pythagoreans tried to explain natural events according to mathematics (geometry). They associated the motions of the heavenly bodies with sounds in such a way that there resulted a "harmony of the spheres" much like musical harmonies. They believed that a divine plan of creation had imposed a mathematical pattern upon a formless primordial matter. The scientist's task was to discover the mathematical pattern of the universe, which was God's language—hence their preoccupation with mathematics. In the 16th century AD, Copernicus revised existing mathematical models of the celestial system and found that the facts were better accounted for by a sun-centred system of the universe than by a theory of harmony of the spheres.

This example serves to illustrate that scientific knowledge is often acquired in incremental steps. The steps may span many decades or centuries before a phenomenon is understood. Sometimes advances in an area of study can be delayed until there have been new technological advances (e.g., telescope, microscope).

In speech and language therapy, it has been several decades since the 1950s, when the developmental stages of children's articulation were systematically described, yet we are still nowhere near fully understanding (let alone being able to explain) many children's speech production problems. Consequently, it is unlikely that one research study, no matter how well performed, will provide a definitive answer on its own. In reality, it usually takes multiple studies addressing the same issue again and again until the weight of evidence builds a picture of what is happening or tips an argument in favor of one theory over others. This is why replication of research is important in science.

SCIENTIFIC EXPLANATION

We have said that science is about seeking causal explanations. Causal explanations can appear in two different deductive forms: the superordinate principle and the intermediate mechanism.

The superordinate principle states the following:

a' causes b'.
if a is a special case of a', and
if b is a special case of b',
then a causes b.

Example

The longer the child worked on the task, the more mistakes he made. (Time [a] *is reflected in* attention [a'], *and* number of mistakes [b] *is reflected in performance* [b'].)

We can derive an explanation for the preceding example by appealing to a principle of arousal which states that the length of time affects attention (i.e., the longer we attend to something, the more we habituate to it) and then performance declines. On the basis of this principle, we can conclude that the more time the child spends on a problem (a), the more mistakes he will produce (b).

The intermediate mechanism form states the following:

a causes x, and
x causes b.
Therefore, a causes b.

Clinical Example

Vascular disease can cause a stroke.
A stroke can cause aphasia.
Therefore, vascular disease can cause aphasia.

As stated in Chapter 3, deductive arguments are preferred as scientific explanations because of their logical form. These arguments are valued because if the premises are true, then logical forms of the arguments can lead to only one conclusion (i.e., determined outcome). This, in turn, leads to the formulation of predictions that in turn guide the investigator's search for evidence to confirm or disconfirm the hypothesis.

Deductive Versus Inductive Explanations

An inductive argument is a generalization from a specific event, to a general observation but it does not explain the event. Most philosophers of science hold the view that inductive arguments cannot offer explanations (Lambert & Brittan, 1992).

Example

Many head-injured individuals show pragmatic deficits in social interactions. Susie presents with pragmatic deficits because she has a head injury. (*The argument is inductive and it cannot explain Susie's problems (i.e.,why she shows these deficits?). An explanation for Susie's problem will have to at least give an account that includes how the neuropathology of head injury is related to producing pragmatic deficits. Furthermore, Susie may have pragmatic deficits for other reasons*).

Novice researchers can become entangled in the deductive and inductive arguments. It is a problem when individuals are not aware of this distinction and the limitations each mode of reasoning imposes on explanations.

Clinical Example

I observe that all my research participants produce shorter vowels after a voiced consonant. (*What is driving this observation? Why should this be interesting or even important to know in theoretical terms?*)

I hypothesize that voiced consonants carry some of their voicing into a vowel, and that's why they're shorter; it's a case of assimilation.(*This is okay if it is followed by another experiment to test this hypothesis.*)

I conclude that the voiced/voiceless distinction of a consonant is important in determining the length of a vowel in production. (*There can be no valid conclusion about the relationship between vowels and consonants on the basis of this argument because there is no mention of a control comparison. The possibility that the same phenomenon may be observed in other sound environments cannot be excluded on the basis of this observation.*)

When an investigator knows little about a subject, an initial response is to gather data, examine them for patterns and trends, and then make some suggestions about potentially meaningful relationships between events shown by the data. Inductive reasoning can be useful in generating hypotheses for testing later. Unfortunately, some investigators may be drawn to interpreting mere suggestive trends in the data as conclusions and so end up formulating an inductive explanation of the data. Again, this type of explanation is not viewed as a scientific explanation because it has not been directly tested.

Figure 5.3 illustrates how conclusions are derived from inductive and deductive reasoning. A researcher in the course of interviewing different criminal types observes that many of the prisoners serving jail time for assault have communication problems associated with being learning disabled. If the researcher reasons inductively, he may conclude that communication problems in learning disabled people lead to assault attacks. In contrast, a researcher who reasons deductively about this observation might formulate a hypothesis which states that communication impairments in learning disabled people result in increased

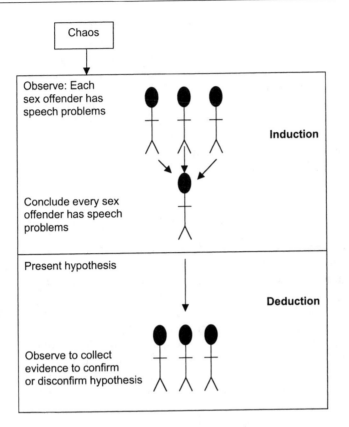

FIG. 5.3. Inductive and deductive reasoning in hypothesis testing.

frustration, which is expressed by an assault on a conversation partner. The researcher will then submit the hypothesis to new research that tests this hypothesis. The hypothesis could be tested by comparing the number of assaults committed by learning disabled individuals who have communication impairments with the number observed in two control groups. One control group may consist of non-learning disabled individuals with communication impairments (CI) and the other control group could be learning disabled people without communication impairments (LD). If the incidence of assaults is the same in all groups, then it can be concluded that there is no relationship between assaults committed and whether a person is learning disabled or communicatively impaired. In contrast, if the incidence of assaults is higher in the both groups compared to control group CI, then we conclude that it is the presence of a learning disability and not a communication impairment that determines the likelihood of an assault on a communication partner.

Inductive reasoning is generally regarded as nonscientific reasoning, largely because an outcome cannot be guaranteed with this type of argument (Bird, 1998). Furthermore, the principles guiding the inductive process of investigating data cannot be considered reliable as they may not be known and can vary across researchers (Lipton, 1998). In practice, inductive and deductive reasoning are iterative, and it remains common for observations to inform the formulation of hypotheses and for hypotheses to inform observations. When events are not observable, induction is limited in what it can offer, and progress depends on using laws to predict events (Curd & Cover, 1998). It is still considered important in scientific research to test hypotheses or predictions before suggesting causal links between events.

Levels of Explanations: Reductionism

As can seen from the earlier examples, there are different ways or levels in which one can explain how John acquired a bruise. The bruise can be explained at a biological level (i.e., an explanation about the cell wall being damaged and that cellular fluid and blood collecting in a tissue space). It can also be explained at a sociological level (i.e., the bruise was caused by being bullied at school). And we can explain a man's speech problem at a physiological level (i.e., a clot formed in the middle cerebral artery in the left hemisphere, causing the surrounding areas of the brain to become starved of oxygen, which led to tissue death of the areas that support language). Alternatively, an explanation at a linguistic level might state that the man's speech problem is due to a preservation of the ability to produce syntactic structure but not content words.

In science, there is a general aim to try to arrive at the finest resolution possible in explaining phenomena. This means there is a view of what an ideal in our understanding of the world will be. It is represented by as few axioms (i.e., laws) as possible. These axioms unify knowledge from all sorts of fields and disciplines. If what we see is chaos, then we are still a long way from understanding our world. The assumption is that truth has a parsimonious explanation (i.e., it is explained in the simplest form possible). Our task as scientists is to discover this simplicity in explaining our world. Ultimately, the aim is to be able to explain all similar events by a simple natural law (e.g., law of gravity). This is considered to be the way we will come close to discovering the cause of events. The cause of an event will be a mechanism that reliably brings about the given result or outcome. However, in some fields, it is not easy to see how one can go beyond a certain level of explanation (e.g., try explaining social class [an abstract concept] in terms of neurones [physical matter] or a stutter [a behavior] in terms of atoms [physical matter]). In the social sciences, such as speech and language therapy, we rarely contemplate causes of what we observe because we often work at a gross level of description (compared, for example, to physicists). At best, we can say that some events are associated with other events (i.e., correlated events).

CORRELATION VERSUS CAUSATION

It is important to remember that just because two things occur one after another does not mean that one caused the other to occur. It could be coincidence that the two events occurred together, or it could mean that both events were caused by a third, yet-unknown, factor.

In the social sciences, it is very common to be confronted with events that are correlated. In order to show that one has caused the other, we need to show that varying one variable will reliably produce a change in the other variable. For example, we might observe that varying levels of attention (one variable) paid to a child has proportional changes in how long the child stays seated (a second variable) in his chair in class. Only when we can predict how one will vary when the other event is changed can we suggest that two events are causally related and not just correlated (see Fig. 5.4). This means that if we can predict how long a child will stay in his chair based on how long we attend to him, we are much closer to claiming that the length of time the child stays seated is caused by how much attention he receives.

In another example (see Fig. 5.4), we might be tempted to conclude the obvious: that poverty causes poor educational achievement. However, we know that poverty also co-occurs (or is correlated) with other factors, such as low self-esteem, low aspirations, poor health, and absence of models of educational success in the family. Any or all of these factors could be responsible for causing a poor educational outcome. Sometimes, however, we might not even be aware of

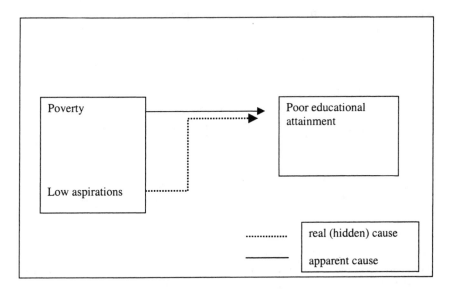

FIG. 5.4. Correlation versus causation in learning.

other factors co-occurring with the events of interest to us. These unknown factors are euphemistically referred to as the "third, unknown factor." In the case of the relationship between poverty and poor educational success, poverty need not be the cause. Poor educational success could be caused by low parental expectations of academic achievement. Low parental aspiration of academic success is higher among the poor in the community, but a similar outcome is observed the very wealthy classes, where people who have little need for academic success also attain low academic success.

In speech and language therapy, another example for distinguishing between correlation and causation can be viewed in terms of the relationship between therapeutic administrations and the patient's outcome. It would not be surprising if a clinician were to conclude that the patient's poor outcome were caused by the therapy program being ineffective or the patient being unsuitable for the type of therapy. However, the real basis for the patient's lack of progress may be due to his poor regard for the clinician. Since the patient's feelings toward the clinician are rarely considered in any evaluation of treatment, this factor could remain undisclosed until it is considered.

Apart from the examples above, it is important to also note that it is not always easy to identify the cause of an event. For example, who would you say caused the murder of a shopkeeper? The man who shot the shopkeeper? or the man who sold the gun to the shopkeeper? What about the case of smoking? Does smoking cause cancer or any other disease? It has taken several decades for a government and cigarette companies to get even remotely close to accepting that there is the possibility of a relationship between smoking and cancer. Why? It was partly because there was always the 90-year-old who had smoked all his life and did not have cancer and there were individuals who contracted cancer but had never smoked. Both parties could see that smoking and cancer were statistically correlated, but this did not mean one caused the other. Tobacco companies were naturally reluctant to be held responsible for the damage caused by smoking because of public liability issues. To demonstrate a causal link, it is necessary to demonstrate that the carcinogens in tobacco reliably produce cancer.

Cause is a word often used casually in conversation. In reality, it is not easy to identify the cause of anything. At best, things are usually *associated* (i.e., correlated).

HOW SPEECH AND LANGUAGE THERAPISTS EXPLAIN WHAT THEY KNOW AND DO?

The speech and language therapy profession has access to a rich knowledge base, largely grounded in the fields of medicine, psychology, and linguistics. Researchers in these fields strive to seek answers to questions "How do we understand and produce language? How is language represented in the brain?

How are concepts acquired? How is speech processed?" These researchers' endeavors focus to a great extent on what happens in normal function—say, in speech comprehension, in speech processing, in memory—and their research is a long-term process. In contrast, clinicians want answers or solutions to their patients' communication disorders and, hence, research that is directly related to patient care is popular with the clinical community (i.e., applied research). Herein lies a problem. If those who are doing basic research still do not have the answers to how normal people do what they do, how can clinicians explain what patients do? It is not possible for clinicians to sit around and wait for those disciplines to deliver the knowledge required because patients need help right away.

Indeed, with communication disorders, in many instances it is simply not possible to explain why things happen the way they do. By and large, patients tend not to ask how therapy works or even why. The most common question is, "Will therapy make the patient better?" When there is an absence of factual and reliable information to guide our thinking and clinical decisions, we should perhaps be honest and say to the patient that we do not know the answer to that question and that research has to be done before answers become available. This level of honesty in communication happens frequently, but the temptation to offer an authoritative account (based on experience) exists, making it difficult to avoid posing arguments from authority or experience. This is elaborated on in Chapter 3, but, briefly, this means that a clinician attempts to persuade another of the correctness of his or her conclusions by citing experience as a reason for what is believed.

Explanation from authority is often anchored in the experience and authority status of the person providing the explanation (i.e., usually someone who has achieved guru status in the field or profession). For the layperson, a common figure of authority is a medical clinician. For the student clinician, the most common figures of authority tend to be the lecturers and clinicians encountered during training. In the case of the lecturers and clinicians, the authority figure can be anyone perceived to have received wide recognition by the professional and/or scientific community. Who is the figure of authority for the patient? We often encounter arguments from authority, and here is one example: Jane might argue that it is therapeutic to tell a patient that what he is saying does not make sense because it helps him to self-monitor his speech and this will increase the likelihood that he will self-correct his speech. Sue, however, thinks that helping a patient acquire insight into his speech problem is not desirable because this will cause the patient to become depressed and remain so, as there is no guarantee that his speech will improve. Since Jane has worked with aphasic patients for 10 years, it appears that she might know what she is talking about compared to Sue, who has only has 2 years' experience with this patient group. In this example, Jane is relying on an argument that says "I have more experience than Sue; therefore, I have more authority to speak on this subject than Sue and I know what is best for the patient." On this basis (i.e., counting experience), Sue will always be deemed to be correct in a debate because Jane will never have more experience than Sue. This is a weak argument because experience alone is neither evidence nor an explanation for how and what role is played by self-monitoring in speech.

There are costs to accepting that knowledge is derived through arguments based on authority. Take for example, the lobotomy operations that were popularized by Antônio Egas Moniz (1874–1955) of Portugal, as psychosurgery for alleviating mental illness. The *Science Odyssey* TV series funded by the National Science Foundation provides one description of how Moniz was able to have such an impact on health care practice, despite rather questionable methods and results. Their report is as follows:

Antônio Egas Moniz (1874–1955) of Portugal was an ambitious and multitalented person—a neurologist, political figure, and man of letters. By the 1930s he was already known for his successful refinement of techniques enabling doctors to visualize blood vessels in the brain by using radioactive tracers. He had hoped and perhaps expected to receive the Nobel Prize for this work and was disappointed when he realized he would not.

In 1935 at an international neurology conference he saw a presentation on the frontal lobes of the brain and the effects of removing them from chimpanzees. Moniz later claimed he had been thinking about similar methods before the conference, but it went into scientific mythology that the calm behavior of the presenter's formerly temperamental chimp had inspired him to develop the lobotomy to treat mental illness.

Moniz had an idea that some forms of mental illness were caused by an abnormal sort of stickiness in nerve cells, causing neural impulses to get stuck and the patient to repeatedly experience the same pathological ideas. There was no empirical evidence for his theory, but Moniz pressed on. If the nerve fibers causing these morbidly fixed ideas could be destroyed, the patient might improve. In November 1935, he and his assistants made the first attempts at this type of psychosurgery. First they gave a series of alcohol injections to the frontal lobe (through holes drilled in the skull). After seven patients, they switched to cutting the lobe with a wire. Nothing was removed; connections were just severed.

In 1936 Moniz published the very positive results of his first 20 operations on patients who had suffered from anxiety, depression, and schizophrenia. Though his follow-up was mainly within the first few days of surgery and his determination of "improvement" rather subjective, his publication was well received. It seemed to offer evidence of the benefits of psychosurgery. For example, Moniz's first patient was less agitated and less overtly paranoid than she had been before, although she was also more apathetic and in fact duller than Moniz had hoped. She had a few physical side effects such as nausea and disorientation but overall struck Moniz as much improved. In the 1930s diagnoses of serious mental illness were increasing, and yet knowledge of its causes or how to treat it was not. Doctors were sometimes willing to try anything to help their most desperately ill patients. This terrible need for treatment cleared the path for widespread acceptance of such radical treatments as shock therapy and lobotomy.

In the United States, neurology professor Walter Freeman threw himself into lobotomy practice and promotion with an unmatched fervor. Within a year of reading Moniz's publication, he and an assistant had performed 20 lobotomies. They wrote, "In all our patients there was a common denominator of worry, apprehension, anxiety, insomnia and nervous tension, and in all of them these particular symptoms have been relieved to a greater or lesser extent." They also claimed that disorientation, confusion, phobias, hallucinations, and delusions had been relieved or erased entirely in some patients. But they also noted, "Every patient probably loses something by this operation, some spontaneity, some sparkle, some flavor of the personality." In 1942 they published an influential book promoting the practice. In the United States the number of lobotomies performed per year went from 100 in 1946 to 5,000 in 1949. That year Moniz won the Nobel Prize in physiology/ medicine for his contribution.

The popularity of the procedure declined drastically in the 1950s and beyond. Evidence of serious side effects mounted with long-term studies. The use of newly developed Thorazine, the first nonsedating tranquilliser, reduced the perceived need for most lobotomies. (www.pbs.org)

FURTHER READING

Anderson (1971) offers information on scientific method and description.
Lambert & Brittan (1992) provide a very accessible account on scientific explanation.
Richards (1987) Chapter 2.
Schmidt & Lee (1999) provide a non-speech therapy perspective on scientific description.

GRADUATE READING

Blake et al. (1989) provide an account of Hume's causal explanation.

6

Models, Hypotheses, Theories, and Laws

Anecdotes do not make a science.

—Shermer, 1997

The terms *model, hypothesis, theory,* and *laws* are encountered often when reading literature in scientific journals. So what do they mean and where do they fit in the scheme of things?

We can start with describing an experiment. An experiment is the study of an event under controlled conditions. It usually consists of a theory and/or a hypothesis, participants, independent variables (i.e., things you manipulate or vary to assess their effects), dependent variables (i.e., outcomes you measure), and a conclusion about whether the hypothesis was supported by the data.

A well-designed experiment is capable of informing about:

- whether the events we observe are real and not just due to the product of our imagination, wishful thinking, and so forth. *(Empirical evidence)*
- whether what we have observed can be applied to other people, places, and conditions. *(Generalizable)*
- whether what we have observed is a genuine effect. *(Replicable)*

All this information gleaned from experiments can be collated, and it might be possible to represent the information in the form of a model.

MODELS

The purpose of a model is to represent and possibly explain various aspects of a phenomenon. A model is typically a simplified, schematic abstraction of what it represents. No one actually expects a model to represent how things really work. Models are shorthand ways to represent what one is talking about to aid the communication of ideas. In speech and language therapy, many of the models we use are psychological and linguistic models. They provide a schematic framework on which to hang what one knows about a particular process in speech processing. They are useful devices for communicating what is known. There are, however, differences between various types of model. Some models are produced without the support of empirical evidence: anyone can draw a model to represent what one is thinking. Other models are produced only on the basis of available empirical evidence.

In general, no one really expects a model to be an actual representation of the real thing. For example, a plastic model of an airplane is intended to represent a real airplane, but no one expects the model to be an exact reproduction of the actual airplane, with movable parts and an engine. An architect's model is usually a miniature construction of the actual house to be built, but without working parts. Models can appear in several forms, and they are almost always abstract representations of what is represented.

For example, Fig. 6.1 shows a plastic model of how human vocal folds move on phonation.

A model can also be a formula that defines voice production in terms of how much air supply is available as a function of time:

$$\text{Phonation quotient (PQ)} = \frac{\text{Vital capacity (VC)}}{\text{Maximum phonation time (MPT)}}$$

Sometimes, models are expressed as syllogisms. Syllogisms capture a particular form of reasoning or argument. For example,

Increased muscle tension causes increased vocal fold.
Vocal fold adduction results in voice production adduction.
Therefore, increased tension must increase certain aspects of vocal production.

Computer programs can model (or simulate) how the vocal mechanism works with various physiological events. Figure 6.2 shows a computer-based simulated model of the larynx.

Another type of model often used to describe language and speech processing is an information-processing model (Patterson & Schewell, 1987). A box-and-arrow

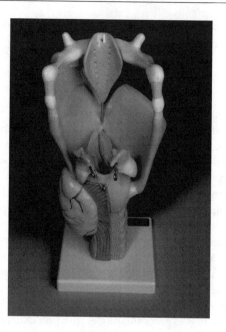

Fig. 6.1.   A model of the larynx.

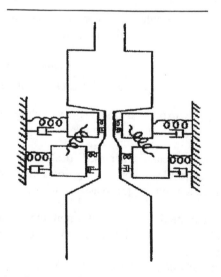

Fig. 6.2.   Computer-based simulation of the larynx.

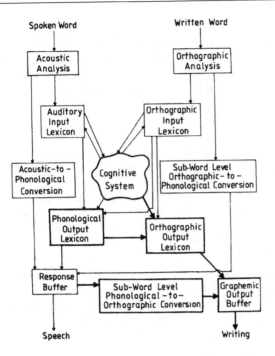

FIG. 6.3. A simple process model for the recognition, comprehension, and production of spoken and written words. (Source: Patterson, K., & Shewell, C. (1987). Speak and spell: Disociations and word-class effects. In M. Coltheart, R. Job & G. Sartori (Eds.), *The cognitive neuropsychology of language* (pp. 273–294). NJ: Lawrence Earlbaum Associates.)

diagram is used to represent the different components and the direction of information flow between these components (see Fig. 6.3).

What Must a Model Have?

A model can be simple or complex (i.e., showing many features) and still be a representation of the same object or process. What it includes depends on what the designer wants it to have and wants to emphasize.

Models are very useful. They are a very good source for generating hypotheses or predictions. Then enable one to plan an experiment that will test a hypothesis or prediction. Models can guide the hypotheses or predictions formulated in experiments.

HYPOTHESES

Anderson (1971) defined a hypothesis as a statement, either descriptively or explanatory, that has not been adequately tested. It can also be thought of as a hunch about something. Polgar and Thomas (2000) refered to hypotheses as statements that state the nature of the relationship between two or more sets of observations or measurements. It is important that all the terms and referents in a hypothesis be clearly articulated to minimize ambiguity about the intended meaning. In other words, the terms in the hypothesis must be operationally defined. (Further explanation is provided in Chapter 7.)

Clinical Example

John, age 5 years, was tested and found to have delayed language development. As his medical history showed, he was often ill and suffered ear infections. The clinician hypothesised that chronic ear infections were likely to be responsible for John's failure to achieve language levels commensurate with his chronological age.

Research Example

There is a hypothesis that the age at which a child learns a word has an effect on how easily he or she is able to reproduce this word after sustaining brain damage as an adult. The investigator hypothesizes that the degree of picture naming accuracy will increase as the age of acquisition ratings for the pictures become smaller.

Null and Alternative Hypotheses

In scientific reasoning, the investigator does not set out to prove that hypotheses such as the ear infection and age-of-acquisition hypotheses are correct. These are called the *alternative hypotheses*. It is important that an investigator (i.e., a scientific investigator) display both skepticism and open-mindedness to new ideas. Rather than try to prove the alternative hypothesis (i.e., that ear infections impede language development in children), the investigator sets out to demonstrate that the *null hypothesis* is true (i.e., that there is no difference between the two conditions). This means there is *no difference* between children with and children without ear infections in their levels of language development. In the case of the age-of-acquisition hypothesis, the null hypothesis states that the patients will show no differences in naming pictures with high or low age of acquisition ratings. When findings from a study do not allow an investigator to reject the null hypothesis, we say that the results failed to support the null hypothesis (i.e., no difference). We do not then say that the findings proved the experimental, or alternative, hypothesis. This is because the same set of results might be accounted for by two separate theories. Both hypotheses or theories cannot be true at the same time.

So we have experiments and models to generate hypotheses for experimental testing. Where does all this information lead? In time, a bank of data will accumulate from various experiments. Reviewers may observe that many studies on the same issue conducted by independent researchers have reported similar results. Someone may then attempt to formulate a theory or a law which states that some outcomes will always be observed under certain conditions. One of the problems in practice is that very few studies are replicated. This is partly due to the fact that after one replication study, many journal editors and readers would find it uninteresting to read yet another study that reports the same results as another, already published, study. Furthermore, grant-funding bodies seem to tend to fund research of new ideas rather than replication studies.

Statistical and Theoretical Hypotheses

With *statistical hypotheses*, every time a researcher obtains a result, it is necessary to test whether the obtained result has happened by pure chance or whether it reflects a true effect of the event under study. This is why we see many statistical procedures called "tests" (e.g., t test, McNemar test, chi-square test). These statistical procedures test the probability of a given result arising by chance. There is no guarantee that you will get the same results every time you conduct a study. Sometimes, your findings might erroneously say that there is a true effect (or difference) when in reality these results happened to arise just by chance. Sometimes, the reverse may occur: There is a true effect, but the finding erroneously states that there is no effect.

Testing a statistical hypothesis is based on testing your result against a set of (already worked out) probabilities for when such a result might happen by chance. A statistical hypothesis runs something like this: We know the calculate values (e.g., t values or chi-square values) of a hypothetical distribution. We hypothesize that the result from the analysis (e.g., t statistic) comes from the same distribution of values that occur when there is no effect happening in the study (null hypothesis). This hypothesis states that there is no significance difference between my derived value and the values found in the hypothetical distribution. If I find, however, that my result occurs in less than 5% of the values in this distribution, then my result is significantly different from the values in the hypothetical distribution. My result must then have a higher probability of representing values from a different distribution (i.e., a different population). A real effect has been observed and the probability of my result arising by chance alone is less than 5%. We therefore have to reject the null hypothesis.

Theoretical hypotheses are familiar to most people. These are hypotheses couched in language that refers to some idea about how certain variables are related. For example, I hypothesize that individuals with high IQ scores will show a higher speed of processing than people with low IQ scores. As you can see, statistical hypotheses are used to verify theoretical hypotheses. For example, the following are a theoretical and a statistical hypothesis:

- Individuals with high IQs have higher processing speed than individuals with low IQs. *(Theoretical hypothesis)*
- People with high IQs do have higher speeds of processing. *(Observed result)*

If the finding from study is due to chance, then there will not be a statistically significant difference between this study's finding and what could have occurred by chance. If a statistically significant difference is observed, then this finding reflects a true effect (or real difference) in this sample (statistical hypothesis).

THEORIES

A theory is a universal statement that allows a large number of observations to be summarized (e.g., evolutionary theory, germ theory). Chalmers (1999) suggested a comparison between two types of statements (i.e. observational statements and universal statements) to clarify this distinction:

- *Observational statements* are statements that refer to specific events or particular sets of circumstances at a specific time.
- *Universal statements* are statements that refer to all events of a certain kind that occur at all places and at all times.

Example
That stick, partially immersed in water, appears bent. Mr. Smith struck his wife. The litmus paper turned red when immersed in the liquid. The intonation of Mrs. Jones's speech has altered after 20 years of profound deafness. *(Observational statements)*
All planets, wherever they are, will always move around a sun. A profoundly deaf person who is deprived of auditory feedback will always show a departure from a normal intonation pattern. *(Universal statements)*

According to Chalmers (1999), universal statements are the laws and theories that inform scientific knowledge.

What is a good theory? A good theory accounts for all existing data, predicts new observations, and is testable. An example of an untestable theory is Freud's theory of the unconscious. This theory states that human behavior is influenced by unconscious thoughts that are not known to us. These unconscious thoughts can be of a sexual, an aggressive, or a repressive nature, and nothing that is said or done can be without meaning. The problem with this theory is the circularity of its argument:

Question: Why did the President George Bush say, "We have sex . . . set plans" during a speech?

Answer: What he said was driven by his repressed thoughts about sex in the White House.

Question: How do we know these thoughts are what you claim they represent?

Answer: We don't. These thoughts are unconscious.

Another unfalsifiable account is astrology because it makes predictions so vague as to be irrefutable (e.g., you will travel this month; you will have conflict with your colleagues) The claims that behavior is determined by unconscious thoughts and that personality is influenced by the alignment of astrological bodies are examples of untestable theories.

LAWS

After a time, the bulk of accumulated research evidence gathered from a variety of disciplines about conditions and events can lead to a formulation of a law. A *law* states that there is a regularity in the way something works, regardless of who, what, or where this event occurs. The formulation of a theory can emerge as a result of a scientist having a unique insight or as a result of being informed by the results of previous research and theories.

Laws are statements that express regularities. As hypotheses gain increasing empirical support, it sometimes becomes possible to subsume the research findings under a law. Laws do not address specific individual events. They are statements that are thought of as laws of nature or natural laws in the physical sciences. This type of statement says that a particular phenomenon will always occur if certain conditions are met.

In physics, one single law, the law of gravity, explains the falling and movement of all sorts of objects anywhere in the world. In psychology, Thorndike's law of effect states that learning is strengthened each time a response is followed by a satisfying state of affairs. So if hitting the TV makes the picture stand still, the viewer is likely to hit the TV. Similarly, a clinician trying a new technique is more likely to try it again if the first patient she tried it on acted favorably toward her when she used it. The Yerkes-Dodson law (also called the inverted U law) states that the best performance is obtained when the level of arousal is optimal for a given task. The optimal level varies for different tasks. For example, arousal needs to be *high* for a gross motor task but *low* for a fine motor task. For example, a high level of arousal is needed to play football, whereas a lower level of arousal is needed to thread a needle. It would be quite difficult for someone coming straight off a football field to be able to thread a needle without shifting down his arousal state.

All scientific endeavors aim to arrive at laws. A law is, in effect, a single rule that can be generalized to all events. Laws serve to provide a parsimonious description of all observations.

FURTHER READING

Breakwell, Hammond, & Fife-Schaw (2000) gives an account on theory in easy to understand terms.
Coolican (1996) presents a section on the types and meaning of hypotheses.
Richards (1987) is a useful source on laws and theory.
Schmidt & Lee (1999) offers a chapter on laws and theory regarding the topic of motor performance.

GRADUATE READING

Giere (1997) describes authentic accounts of early scientific discoveries.

7

The Scientific Method

Psychiatrists classify a person as neurotic if he suffers from his problems in living, and as a psychotic if he makes others suffer.

— T. Szaz, 1920

The scientific method can be thought of as a method for describing and explaining phenomena. Of course, there is nothing to explain about a phenomenon until it has first been described. It is commonly understood by philosophers of and educators in science that there are several scientific methods (Anderson, 1971; Gowers, 1997; Grinnell, 1992; Pannbacker & Middleton, 1994). Despite variation, there are some common agreements and shared rules about what constitutes a scientific method in the empirical sciences. In 1971, Anderson described five principles of the scientific method, and although the same ideas have been echoed by many other authors (Coolican, 1996a; Gower, 1997; Grinnell, 1992), Anderson's structure of these abstract ideas is useful.

The scientific method involves a set of rules for attaining goals in scientific research. These rules constrain how we describe and explain phenomena and are necessary to distinguish a scientific approach from other research approaches that characterize fields of study such as philosophy and pseudosciences (e.g., astrology, phrenology), alternative medicine (e.g., homeopathy, aromatherapy), and some cult movements.

THE FIVE PRINCIPLES OF THE SCIENTIFIC METHOD

The scientific method is a set of rules or standards that constrain and guide research to optimize the likelihood of arriving at a scientific understanding of the targeted event. The five principles of the scientific method encompass four principles for description and one for explanation:

- Empirical verification
- Operational definition
- Controlled observation
- Statistical generalization
- Empirical confirmation

Empirical Verification

The principle of empirical verification states that the investigator must provide evidence that there is a correspondence between what is described and what is observed in reality. This major principle of the scientific method states that a descriptive statement is regarded as true if it corresponds to observed reality. Observed reality is defined to mean observation based on sensation such as touch, smell, and hearing (but not intuition) and observations about which others agreed (and therefore not hallucinations). To satisfy the principle of empirical verification, the researcher must provide evidence that there has been a careful examination of the correspondence between a descriptive statement and reality. The objective of the investigator is to describe fully the conditions and process under which these observations took place. This minimizes any tendency to argue for the observed facts from authority or to guess what happened.

Example

If it is claimed that the labial sounds /p/ and /b/ are acquired by a child before the fricatives /f/ and /v/, then the investigator needs to provide evidence that

- The children do acquire these sounds.
- The order in which these sounds are acquired is as the descriptive statement claims.
- Independent observers have made the same observations and agree with the descriptive statement made by the investigator.

Operational Definition

The principle of operational definition states that the investigator is required to define all the terms of the operations involved in manipulating and observing whatever is under study. Operational definitions ensure that all observations are testable. Only testable statements are considered scientific. An operational definition can be thought of as a set of instructions like a recipe that describes what the investigator did and how he or she went about studying what he or she investigated. An analogy to help visualize this is to think of the common kitchen (i.e., the laboratory) and the problem of baking a cake. The recipe must be written with a set of instructions so clear that it would be impossible for someone else not to reproduce the same cake. These instructions operationally define the cake and must be so explicitly clear that we arrive at the result we desire (i.e., a chocolate cake and not chocolate fudge). To satisfy this principle, an operational definition should consist of a set of unambiguous statements that specify what will be observed and under what particular conditions. Complying with this principle ensures that the events that are observed can be shared with other observers because it forces us to communicate explicitly about what we witness to others. Without an operational definition, it would be very difficult for anyone to replicate a study. Take this descriptive statement:

Patients find it easy to say a word after a cuing phrase.

This statement is ambiguous because we do not know what is encompassed in the term *patients*. Does *patients* refer to all kinds or just one kind of speech-disordered patients (e.g., aphasic patients)? *Easy* is a relative term. Observers can disagree about whether an outcome came about easily for a given patient. A clinician who has seen many patients might, relative to all the patients she has seen, consider this particular performance to have been easily achieved by a patient. A less experienced clinician might think that the effort was too great and that the outcome was achieved with difficulty. To avoid ambiguity of the term *easy*, it must be operationally defined as "when there are more correct responses than incorrect responses in naming a picture after a cuing phrase". Furthermore, *Word* is also an ambiguous term. Are we talking about nouns, adjectives, adverbs, long words, short words, or monosyllabic words? A clear definition of the term *word* can be that it is "the target name of the picture". *Cueing phrase* also needs to be defined, and stating the name of the object pictured in the stimulus can state this.

Defining all the key terms of a descriptive statement described here ensures that the whole operation involved with patient naming is communicated without ambiguity. A check on whether a definition is operationally defined is to ask "Is there any room for disagreement about the intended meaning in this event or phenomenon?" If the answer is yes, then we have not provided an operational definition. It pays to remember that there are many terms that are difficult to define, even though many people think there is nothing terribly unclear about terms such as *correct, normal,* and *impairment.* There are events that defy good scientific definition. When something is not operationally defined, it can be difficult to study and communicate to other people.

Students often confuse the issues surrounding operational definitions with validity. It is important to remember that the whole purpose of defining something operationally is to be able to communicate explicitly to another person about events we have experienced. What we experience must accord with reality (i.e., it must be experienced in the sense of what we can touch, see, or hear). This is necessary so that what we describe can be measured or replicated by another person. The experiences defined must be public. For example, we may choose to describe someone of average intelligence as a person who scores an IQ of 100 or more on a test of intelligence. In this case, we are using the person's performance on a set of test tasks to define that person's intelligence.

Some people disagree with this very restricted sense of what it means to be intelligent. They may consider that intelligence encompasses more than just being able to perform of a set of tasks that happen to be called "intelligence tests." Another issue is that there may be a number of types of intelligence. Are there separate specialized types of intelligence for different skills (e.g., language, numbers, spatial appreciation), or is there a single mental faculty encompassing

FIG. 7.1. Operational definitions need not necessarily represent the true state.

all these skills? This kind of debate deals with the truth-value (i.e., validity) of what is intelligence. Despite these debates, we can define intelligence on the basis of an IQ score, even though such a definition of intelligence may be considered invalid (i.e., untrue).

To further illustrate this distinction, we can choose to define intelligence according to how long one can hold one's breath. As long as we can observe and measure the length of time one holds one's breath, we have an operational definition of intelligence in this case. Whether breath holding is an indicator of intelligence is another matter—a matter of truth or validity (see Fig. 7.1).

Controlled Observation

The principle of controlled observation states that it is necessary to demonstrate the evidence for a statement that claims "X causes Y" (e.g., sugar causes tooth decay). If sugar does indeed cause tooth decay, then we need to show that whenever the values on the variable sugar consumption change (sugar–no sugar), the values on the variable tooth decay (decay–no decay) change, too. We also need to show that no other variables besides sugar produce the observed result. So, we can only claim that sugar causes tooth decay when all other variables (e.g., diet, hereditary factors) have been discounted.

This principle relates to what Campbell and Stanley (1963) termed "internal validity." Anderson (1971) stated that there are five ways to control a situation so that one can discount the variables, that confound the claim that X causes Y:

- Experimental control
- Statistical control
- Assumed invariance
- Assumed irrelevance
- Randomization

Experimental Control.   Experimental control means that one variable is held constant while other variables are free to vary or are manipulated systematically in some way. Variables that do not change cannot produce changes on other variables, so holding one variable constant eliminates its effect on other variables.

Assume that someone claims that, after a course of speech therapy, a child improves in his ability to name objects around the house. What is wrong with this statement?

We all know that children, including disabled children, grow and mature. How can we exclude the possibility that the child's improvement was due to developmental maturation? The child might have had a developmental spurt just after therapy started. To be able to claim that therapy *and only therapy* was responsible for the child's improvement, we need to exclude maturation as the factor responsible for the child's improvement. Alternatively, we can express this relationship by saying that we need to demonstrate that therapy produced improvement in the child over and above normal maturation.

We can do this through experimental control. We need to build in a control task (i.e., a task on which the child is only measured before and after therapy, *without* involving treatment). Let's say you decide to treat a child's speech problem. You are an astute clinician and you are aware that the child will be developing all through the time he is in treatment with you. You may decide to use a spelling task as a control task (i.e., a task on which you measure the child's performance but you do not provide any therapy in spelling). If your therapy were effective, then you would predict that the child would show an improvement in his speech (brought about by therapy) but not in spelling because therapy was not directed at spelling performance. Three outcomes are possible:

1. If therapy alone has an effect, then we should see improvement only on the treatment and not on the control (i.e., untreated) task.
2. If therapy has no effect but maturation is present, then we should see an improvement on both the treated and the control (i.e., untreated) tasks.
3. If therapy has an effect and maturation has an effect, too, then we might see an improvement on the therapy task, but it might have a greater improvement level than the improvement recorded for the control (i.e., untreated) task (see Fig. 7.2).

Statistical Control.   Statistical control refers to using arithmetic for working out the probability of getting an observed result just by chance.

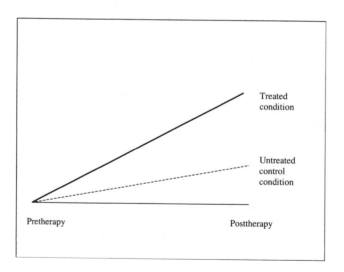

FIG. 7.2.   Therapy effect over and above maturation or recovery effects.

Let's say we do one procedure exactly the same way with 100 children. Sometimes we would record an improvement when it had really occurred, but other times, when nothing happened, we might still think the patient had improved. So we have several possible outcomes:

1. After therapy, there is measurable improvement, and the patient really has changed. (*True*)
2. After therapy, there is measurable improvement, but the patient really has not changed. (*Type I error*)
3. After therapy, there is no measurable improvement, and the patient really has not changed. (*True*)
4. After therapy, there is no measurable improvement, but the patient really has changed. (*Type II error*)

Assumed Invariance.   As the term *assumed invariance* suggests, the investigator neither measures nor controls the variable. One simply assumes that the variable is naturally unchanging or invariant. For example, we know that changes in temperature can affect a patient's level of comfort. However, if temperature changes normally vary minimally during the course of a treatment session or a research study, we can assume that the variable (temperature change) is functioning as a constant.

Assumed Irrelevance.   The term *assumed irrelevance* refers to a situation in which an investigator considers a variable to be irrelevant and so there is no need to control or measure it. In this case, it would not matter if this variable changed because, being irrelevant, it has no effect on what you are observing.

For example, if we were interested in assessing the effect of a metronome on the number of dysfluencies exhibited by a stuttering patient, then whether the metronome's wooden case was black or brown would be considered irrelevant.

Randomization.   Randomization is an important technique for controlling an extraneous or a confounding variable (i.e., one that confounds the statement that X causes Y). Often, when we cannot eliminate the influence of an extraneous variable, the next best thing to do is to distribute its effects. This is done in order to minimize the biasing effect it has on what we are interested in observing. The term for the distribution of participants to different groups without intended bias is *randomization.*

For example, we know that motivation can make a big difference in how an individual responds to therapy. A highly motivated patient will tend to achieve more than others because he or she practices more often, tries harder, and so on. If we were interested in comparing the effect of therapy X with a no-therapy condition, we would need to randomly assign patients, as they are referred to one group or the other. One group will receive Therapy X (i.e., experimental group), and the other group will receive no therapy (i.e., control group). Random assign-ment increases the likelihood (but does not guarantee) that highly motivated or apathetic patients will be distributed equally in both groups. In this way, we have minimized the possibility of motivation confounding the interpretation of the study's finding (i.e., that therapy improves patient performance).

Statistical Generalization

The principle of statistical generalization states that if you want to generalize findings to individuals or conditions you have not studied or treated, then your generalizations will be valid if the original observation is representative of the conditions you have not observed. Representativeness can be improved by mak-ing sure that there has been adequate sampling from the range of conditions to which you want to generalize your observations.

Generalization to unstudied or untreated conditions can be taken to mean generalization of the results of a study to different subjects (people), to different categories of words (grammatical categories of words), or to different social contexts (different environments). This principle relates to what Campbell and Stanley (1963) referred to as "external validity".

For example, say that a clinician, Jane, observes that John, after a course of therapy, is able to produce /s/ when it occurs in the initial position in a noun. No changes were measured on a control task. The highly specific nature of the therapy (i.e., John produces /s/ in the initial position and only in the context of single nouns, with Jane) means it would not be valid for Jane to claim that this therapy is effective with treating /s/ production in all classes of words. The same would apply to variations in location (e.g., home, clinic) or that every other clinician and other speech-disordered children would be able to use and benefit from this therapy. This is because the new conditions we are interested in were not represented in the original therapy study. The only valid claim Jane can make is that this therapy was effective in treating /s/ in the initial position in nouns in children like John.

To be able to generalize the finding of this therapy study to other conditions, it is necessary to demonstrate that John is able to produce /s/ in a variety of grammatical classes of words, at home, in the clinic, and with different clini-cians. To be able to generalize this therapy to other children, it is necessary for the clinician to demonstrate the same therapy effects in another child who may or may not have the same individual characteristics as John.

Empirical Confirmation

The probability of something being true increases the more times you can consis-tently predict the finding. The argument goes like this:

If A then B,
Not B,

Then, not A.
I predict that when there is A, there will be B.

Example

When John concentrates, he speaks intelligibly.

John is not intelligible.

Therefore, John is not concentrating.

I predict that when John is distracted, he will speak unintelligibly.

Although the example seems to suggest that A causes B (concentration improves intelligibility), there can be other reasons for John speaking unintelligibly (e.g., the sentence is too long, the sounds in the sentence are too complex to articulate easily).

So what must be done before we can conclude with a high degree of certainty that concentration does indeed cause improved speech intelligibility? Basically, the more successful we are in being able to predict an outcome of an antecedent event (i.e., that if John concentrates, his speech will become intelligible), the more we confirm our account of the relationship between the antecedent (concentration) event and the outcome (intelligibility) as being correct.

FURTHER READING

Coolican (1996) offers a brief commentary on empirical verification operation definition and a good example of controlled observation.

Halpern (1996) presents these topics within the context of hypothesis testing.

Lambert & Brittan (1992) offer on alternative source for reading about statistical generalization and empirical confirmation.

Polgar & Thomas (2000) provide brief but easy to follow accounts on empirical verification and operational definition.

GRADUATE READING

Grinnell (1992) provides an overview of all the principles of the scientific method.

Gower (1997) describes the scientific method.

8

Chance, Probability, and Sampling

What men want is not knowledge but certainty

— B. Russell, 1872–1970

CHANCE

It has often been said that only two things are certain in life: death and taxes. Everything else in life has a chance of either happening or not happening. Some-times things (e.g., going to work) happen with such regularity that it is difficult to think of these events being subject to chance. When events occur at chance (i.e., at random), most people find it very difficult to resist forming an association between the events. It is usual to think if two random events co-occur together, one caused the other, or at the two are related to each other in some yet-to-be-discovered way. In reality, the two events may be random i.e. there is no relationship. Halpern (1996) told a rather charming story from Munson (1976) to illustrate this:

> A farmer was travelling with his wife on a train when he saw a man across the aisle take something out of a bag and begin eating it. "Say, mister" he asked, "What's that thing you're eating?"
> "Its a banana," the man said. "Here, tryone."

The farmer took it, peeled it, and just as he swallowed the first bite the train roared into a tunnel. "Don't eat any, Maude," he yelled to his wife. "It'll make you go blind!" (pp. 277)

We can observe similar situations arising in clinical work. For example, a new computer exercise is presented to help develop John's written communication. After two sessions, the clinician observes that John has written more sentences than previously. She concludes that the computer exercise has caused John's written communication to improve.

You may wonder what could be wrong with this conclusion about John's written expression. After all, these are the types of conclusions we draw all the time in the clinic. There are several problems:

- There is no empirical evidence that this particular computer exercise has an effect on the patient's written communication.
- We have no basis for scientifically explaining why this exercise should have worked.
- John may have been improving spontaneously anyway, independently of the computer exercise. Hawthorne or placebo effects could also account for this outcome.
- It could have happened by chance (i.e., John's writing is variable up and down). He might have felt particularly good or highly motivated on the day.

PROBABILITY

Chance is commonly described in terms of probability in most statistics books. Probability is about likelihood and uncertainty. However, there are two nuances to the word *probability*: a mathematically derived figure such as a percentage or a fraction (i.e., objective probability) and a belief about whether an event will happen or not (i.e., subjective probability). In research, objective probability is used. Objective probability is mathematically derived, and probability estimates range from 0 (never happens) to 1 (always happens). If out of two events either event is likely to happen or not happen, then the probability of one event happening is .5, or 50%. However, when we express subjective probability, which is common in our daily conversations, we might say that he has a 50–50 chance of getting through an exam or the probability of getting the job is 80%. Subjective probability is based on personal estimates. Studies of human judgment guided by subjective probability commonly report that these judgments are highly fallible.

Fallacies in Probabilistic Reasoning

Research on probabilistic reasoning has shown that there are a couple common fallacies.

Gambler's Fallacy. Gambler's fallacy refers to a typical misconception about how likely an event is to occur. Let's say you and a friend go to the casino and play roulette. You keep a record of all the winning numbers over 2 hours, while your friend plays. Your record shows that the number 15 has not appeared as a winning number. So you advise your friend to bet heavily on 15 because you believe it has to appear as a winning number soon. Should your friend take your advice?

The answer is no, or you will fall for the gambler's fallacy. The roulette wheel does not have a memory of the numbers that have won, and neither does it have a basis for deciding which numbers should be selected on the basis of which numbers have or have not appeared before. So the chances of 15 appearing is no greater or less than the chances of any other number appearing.

Example

When people buy lottery numbers, many people prefer to select their own numbers rather than buy computer-generated numbers. They do this because most people overestimate how much control they have over uncertain events. In real terms, the probability of a string of numbers chosen by oneself and one generated by the computer is equal. Yet, people an encouraged to think that they can exercise some control over winning the lottery (a random event). When a lottery agent tries to attract customers, are advertises that it alone was associated with two or three major prize winners who bought their tickets at the agency's shop. It is worth remembering that the likelihood of the sequence 1, 2, 3, 4, 5, 6 is just as likely an event as the likelihood of 3, 8, 9, 13, 22, 40 showing up.

Nonrandom Streaks Fallacy. The fallacy of nonrandom streaks refers to people's misconception that winners keep winning and losers keep losing in gambling (i.e., a belief in "runs" of events). This gives rise to the notion of a run of bad luck or good luck. In reality, there is no greater or lesser likelihood of an event occurring again and again just because things have been going that way.

Suppose you feel you have been surprisingly successful in getting several dysphagic patients to resume swallowing again. You might be more inclined to accept a referral of a difficult patient because you have had a spate of good luck lately in getting these patients through their difficulties. Alternatively, if you have had a run of unsuccessful cases, you might be reluctant to take on such a referral. Although these cases are unconnected to each other, the fact that you have experienced a sequence of good or bad cases has left you believing that the next one is likely to be similar.

Rules About Probability

AND Rule. If two events are independent (i.e., either event is possible), then to work out the probability of both events occurring together, you multiply the probabilities of each event. For example, if the probability of an individual being speech impaired is .08 (8%) AND the probability of being blind is .02 (2%), then the probability of a person being both speech impaired and blind is .08 × .02 = .0016 (i.e., less than .1%—(a low rate of occurrence).

OR Rule.   If we were to ask what is the rate of occurrence for an individual to have either a speech impairment OR be blind? In this case, we have to add the probabilities together, that is, .08 (8%) plus .02 (2%) = .1 (10%). The likelihood of an individual presenting with one or the other disability is then higher than for two disabilities occurring together in the same individual.

The Role of Probability in Speech and Language Therapy Practice

Testing.   Say you give a patient a 20-item test on word meaning. Each test item requires the patient to answer yes or no. You score the test and find that the patient passed 9 out of 20 items. Can you conclude that the patient has some knowledge about word meanings? If the patient were to guess the answers to the questions, he would have 50% chance of answering the test items correctly. This is the case because he has to decide between only two chances—yes and no—and the probability of him choosing the right answer is 50%. On this basis we can say he will get 10 of 20 items correct just by guessing (i.e., by chance). So, if the patient correctly answers only 9 out of 20 items you cannot say that the patient has knowledge about word meanings. What if the test gives the patient a three-response choice? What is the chance level of correctly-responding to test items?

Understanding Patient Disorders (Base-Rate Neglect).   Base-rate neglect refers to initial or prior probabilities of an event happening. For example, you might believe that swallowing disorders lead to an increased incidence of pneumonia in patients. You find that the incidence of pneumonia among patients with swallowing difficulties is also 2% within the past year. However, when you survey a group of elderly people without swallowing disorders, you find that 2% of the group reported having pneumonia within the past year (i.e., the base rate). Consequently, before forming any ideas about the relationship between swallowing problems and their relationship to the risk of pneumonia, it is important to establish the base rate for these events. Typically, people focus only on patient-related events and forget to determine the incidence of this event in the general population.

Decision Making.   There is an approach to decision making that involves assessing the risks or outcomes of certain events happening. It is based on working out the probabilities of single events occurring. Some of this preliminary information about specific probabilities can be obtained from epidemiological studies or be based on pilot studies. This type of research is generally referred to as *decision theory* or *risk assessment* (Riegelman & Hirsch, 2000). Periodicals such as *Theoretical Surgery: A Journal of Decision Making in Surgery, Anaesthesia and Intensive Care* are devoted to this subject. Using this periodicals surgeons can work out what might be the risk or outcome of a 70-year-old alcoholic smoker having a cardiac bypass operation.

SAMPLING

When we decide to conduct an investigation, it is usual to gather a group of participants (i.e., a group of children with language delay, a group of adults with voice problems, a group of aphasics, a group of speech clinicians or speech therapy students).

How do we select whom we study? This is an important question because the process we use to select participants can inadvertently influence the results of our study.

There are two basic approaches we can use to select participants

- *Nonrandom sample*—This means we just study the group of participants available to us. It could be all the children with language delay in a given school or all the laryngectomy patients in a given hospital
- *Random sample*—There are different ways one can achieve a random sample, but for the sake of keeping things simple, only few ideas are described here. To obtain a random sample of speech therapy students, an investigator could select every third student from a list of names. Or, an investigator could put all the students' matriculation numbers in a bag, and without looking, select 20 numbers, each representing a student to be included in the sample. Or, an investigator use a random-number generator on a computer or a random numbers table. Let's say the random numbers range from 0 to 2. We assign a number to each student in consecutive order (i.e., 0, 1, 2, 0, 1, 2, etc). We put the list aside, and then read off the numbers generated by the random numbers table by taking down the order in which the numbers occur. So we might get 1, 1, 2, 0, 2, 2, 1, 2, 1, 0, etc. Next, we take the first students whose numbers match the ones on the list. We will have to skip over quite a few students, when their numbers don't match the ones on your list. We study only the ones we have selected.

How Investigators Deal with Very Large Samples

In surveys of households, it is not unusual to apply random selection procedures to the electoral register or telephone listings. There are inherent problems, though, as not everyone is listed in the phone book (e.g., because they have unlisted numbers) or the electoral register. This could introduce certain biases in sampling, which could influence the outcome of our study. So investigators of large-scale studies often have to check more than one source to ensure that the group they want to study is well represented in the source they are consulting.

The Reasons for Random Sampling

The main reason for using random sampling is to avoid systematic biases that could have an unwanted influence on the outcome of a study.

Let's say you're interested in studying a group (a sample) of language-delayed children aged 5 to 7 years. It is not practical for you to study *all* the 5 to 7 year-old children with language delay (i.e., the population), so you are going to select a random sample of these children. You want your sample to be as representative of the population as possible. This means that you want whatever characteristics appear in the population to be represented in your sample (e.g., social class, number of siblings, single mothers, premature and full-term birth histories). Why? Because you hope to be able to say at the end of your study that your results can be generalized to the population of these children.

Herein lies the dilemma. Random sampling procedures do not guarantee representativeness. At best, it *optimizes* representatives. So why do it? Mainly because these procedures provide objectivity in the selection process. Without random sampling procedures, the investigator would be forced to rely on his or her own judgment about who to include in the study. This judgment could reflect personal biases of the investigator that could jeopardize the study. Random sampling allows better generalization of results when the population under study is relatively *homogeneous* (i.e., individuals do not vary wildly from one another in important ways).

So, going back to the example of a study of 5- to 7- year-old children with language delay. What can happen when you are sampling from a population of these children? Suppose the population of children with language delay aged 5 to 7 years were represented in the circle shown in Fig. 8.1.

The population mean (which is usually not known to the investigator) is 4.5 years. This means that the children in the language-delay group have a level of language performance equivalent to a $4\frac{1}{2}$-year-old child. If the sample we select were to be representative of the population, then we would want the sample to have a mean comparable to the population mean (i.e., 4.5 years). But see what happens with sampling. The children in Sample 2 have a mean of 2.0 years, not 4.5 years. Similarly, the children in Sample 6 have a mean of 6 years.

We observe, though, that as the sample becomes larger, the sample mean is more comparable to the population mean, hence it is more representative. This is partly why many researchers have the view that large samples are better than small samples. But it is also apparent that sampling can result in a range of means, with some being close approximations of the population mean and some not. This effect increases if the population is very heterogeneous (i.e., where the

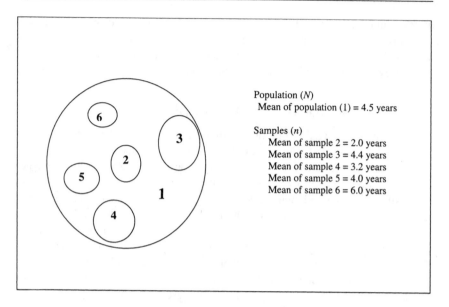

Population (*N*)
  Mean of population (1) = 4.5 years

Samples (*n*)
  Mean of sample 2 = 2.0 years
  Mean of sample 3 = 4.4 years
  Mean of sample 4 = 3.2 years
  Mean of sample 5 = 4.0 years
  Mean of sample 6 = 6.0 years

FIG. 8.1.   Sample size and representativeness.

individuals vary widely from each other in terms of their language-delay problems). A homogeneous population will correspond to less variation in sample
means. Figure 8.2 shows what happens in sampling.

In sampling a given population, it is possible to sample at either end of the
distribution of sample mean. You can see that a study based on such extreme
samples (e.g., mean = 2 or mean = 14) will not generalize to most of the children represented in the population (mean = 8). This is also why it is important in
research to replicate studies as a check on your study.

Sample Size

The size of a sample is important in deciding whether it is the right size to pick
up the true effect of the phenomenon under investigation. A phenomenon with a
very large effect will often need only a small sample to detect its effect. In contrast, a phenomenon with a genuine but small effect will need a much bigger
sample to detect its presence. Sometimes, investigators increase the sizes of their
samples in the hope that this will strengthen the ratio of the signal (i.e., event)
campared to the noise (i.e., contributions of ambient factors). Pilot studies can
also help with planning an experiment by allowing a researcher to measure the
size of the effect of a given phenomenon. This helps the investigator know
whether a given sample size is of the right size to detect genuine but small effect
sizes (Cohen, 1988). The capacity to detect a true effect is called *power*.

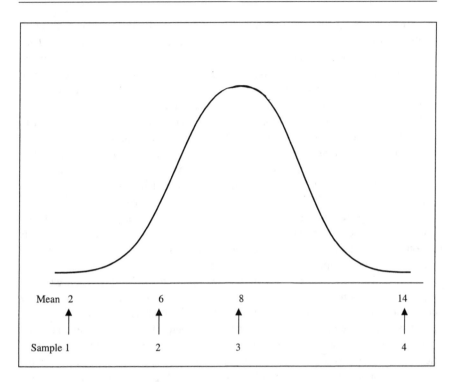

FIG. 8.2. Means of different samples taken from the same population.

Statistical Significance

The term *significance* has a special meaning in the research and statistics literature. It basically refers to a designated level—an alpha value or a significance
level—that determines the likelihood of an observed phenomenon happening
just by chance alone. It is conventional for a value of .05 to be the alpha value
(Tabachnick & Fidell, 1996). It is good if the statistic we calculate is lower than
.05 because this means that the likelihood of the event happening just by chance
is less than 5%. This is called *statistical significance*. The alpha value is an *arbitrary* value, and sometimes scientists might want to be more conservative, particularly if there is a possibility of risk or danger to the public. For example, a
group of scientists might have to decide whether to accept the results of a clinical
trial study which claims that the use of a certain drug is highly effective in de-
stroying tumours and therefore in alleviating some cancers. This is, however, a
controversial drug, quite apart from being a highly toxic drug. The scientists
therefore want to be very sure that these results did not arise simply through
chance factors or error. They select a very conservative alpha rate of .001 (rather
than .05) by which to decide whether to accept the results as being true. An alpha

value of .001 means that the likelihood of these results having arisen through chance factors could only happen in 1 in 1,000 cases which is much more stringent than .05 (5 in 100). Having established that the likelihood of these results being due to chance is less than .001, the scientists may proceed with confidence that they have a truly effective drug that they can consider in later studies in how many and what types of cancers can it help alleviate.

When we rely on a standard like .05 as the criterion for determining whether to accept the null hypothesis, we must remember that there is nothing magical about this value. There seems to be a trade-off between accuracy and convenience. The value .05 is convenient to use. We are, however, required to consider whether the distribution of the sample matches the distribution characteristics of the theoretical (hypothetical) sample. Those who calculated the values for the look-up statistical tables had to make certain assumptions about a hypothetical population distribution. If a sample's distribution characteristics match the characteristics of this hypothetical distribution, then the criterion .05 is likely to accurately reflect the probability value it represents. If the distribution characteristics of a sample and the theoretical distribution do not match, then we cannot really be sure about what .05 really means when applied to the sample. To resolve this problem, some people choose to generate their own theoretical distribution of statistical values on a computer, based on the distribution characteristic of their own sample. They can work out new probability values that take into account the unique distribution characteristics of the sample (see permutation statistics or Edgington's randomization statistics; Clements & Hand, 1985; Edgington, 1995). Others sometimes use a process called *transformations* as a way of mathematically configuring a sample's distribution characteristics to conform to the hypothetical mathematical distribution before they calculate statistics (Malim & Birch, 1997; Tabachnick & Fidell, 1996).

Some authors argue that the unquestioning adoption of an alpha value of .05 undermines the whole purpose of statistical tests (Cohen, 1988). Cohen considersed the size of effect to be the most important aspect of determining the significance of differences between samples. This refers to the fact that some samples have a small effect (i.e., of a difference between samples), and this effect may not manifest as a statistically significant result if the sample is too small for the size of the effect to reveal itself. Cohen described mathematical procedures for determining how large a sample should to be to be a fair test of whether there is a significant effect.

Clinical Significance

Sometimes a mismatch can give rise to what is commonly referred to as *statistical versus clinical significance* (see Figs. 8.3 and 8.4). The term *clinical significance* refers to the difference a treatment has on the patient's daily communication performance, referred to as *functional communication* (Chapey, 1994; Kazdin, 1978). In contrast, statistical significance simply provides a numerical

FIG. 8.3.   Clinical significance without statistical significance.

FIG. 8.4.   Statistical significance without clinical significance.

estimate of how likely it is that one could have obtained this particular pattern of results just by chance (Howell, 1997). Test designers usually design tests that are highly specific in what they are meant to do (i.e., content) and restricted in the, contexts where they can be used and how they can be used (i.e., standardization requirements; Anastasi & Urbina, 1997). The content can also be selected to conform with particular theoretical interpretations of speech and language processes (e.g., Kay, Lesser, & Coltheart, 1992). Consequently, tests tend to capture theoretically motivated behaviors that are easy to observe and measure and that generally consist of behaviors that can be executed in the clinic or in a similar environment. If statistically significant improvements were obtained on posttreatment tests without corresponding changes in the patient's ability to communicate in day-to-day situations, we would describe this test as having minimal ecological validity (Anastasi & Urbina, 1997).

One way to overcome this problem would be for test developers to include information about how performance on their test compares (or statistically correlates) with the person's ability to participate in day-to-day communicative situations outside the clinic. This information can be obtained only if the test developers undertook further investigative development work. There is no real need to directly assess or evaluate so-called functional communication behaviors directly if this information could be reliably inferred from clinic-based tests.

The converse can occur, too: The test can show no significant change, but the patient is reported by others to have improved in the extent to which his communication is functional and useful. There are a few reasons for how this situation could arise. The first refers to observer error. Clinicians who have put hours of work into trying to improve a patient's communication abilities are unconsciously motivated to selectively see behaviors that can be interpreted as improvement. Laypeople, family members, and friends are similarly susceptible to observer bias, as they are untrained observers compared to the clinician. Another reason relates to the sensitivity of the test. Sometimes, there really is improvement, and it is noticed by the various clinicians working with the patient, but this improvement fails to register on the test used. It is possible that the particular method for scoring the patient's responses or behaviors is too gross (e.g., 1 = *independent*, 2 = *a little dependent*, 3 = *dependent*). If a patient starts out with a rating score of 2, and months later, he improves to a rating of 3, the change may not be mathematically great enough to register that significant change has occurred, irrespective of whether the test measures functional communication skills. In other words, this is a range restriction problem (Anastasi & Urbina, 1997; Howell, 1997).

FURTHER READING

Coolican (1996) pp. 143–152.
Halpern (1996) Chapter 7 deals with probability very clearly using everyday examples.
Polgar & Thomas (2000) Chapter 17 covers probability and its calculation.

Shermer (1997) Chapter 4 offers a light-hearted account of probability within the context of paranormal events.

GRADUATE READING

Cohen (1988) provides information on power analysis.

Edgington (1995) introduces the rationale for permulation statistics.

Tabachnick & Fidell (1996) describe other variants to the alpha value of .05. See also Power analysis and Bonferroni method.

O'Hear (1984) offers another source on the topic of probability with a range of examples.

9

Describing and Measuring Events

Two men look out through the same bars. One sees the mud and one sees the stars.
—F. Langbridge, 1849–1923

After obtaining a sample of participants the next thing to do is to describe and measure the events in which the participants will become involved. *Subjectivity* refers to personal impressions or personal judgments, intuitions, or personal or private senses that cannot be shared (or observed) by anyone else. If an examiner, a researcher, or a clinician makes a subjective assessment of an individual, then we would hear judgments like this:

Examiner: "Oh, Susie comes to my class often. I think she is a conscientious student. She is an A student in my books."
Clinician: "I think Johnny (age 6 years) has a sentence comprehension disorder."

Subjective evaluations make it very difficult:

- To know which factors led to the assessor's judgment
- For another person to arrive at the same judgment because there is no common procedure for making this assessment

106

- To replicate the assessment in the same way at a later date.
- To minimize the influences of extraneous factors on observation and assessment.

Objectivity refers to descriptions based on the actual factual aspects of whatever we are observing without reference to the assessor's opinion or feelings on the situation or the object. If we take the preceding examples and render them as objective statements, we will have the following:

Examiner: "Oh, Susie has missed only one class. I say she is a conscientious student as she achieved an A in last term's exam paper."

Clinician: "Johnny (aged 6 years) failed the TROG test of syntax comprehension. His performance on this test was measured at 4.5 years, so he is performing below his age limit."

DESCRIBING EVENTS

Description is a major goal is social science research. Some events we study are covert (e.g., reasoning, speech processing), and other events are overt, or visible (e.g., head-banging behavior, the number of test pictures named incorrectly by an aphasic patient). To describe a particular situation objectively, it is necessary to be able to observe and measure it. The results of these procedures give us *empirical evidence* for the situation we studied. However, it is not enough to observe and measure events. To conduct true scientific observations, it is necessary to do these systematically, and methodically to obtain accurate recordings of what is observed.

As an example of an empirical investigation, if we want to know if the weather affects patient attendance, then an empirical study would involve contacting the weather bureau to obtain a record of all the working days when it rained or didn't rain during regular treatment times. Next, the clinician must count the patients' attendance on rainy and nonrainy days. If it is true that bad weather deters patients from attending the clinic, then we would predict that there will be fewer patients attending on rainy than on good-weather days. The observations derived from systematic recordings qualify these observations as scientific observations. The alternative would be to try to remember the rainy days when the patients did not come to the clinic, and this latter process would yield highly unreliable results.

Observer Expectancy Effects

Clinicians are human observers, subject to the problems of prejudice and expectancy effects like anyone else (i.e., they are prone to seeing what they want or expect to see). Observer bias was shown in a study where teachers were told to watch a group of primary school children, some of whom had been labeled as learning disabled, emotionally retarded, or mentally retarded. The investigators, Foster, Algozzine, and Ysseldyke (1980), found that the teachers all rated the children differently, depending on what each had been told about the children. Observer bias—observers being influenced by stereotyped beliefs about people and situations—is a well-known phenomenon (Coolican, 1999; Coon, 1998; Kearns, 1981; Rosehan, 1973; Rosenthal, 1966).

Whenever a clinician or an investigator wants to control for observer bias (i.e., to minimize its effects), one technique is to ask several independent observers to rate the same individuals. This is known as *interrater agreement* or *interrater reliability*. So, if interrater agreement is 90%, this means that 9 out of 10 times the observations of both observers on the same individual or the same event agree. Observer training can also often help improve the accuracy of measuring observations and for ensuring that more observers are interpreting events in the same way.

The Halo Effect.   A halo effect can be either a positive or a negative halo effect depending on whether the observer is favorably or unfavorably disposed toward the person or situation he or she is observing. Someone who is physically attractive and has fine facial features may be viewed as being more mature and intelligent than he or she actually is (i.e., positive halo effect). Someone who is short and stocky with broad facial features might be perceived as being more uninteresting and unintelligent than he or she really is (i.e., negative halo effect).

Another example comes from a joke told at the Edinburgh Festival by a group of comedian medics called Struck Off and Die. One of the medics told the audience that if anyone thinks he or she might be a candidate for a cardiac arrest, he or she should make sure to be attired well. They claimed that a study showed that paramedics took less time to attend to, and resuscitate a person with a cardiac arrest when the patient appeared in a suit than when the patient looked scruffy. The implication here is that some lives are worth saving more than others, denoted by clothing.

The Rosenthal effect.   Rosenthal (1966) showed that an experimenter's beliefs about how the results of an experiment should turn out had an effect on the data in many ways. A Rosenthal effect occurs when the observer has a preconceived idea about what he or she expects to see or expects might happen. This makes the observer become more sensitive to observations that fulfill those expectations and to be readily dismissive of observations that do not accord with those expectations. This effect is often explained to students in the context of a couple famous studies conducted in the mid-1970s in the United States (Rosehan, 1973, 1975). These studies occurred during a time when there was considerable debate about the meaning of madness and whether it could really be distinguished from sane behavior. Researcher Rosehan (1973) and a group of colleagues set about having themselves committed to psychiatric hospitals. Each researcher feigned one schizophrenic symptom, and 11 out of 12 of them were admitted to the hospitals they approached. These pseudopatients stopped acting after their admission, and they spent between 1 and 7 weeks in the hospital before being discharged. Although the staff did not detect the hoax, some patients did, informing the researcher that they thought the researcher was a journalist. The researchers reported that the treatment of patients, including themselves, involved alienation. Rosehan reported that the staff appeared to perceive the patients as nonpeople, as though they were invisible. Staff members discussed patients in front of other patients, a nurse unbuttoned her uniform to adjust it in front of patients, and one paid attention to Rosenhan's obvious recording and note taking, which the staff took to be a symptom of his illness. Staff ignored him, as they did many patients.

The reason Rosenhan offered for why the staff did not detect the fake patients was due to the fact they presented in the context of a mental ward. Because they were labeled schizophrenic, any odd behavior the staff observed was attributed to this condition. Rosenhan found these results incredible and planned a follow-up study. This time, Rosenhan advised the staff at the hospital that one or more pseudopatients were going to try to be admitted over the next 3 months. Among 193 "patients", 41 fakes were identified by at least one staff member, and another 19 were labeled as suspicious. These findings confirmed Rosenhan's original conclusion because he had not sent any patients or pseudopatients to the hospital.

This tale highlights the significant influence of observer expectations. In this case, the use of labels to communicate a person's disability carries a major social stigma that often prevents others from regarding the person beyond his disability. In clinical work, a parallel would be to label patients by disorder labels (e.g., "He's an aphasic," "He's a spastic"). Currently, this form of address is actively discouraged during training and in the publication of professional and journal literature.

A Rosenthal effect also arises when a clinician compares two treatments in a study and finds that the children treated with Brand X therapy did better than those who received Brand Y therapy. The clinician is happy with this finding because it demonstrates that she was right in thinking that Brand X therapy is more effective than any other form of therapy available. The problem here is that the clinician's belief in the potency of Brand X therapy will influence the way the clinician delivers the two therapies. It is very unlikely that she can be impartial and deliver both therapies with an equal amount of commitment and enthusiasm. The consequence is that children treated with Brand X will be more likely to return good results than those with Brand Y.

Unreliability in Observation.   Observers are human, so they are subject to factors like fatigue, distractibility, and boredom. The number of errors an observer makes can affect the accuracy of the conclusions drawn from a period

FIG. 9.1.   Appreciating interobserver agreement and interobserver reliability.

of observation. Consequently, it is important to use more than one observer to ensure that the observations are accurate (see Fig. 9.1).

Effects of the Observer on What Is Observed.   Often the presence of the observer interferes with what is being observed. In these situations, to minimize the effect of the observer those observed, it is often necessary to conceal the observer (e.g., behind one-way mirrors, by concealing recording equipment; Coolican, 1996b).

Participant Expectancy Effects

The Hawthorne Effect.   The Hawthorne effect was first reported in the 1930s by a group of researchers who were investigating the effect of different variables on worker productivity in an electric works company (Roethlisberger & Dickson, 1939). They manipulated variables such as working hours, lighting, and salary and found that these changes resulted in increased productivity, even when the changes resulted in reinstating the original working conditions. The researchers concluded that when the workers were conscious that they were the objects of attention, they were motivated to work hard. The increased productivity had little to do with the changes in working conditions. It is conceivable that in a clinic, a patient may report feeling improved, may be motivated to show improvement, or might think her child is much better just from being in contact with a clinician, from receiving attention, or from using technological equipment.

The Placebo Effects.   In a clinic, a patient may show improvement quite independently of the treatments the physician or the clinician applies to the patient's condition. The patient may seem to get better just from being in the situation of being cared. The result in this case is similar to the Hawthorne effect; it is the *placebo effect*. A placebo effect is said to have occurred when a patient, in a stable condition, shows improvement when no therapeutic intervention has been given. Often physicians or nurses can, themselves, become placebo agents (i.e., their presence, as well as perhaps the fact that they are wearing white coats; effects a change despite the fact that they have not done anything specific to treat the patient). In many drug trials where the effectiveness of medicines is tested, it is common to use sugar pills (i.e., placebo condition) as a substitute for the real drug. The patient would not know whether he or she received the sugar pill or the real drug. According to Harrington (1997), the effectiveness of placebos can range from approximately 21% to 62%; that is, 21% to 62% of patients may improve when they believed they are being helped or treated. The variation reflects the conditions being studied and the different methods used by investigators. The placebo effect is a very robust effect and it is claimed that it is most effective in studies, that investigate the use of drugs in conditions such as dermatitis and allergies. It is also thought to be highly effective with conditions in which the symptoms wax and wane or belong to an unknown condition. Placebo effects are thought to be least effective in chronic medical conditions and in conditions that normally show little spontaneous remission.

No studies have investigated the relevance of placebo effects to speech and language therapy. However, one could speculate what these effects might be on the basis of the guiding principles about optimal conditions for effective placebos. According to Harrington (1997), medical conditions that are optimal for giving rise to placebo effects seem to include conditions in which the patient is not so ill as to not get better and conditions that have periods of remission (i.e., are not chronic).

It is likely that the treatment of aphasia, learning disabilities, aural rehabilitation, and child phonological and language disorders would be resistant to showing placebo effects simply because these are enduring conditions. In contrast, conditions such as functional voice disorders, stuttering, transient dysphagic conditions, and psychological disorders might be more susceptible to placebo effects.

An argument states that it does not matter if the placebo effect, rather than a therapy effect, is responsible for patient improvement. What is important is that the patient has improved. The problem posed is twofold. First, as a scientific profession we cannot just accept that a placebo effect is at work because we need to be able to explain how it works. Second, it is difficult to explain how placebo effects work. So, why do we not exploit this effect more often? Why do we not make patients believe we are giving them treatment when in fact we are not? The major reason is ethics. Although it was once in the history of medicine accept-able to intentionally administer placebo treatments to patients, this practice is no longer regarded as ethical medical care (Harrington, 1997). It is unethical to "trick" a patient in treatment. In research, this can be circumvented if the patient is informed that some individuals will receive treatment and others will not. In that case, the patient understands the conditions of the research investigation and signs an agreement to participate on that basis. Therapy is different from re-search because the patient has faith or trust that the clinician will be administer-ing an effective treatment to help solve the problem.

MEASURING EVENTS

The following are some examples of events that are measured in speech and lan-guage therapy:

- How often the target behavior occurs (e.g., the frequency with which a child uses the past tense)
- How a patient perceives his or her speech problem (e.g., asking a stutter-ing patient to complete an attitude questionnaire)
- How many pictures a patient can correctly name
- The patient's ability to hear a signal tone
- The volume of the patient's voice
- Whether a patient has changed between two points in time on a task (e.g., before-and-after therapy).

Measurements taken must be accurate in order to lead to the right conclusion. The clinician should be alert to the following potential sources of error in measurement:

- Instrument error
  —Does the machine take time to warm up before working reliably?
  —Is the machine working reliably?
  —Is the machine correctly calibrated for what it has to measure?
- Observer error
  —Have the observers been trained for the task?
  —Are there independent observers to ensure the objectivity of the observations?
  —Is the presence of the observer interfering with the observed event or participant?

- Test design error
  —Are the tests designed to measure what they are used for?
  —Are the tests sensitive to measuring change?
  —Are the tests reliable?
  —Are the tests based on the various cultural background of the participants?

Reliability and Validity in Measurement

There are tests all around us. How do we differentiate between the quiz-type tests found in popular magazines and those found on the back of a cereal box from those in school or job interviews? What makes a test a good test? There are two questions one should ask about a test Is it reliable? and Is it valid? The following material is based largely on the work of Anastasi and Urbina (1997) and Cronbach (1990).

Reliability

For a test to be considered reliable, it should yield the same score or close to the same score each time it is administered to the same individual. A test that is unreliable is useless because we cannot distinguish between variability due to the patient changing (i.e., signal) and that due to the poor design of the test (i.e., noise; Anastasi and Urbina, 1997). If we were measuring a line, we would want our test to behave like a steel measuring tape. An unreliable test would behave like a measurement tape made of elastic (see Fig. 9.2).

Many clinical situations can give rise to unreliable measurements, and are often overlooked as potential sources of error. The following are examples of typical events producing unreliable measurements in the clinic:

- *Using Different presentation modes.* A clinician evaluated the patient for the first time on an audio recorded version of The Yabba-Sentence Test, but when she administered the test again 2 months later, she forgot to bring the tape recorder to the session, so she spoke the sentences to the patient. Speaking the sentences allowed her to modulate the rate of her speech in direct response to the patient, although she was not aware of doing this.
- *Altering the conditions of the test.* The clinician, feeling the patient's frustration and severe difficulty in understanding sentences spoken to him, slows down and repeats the sentence, often two or three times, until the patient comprehends what has been said. She marks these responses as incorrect, even though he eventually gets the right answers through this procedure. Months later, the patient is reassessed on the same test, but this time the clinician is expecting improvement and sensing that the patient is more relaxed with her, so she is disinclined to say sentences repeatedly until the patient comprehends the sentence. When the clinician compares

FIG 9.2.   Reliable and unreliable measuring tools.

the results from both test administrations, she proclaims that the patient
has improved because "although he has made about as many errors, the
patient required fewer repetitions."

- *Giving away clues.* The clinician tests the patient on an auditory-synonym
judgment task. Rather than use the tape recorder to present the test items,
she decides to speak them to the patient herself. After a while she notices
that the patient nearly always questions her after she has spoken the first
item (e.g., "Toast, is it?" or "Er...Brake...did you say brake?") before
she has the chance to present the second word in the paired sets of words.
She also realizes that although she doesn't repeat the word, she tends to
acknowledge his question by saying "Hmm" in a tone that suggests affir-
mation though sometimes, when he is clearly wrong, she does repeat the
word or she remains silent. She notices that the patient also looks hard at
her face for clues as to whether he heard her correctly. A week later, she
decides to reassess him as part of gathering pretherapy base-line data, and
of course, he gets a different result and she is not sure why. Did she say
"Hmm" less the second time?
- *Using Different locations.* The first time the clinician saw James, he was in
the classroom, surrounded by his friends. She was observing him to see
how often he initiated communication or made requests. A month later,

she thought she would reevaluate him, but this time, her busy schedule meant she was forced to observe him during playtime, when he was in the playground. She got different results between the two occasions. What could this mean?

- *Relaxing the test conditions.* When the clinician tested the patient the first time, she gave him full credit for any response that was close to the target response for each test item. She gave full credit for close sound errors, close semantic errors, and test items she repeated that he then answered correctly on a second or third attempt. Some months later, when she reassessed the patient, she assigned scores in much the same casual way and she obtained a similar score to that on the first test. Can she conclude that he has not improved? Will her scoring concessions allow her to recognize real improvement in the patient?

There are a number of types of reliability, as described in the following pages.

Test–Retest Reliability.   Test–retest reliability allows you to assess whether the change in the patient's score is greater than random fluctuations. If a test is poorly designed, the degree of change reported as being due to random variation (i.e., a low reliability correlation coefficient) will be too large to be useful in detecting real changes in the patient's performance. This can happen if the test consists of questions or pictures that are unclear and ambiguous. Poor-quality test items cause the respondent to vary considerable in the answers provided. A respondent's answers can vary from another person's, and a respondent's own answers can also vary from one testing occasion to another. A good reliability index has a correlation value around .9 (i.e., a shared variance between the first and second test of 80%). This means that if we know the patient's first score, we will be able to predict his second score with a high degree of accuracy (if we assume that the patient is in a stable state).

Interrater Reliability.   Interrater reliability allows you to assess whether different assessors will come up with the same results on the same patient. If a test is not well designed, it will be unduly sensitive to different assessors.

Intrarater Reliability.   Intrarater reliability allows you to know whether the same assessor, administering the test twice to the same patient (within a day or so), will yield the same results. A poorly designed test will be not clear enough in what it measures, such that the same assessor has too much freedom to read into the test what he or she will at the time of assessment (e.g., if the ratings of a rating scale are too poorly defined, for the assessor might select a rating of 2 one time and 3 the next). A low intrarater coefficient means there is too much variation due to the clinician being unreliable. The clinician will find it difficult to know whether the patient has really changed or the change simply reflects variation on the part of the assessor.

Split-Half Reliability.   Another check on test reliability is to split the test items in half (e.g., odd-numbered items versus even-numbered items) and compare the results of one half with the results of the other half. A high split-half reliability indicates that the two halves of the test are similar and they must be testing the same thing. Consequently, one half of the test could be administered in place of the whole test. This is also another way of demonstrating that the test items through the test are homogeneous (i.e., similar).

Parallel-Form Reliability.   Sometimes, a test may have parallel forms (i.e., two tests that are different forms of the same test). It is possible to use such tests to compare participants' performance on one form of the test with those on the other form of the test to see if they are equivalent.

An advantage of parallel forms over repeated measures with the same test is that practice effects are vastly reduced. When a second administration of one test is given, there is a confounding effect: one effect due to a change in treatment and another effect due to practice on same test items.

Often these indices are reported in test manuals. Unfortunately, many test developers of tests used in speech and language therapy have not taken steps to address the issue of test reliability, and so we often do not know if tests are reliable measurement tools.

Validity

Validity refers to whether a test is designed to measure what it purports to measure (Anastasi & Urbina, 1997). Anyone can put together 20 pictures, claim that it is a naming test, and use it to assess patients. We are unlikely to accept an optician testing a person's eyesight on the basis of test materials he draws or makes up on the spot in front of the individual. Why then, should we think it is acceptable for a clinician to make up a test in situ? One of the problems with so-called informal tests or homemade tests is that we are not sure what the items are testing. In the case of the informal 20 pictures test, the items may be measuring something other than whether the patient knows the name of the picture. This could inadvertently be a test of the patient's familiarity with the objects rather than his ability to name per se. A test designed to measure object names would need to control other factors (e.g., the familiarity of the objects).

A good test also provides test items that measure a range of difficulty levels so that patients do not find it easy to score top marks on the test (i.e., ceiling performance). A test that allows patients to score too highly (i.e., ceiling scores) is probably too easy. In this case, it is unlikely to discriminate different levels of ability among patients. Ideally, tests should be standardized, and the conditions under which this occurred should be made public via the test manual.

Concerns about validity also appear in typical clinical situations. As with issues related to reliability, naïve students often also overlook many situations that jeopardize the validity of measurement. The following are some examples.

- Failing to account for all the demands of a task. The doctor reviews all the patients on his list every month. James is an aphasic patient. To see if he has improved, and lacking a test to hand, the doctor grabs the nearest thing he can find—the telephone book—and asks James to read it. He later reports that James is not greatly improved as he still has problems reading the names listed in the phone book.
- Failing to account for all the demands of a task (again). The Raven test of the syntax comprehension. James is administered this test and he fails. The student concludes that James has a syntactic problem. The clinician reminds the student to analyze all the processing components that contribute to a successful performance on this task (i.e., vision, short-term memory, audition, meaning of words, knowledge of syntax). They later learn that James is very near sighted and was unable to see the pictures in the test clearly.
- Using wrong norms. The Yabba-Sentence test was initially designed to evaluate the performance of elderly aphasic people with 14 years of education and normed accordingly. The clinician working at the Bethesda Hospital used this test to evaluate young head-injured patients because there was nothing else suitable to test them. She realized that the younger patients were different from the older folks in terms of education, life experiences, and so on, but she didn't know how this affected their performance on the test.

There are a number of types of validity, as described in the following pages.

Concurrent Validity.   To establish that a new naming test is a valid test of naming, we could compare a patient's performance on the new naming test with his performance on an established naming test. If the new test is indeed a naming test, then the patient's performance will be very similar on both naming tests.

A clinician might, for example, want to use an American test with a caseload of British patients. If the American test contained words that British patients find unusual—such as pretzel, faucet, and wagon—she might replace these with more culturally relevant items for a British patient. She might also think that the norms do not apply to her caseload. In this situation, it would be appropriate for her to renorm the test on British people. The clinician would then administer the test items to perhaps 20 people in her local community and obtain British norms on this basis. Another example of when a clinician might want to design a new test is when the norms of a test apply to younger or older individuals than those targeted in the study.

Face Validity.   Face validity is a type of validity based on nothing more than the fact that the contents of a test look appropriate for what it claims to test. For example, face validity is satisfied if an assessment of a patient's outcome is based on questions about the patient's level of functioning and abilities in speech, physical activities, and activities of daily living. This is the least useful of all the types of validity.

Construct Validity.   Construct validity refers to whether a test measures what the researcher claims it measures. For example, a task that clearly measures the participant's verbal memory but is described as a test of spelling skills has a problem with construct validity. If a short-screening test can be shown to be highly correlated with a longer test of the same kind, then the screening test is said to have construct validity (i.e., it is measuring the same skills or knowledge as the longer test). In this case, we would be justified in choosing to use the short over the longer test because it has a high construct validity coefficient (or correlation index).

Internal Validity.   Often when we conduct studies, we try to isolate the variables that cause certain outcomes to occur. This is often quite difficult to achieve if a study is poorly designed or has many methodological problems. However, when a study can show a clear connection between two or more events (e.g., genetic status) and the outcome (e.g., speech problem), then we say the study has good internal validity (Campbell & Stanley, 1963).

External Validity.   It is important that the findings from a research study can be generalized to other people who were not participants in the study or to situations not covered in the study. If the findings can be generalized, then we say that the study has external validity (Campbell & Stanley, 1963).

The Relationship Between Reliability and Validity

The following quote by Einstein sums up the nature of the dilemma between reliability and validity succinctly.

> "As far as the laws of mathematics refer to reality, they are certain, and as far as they are certain, they do not refer to reality." (Cited by Capra, *1992*, p. *49*).

Every researcher has to balance the need to develop procedures that are highly reliable with maintaining their validity. If a procedure is highly reliable, then it may be too reliable to be a true reflection of the real state of events—so validity is lost. The converse can also occur. For example, a researcher might measure particular language behaviour of nonverbal communication in the clinic under highly controlled clinical conditions. This improves the chances of being able to replicate the same procedure and derive the same findings at another time. The more controlled the conditions, however, the less likely the conditions are to resemble the environment in which the patient has to use the communication. This raises the question of the validity of what has been measured of the patient's communication.

Validity Compromised in Practice

Sometimes, clinicians argue that a lack of time or an unwillingness to subject the patient to a repeat of a whole test justifies administering to patients small sections of a standardized test. But doing this invalidates the test because the test was standardized under conditions in which the whole test was administered to patients. If special situations are inevitable, then it would be preferable if the clinician made up short screening tasks to monitor the day-to-day progress of a patient for a given task. The clinician could then retain the use of the standardized test when he or she reevaluated the patient at the end of treatment on the whole test.

FURTHER READING

Anastasi & Urbina, (1997) pp. 109, 116–122, 139–164 in relation to tests, validity & reliability.
Coolican (1996) Chapter 3 on validity.
Coolican (1996) Chapter 5 on objectivity in observation.
Cronbach (1990) pp. 32–33 on objectivity in testing.
Kelly (1969) Chapter 4 and 6 in relation to assessment.
Malim & Birch (1997) pp. 46–50 on validity.
Payton (1994) on validity.

GRADUATE READING

Harrington (1997) presents a good overview of the meaning of a placebo effect in the introduction and in Chapter 1.

10

Types of Research

Experience is the name everyone gives to their mistakes.
—O. Wilde, 1854–1900

DESCRIPTIVE AND EXPERIMENTAL RESEARCH

Scientific research is sometimes described as being either descriptive or experimental research. It is useful to appreciate the distinction since research is not always motivated by hypotheses or theories or is it necessarily concerned with testing how particular conditions or situations affect the outcome of an event. The distinction is made thus:

- Descriptive research is used to describe events.
- Experimental research is used to test theories or hypotheses by manipulating events to observe the effects.

120

Example

Early studies focused on describing events or conditions associated with sudden infant death syndrome, or cot death (e.g., contact with animals, material of bedding, maturity of baby). The next factor implicated in cot death was the posture of the child. Until then it was always considered desirable to have the child lie in a prone posture to minimize the risk of asphyxiation caused by swallowing regurgitated milk. Lying in a prone posture was positively correlated with the incidence of cot death. So it was concluded that the child's sleeping position might be a contributing factor to cot death, although no one was quite sure how. Now, it is fashionable to lay a baby on his or her back as this is now considered to carry less risk in regard to causing cot death. *(Descriptive research)*

Clinical Example

Early studies described the ages when children typically produce specific speech sounds in response to a speech-elicitation task. The investigator systematically recorded the children's speech and was able to say that the order of the first sounds acquired by normal children are the labial sounds /b/, /p/, and /m/, followed by the sibilant sounds /s/, /z/, and so forth. *(Descriptive research)*

Descriptive Research

We do descriptive research in a number of cases:

- Usually, when we do not know enough about something to be able to say which variables are relevant or which factors are important in regard to a particular phenomenon.
- When we simply want to know when events happen and/or the circumstances or antecedent conditions leading to when these events arise.
- When we want to generate hypotheses for testing later in more formal studies.

We conduct descriptive research by making systematic observations under controlled conditions and describe what we observe. No theories or hypotheses are tested. There is no need for interpretation; the minimum requirement is a statement that describes what was observed and the conditions under which these observations arose. Descriptive studies can provide a rich basis for speculation that can lead to the development of theories or hypotheses that are subsequently tested under experimental conditions.

Experimental Research

Experimental research has several characteristic elements:

- A theory or a hypothesis is posed.
- A statement specifies the predicted outcome of the experiment.

- The experimental task and procedures are listed.
- Independent variable(s), the variables the investigator will manipulate (or vary), are described.
- Dependent variable(s), the variables the experimenter will measure to assess the effect of the independent variables, are described.

For example, a research clinician might be interested in the effect of specific attributes of words and how they affect reading performance in a brain-injured adult who has lost some ability to read aloud.

The following terms associated with experimental research are described in relation to this example:

- *Theory*—Words encountered often and that are easy to picture in one's mind will be read more accurately than infrequently occurring, abstract words.
- *Hypothesis*—A brain-injured adult will read high-frequency and highly imageable words more accurately than low-frequency and low imageability words.
- *Experimental task*—A list of 30 printed words consisting of high- and low-frequency words and high- and low-imageability words.
- *Independent variables*—Word frequency and word imageability.
- *Dependent variables*—Reading accuracy and time taken to read the word.

The idea behind formulating predictions in experiments is that if the experimenter can reliably predict the individual's performance, given particular antecedent conditions, then the experimenter is closer to discovering or understanding the conditions that result in the individual finding some words easier to read than others. This is still a long way from being able to say what causes the individual's reading problem, but it is a good start to getting to the heart of what is causing or affecting the reading of words.

Experimental research is often linked with the term *quantitative research*. This association can be traced back to the traditions of basic or natural scientific research (e.g., physics, chemistry), though these methods are also used in other disciplines (e.g., medicine, psychology, education; Lambert & Brittan, 1992). The idea of quantification arises because in this type of research events are measured to allow them to be described objectively and calculations (e.g., statistics, mathematical equations) are derived as a way of testing or expressing relationships among the relevant factors. Quantification is also one outcome of a particular perspective on research that is shared by all the so-called quantitative research fields. This perspective is known as *positivism, realism,* or *rational* science (Palys, 1997). These ideas are easier to grasp when explored within the context of distinguishing between quantitative and qualitative approaches to research.

QUANTITATIVE AND QUALITATIVE
RESEARCH

Quantitative research is typically associated with fields such as physics, chemistry, biology, and biomedicine, and with some branches of psychology (e.g., experimental psychology). Other fields such as speech and language therapy and physiotherapy have acquired the characteristics of quantitative research largely because they inherit knowledge founded on the research efforts of more primary fields (e.g., medicine, biology, psychology). Fields that are characterized by qualitative approaches are sociology and anthropology, and some fields incorporate both approaches and give rise to branches of study (e.g., linguistics, sociolinguistics, social psychology, counseling psychology, evolutionary psychology). In speech and language therapy, interest in qualitative research is usually linked to the study of sociological perspectives of communication, resulting in the adoption of methods such as conversation or discourse analysis.

Textbook descriptions of research tend to present and describe various approaches to research as dichotomous categories (e.g., descriptive versus experimental research, qualitative versus quantitative research, single-case versus group research). Such a characterization of research tends to persuade the reader toward thinking that researchers work in either one or the other tradition. This perception does, however, have some basis in reality because many investigators show a preference for one perspective or approach to research over another. Some investigators are happy to work with both approaches.

Many investigators prefer to work within a community of like-minded individuals, who affirm each other's views and simultaneously distrust the methods of those who work outside this community. Kidder and Fine (1987) referred to the relationship between qualitative and quantitative researchers with a hint of amusement. They noted that quantitative researchers perceive their objectives in terms of seeking "numerical precision" and that qualitative researchers spend time "naval gazing." In contrast, Kidder and Fine said, qualitative researchers perceive their data as being "rich in detail," and quantitative researchers are "number crunchers." Terms like *hard science* and *soft science* also tend to capture this distinction, though these are commonly used to distinguish between the physical sciences and the social sciences, respectively, rather than quantitative or qualitative research.

The "touchy-feely" qualitative researchers and the "cold, clinical, heartless" quantitative researchers are common stereotype images that, like all stereotypes, foster prejudice among researchers about the motivations for research. The distinction between quantitative and qualitative research is not so superficial, however, as to be simply about an investigator's personal tastes in research. Rather, the distinction is based on very deep epistemological or philosophical divisions related to what constitutes fact, truth, knowledge, and how one should investigate a problem to establish these. Unfortunately, these topics are usually absent in the texts read by speech and language therapists and students. These texts tend to focus solely on the methods or procedures of data analysis (e.g., experimental design, statistical analyses, participant observation, discourse analysis). Clinicians or students have limited opportunity, therefore, to appreciate the philosophical distinctions underlying the various research methods (quantitative or qualitative) presented to them.

To understand quantitative and qualitative research, it is necessary to comprehend one major fundamental difference between these two research camps: what should define truth and reality and how one investigates a problem in search of new knowledge.

Basically, qualitative research exists as a direct expression of a reaction to the *naturalistic* position on the study of human behavior (Salmon, 1992). They adopt a *nonrational* philosophical position toward the study of human behavior. This position refers to the nonacceptance of John Mill's claim that all human behavior can be studied as is done in the science of physical objects (Robson, 1996). In other words, qualitative research is a reaction against the *rational*, or *positivist*, view that human behavior can be reduced to and explained by a few axiomatic principles (e.g., the law of gravity) in the same way that all physical events in the world can be explained. One of the best examples of the positivist position is Darwin's theory of natural selection, which illustrates how our knowledge of human behavior was advanced when humans were regarded along the same plane as animals. The qualitative researcher believes that it is not possible to understand human behavior without also taking into account the participant's perceptions or understanding of events because these perceptions may in themselves contribute to the participant's experience and therefore cause of events.

The following information on quantitative and qualitative research is a very simplified version to suit the novice research reader.

Quantitative Research

The Nature of Quantitative Research

Origins.   Quantitative research has a long philosophical tradition, dating back to Aristotle, though its modern form owes its existence to the ideas of scientific thinkers in the mid-19th century. The significant advances of scientific knowledge in the natural or physical sciences (e.g., physics, chemistry) were attributed in part to the methods used in their investigation.

The Model Adopted in Research.   The scientific success of the natural sciences forged a template for the investigation of all manner of things and event. This template is known as the *natural science model* (Palys, 1997). Advocates of the natural science model hold the view that everything, including human behavior, will ultimately be explained and understood in the same way that the natural sciences have been explained.

Philosophical Position on Truth and Reality.   Quantitative researchers adopt an epistemology position on truth and reality that is known as *positivist realism*. Positivism is a view of the world which says that the world consists of real events that behave in a precise, certain, and useful way. Realism refers to a perspective that says there exists a reality that can be sampled, studied, and understood. The positivist's task, therefore, is to study the facts and discover the principles governing these facts and causing them to behave in a lawful way (Palys, 1997). In traditional positivist research, researchers collect data, measure it, conduct statistical analyses of the data, and report the results of the analyses. The cumulative results of research can generate laws or theories that should ideally be able to explain everything from the most awe-inspiring event (e.g., why a 500-passenger airplane stays up in the sky) to the most trivial event (e.g., why my hair flies in the wind). In regard to studying human behavior, positivists would argue that human behavior is also explicable through methods and laws that so usefully explain physical events in the world (Davidson, 1980; Denzin & Lincoln, 1998).

Causation and Objectivism.   Four main criteria are associated with positivism: internal validity, external validity, reliability, and objectivity (Denzin & Lincoln, 2000). These four criteria basically answer questions on causation:

- *Internal validity*—Does Event A cause Event B to happen?
- *External validity*—Can I apply the findings of my study to people or events I did not actually include in my study?
- *Reliability*—Do I consistently get the same results?
- *Objectivity*—Is this information factual and verifiable by others?

The search for objective truth (objectivism) requires that things exist and are defined independently of personal experience. The positivist observer is dispassionate about, or detached from, what is being observed. Knowledge, if it is to be depended on, should not rely on what an individual feels or has experienced (e.g., subjectivity; Punch, 1998). Extreme positivists maintain that it is possible to understand events without involving the participant's views or inner experiences. They observe the antecedent events and the outcome on behavior. This early perspective on human behavior was the founding basis of behaviorism.

Aggregated Representativeness.   Quantitative researchers typically seek to discover how typical (or average) events work. To achieve this, they aggregate (or pool) everyone's data to derive a general pattern or trend. Anyone with extremely high or low values (or scores), at either end of the average, is thought to cancel out others' extreme effects, leaving scores representing the average general trend. Palys (1997) referred to this process as the *nomothethic analysis*. Researchers working in this tradition would hold that it is important to study people who are representative of the majority of the population and to exclude minority groups or unusual individuals from the research (Denzin & Lincoln, 1998).

Types of Reasoning Applied in Scientific Research. Deductive reasoning is the preferred style of argument in quantitative research. The idea is that ideally, one starts out with reliable, factual premises from which one can deduce certain outcomes (or predictions). Predictions are very important in this type of research because the more reliable one's predictions become, the more likely it is that one has understood the factors responsible for causing the event to occur. Typically, a theory or hypothesis is proposed that lends itself to formulating specific predictions about how events would turn out if the theory were true. The theory or hypothesis is tested, and in order to test the isolated effects of some particular condition, all other irrelevant or distracting events are kept to a minimum. Hence, quantitative researchers prefer experiments conducted in laboratory conditions where these distractions are kept to a minimum.

Qualitative Research

The Nature of Qualitative Research

Origins. It is claimed that the first questions raised about the nature of humankind occurred when the great expeditions to the New World discovered new societies, races, and social and cultural practices of tribes and communities unknown to the West. The discovery of such variation among people and their societies and customs posed a problem for Old Testament accounts of humans that claimed the creation of man by God (Denzin & Lincoln, 1998). These questions are identified with anthropology, and anthropology is often identified with the inception of qualitative research as its researchers are interested in answering questions about everyday situations in foreign settings, particularly events related to cultural practices and to social customs and their influence on human behavior and organization (Bernard, 1998; Richardson, 1996). The origins of qualitative research, therefore, lie in the history of sociology and anthropology.

The Model Adopted in Research. Unlike quantitative researchers, qualitative researchers choose to work from a humanistic perspective (Polgar & Thomas, 2000) or a phenomenological position (Palys, 1997). *Phenomenology* is the idea that people (researchers and participants alike) can never directly experience an event without also bringing to the situation their own personal experiences. Qualitative researchers who adopt an extreme expression of phenomenologism would focus most of their research efforts on studying people's perceptions of events. They view people's perception as possessing its own reality as well as being able to influence how reality is perceived. Philosophers would, of course, argue about whether it is possible to have a reality independent of one's perceptions. One consequence of phenomelogism in qualitative research is the notion of constructing the participant's reality, called constructivism.

Philosophical Position on Truth and Reality. In contrast to quantitative research, the qualitative research definition of reality in anchored in phenomenologism—reality from the point of view of the experiencer (e.g., participants, researchers) and the effect that the experience has on events. As described later in this chapter, qualitative research varies in how close researchers seek to be to their participants in an effort to access their participants' realities or perceptions.

Verstehan and Constructivism. In quantitative research, great importance is attached to researchers remaining detached from the events they study. This helps minimize any possibility of the researcher influencing the outcome of the study or the results. In contrast, qualitative researchers who lean toward phenomelogism attach importance to getting involved with the people they study because they want to discover how that individual's sense of reality is constructed (Palys, 1997). *Constructivism* holds that things have meaning through the personal experience of the researcher or the people one is interested in studying in relationship to the event. Crotty (1998) captured the essence of constructivism by stating

> All knowledge and meaningful reality is contingent upon human practice, being construed in and out of interaction between human beings and their worlds, and developed and transmitted within an essentially social context. (p. 42)

To achieve verstehan, the researcher does need to get close to or be intimate with the participants to get to know them and to learn how they feel and think about matters. The state in which a researcher thinks he or she can see events through the eyes of the participant (i.e., can empathize) is identified in German as *verstehan* (Schwandt, 1998). Acquiring a state of *verstehan* is taken to mean that the researcher understands the conditions and the participant's reactions to them from an inner rather than from an outer perspective. Extreme expressions of verstehan could involve the researcher being or emulating the people he or she is attempting to research. For example, if a researcher wanted to learn about how society regarded elderly people, the researcher could disguise herself as an elderly person and conduct her life as that person for some months to see how she would be treated by those she met in the course of her daily activities. The goal in qualitative research is to achieve *verstehan*, whereas in quantitative research, understanding is thought to emerge when the researcher is able to predict to a high degree of statistical probability that a given set of conditions would lead to particular events occurring.

For example, if an observer merely observes an action, such as, "A patient with aphasia puts his hand over his mouth occasionally during conversation," we cannot tell just by observing this action whether the patient

- Is gesturing that he cannot speak.
- Is covering his mouth through embarrassment.

- Thinks he has halitosis.
- Is a cultural practice when speaking to people in authority.

In other words, to identify the causes and explanations of this patient's behavior, it is argued that we need to do more than observe. We need to inquire into the person's motives, culture, and history to discover the reasons for his behavior. This inquiry leads to a construction of the patient's reality.

Aggregated Representativeness. Qualitative researchers can go further and reject positivism altogether. Researchers working at this end of the qualitative research continuum are often investigating social research problems (e.g., oppression, emotionality, ethics in caring, personal responsibility). They reject the criteria of positivism and often include in their studies social groups that positivists might exclude in a bid to make their studies more representative of the population at large. Postmodernists are therefore more likely than others to include minority groups (e.g., gays, ethnic minorities, disabled individuals) in their studies. They seek to investigate social problems from several perspectives. For example, if oppression were the subject of study, then the postmodern researcher would consider oppression from the viewpoints of various ethnic, racial, gender, social class, language, and other minority groups and how these all contribute to the experience of oppression (see Fig. 10.1). Unlike many quantitative researchers, qualitative researchers do not subscribe to this method of aggregating data. They hold that grouping people and referring to their behaviors

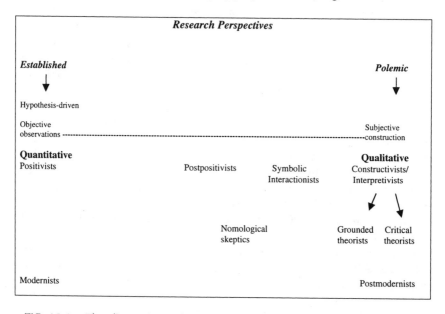

FIG. 10.1. The dimensions of quantitative and qualitative research along a continuum.

through numbers and mathematical models creates a distance between the researcher and the participants to the extent that it invalidates the essence of what it being studied (Palys, 1997).

Types of Reasoning Applied in Research.   Quantitative research favors deductive reasoning. In qualitative research, there is a great tolerance of arguments based on inductive reasoning. This is particularly evident with qualitative researchers work from either or both positions of being grounded theorists (i.e., data, not hypothesis-led investigations). Working inductively is associated with pretheory investigations. Instead of having a theory available to guide the overall interpretation and accounting of the data, the researcher studies each participant individually. The issues of generalization are not high priority until it is time to start trying to reconcile all the data into a theory (i.e., build rather than test a theory).

Qualitative research basically refers to the adoption of a nonrational philosophical position in regard to science. A rational position posits that all human behavior can be studied as is done in the science of physical objects. The qualitative researcher believes that it is not possible to understand human behavior without also taking into account the participants' perceptions or understanding of events because these perceptions may in themselves contribute to the participants' experiences and therefore, to causes of events.

Forms of Qualitative Research

There are various forms of qualitative research (e.g., interpretivism, symbolic interactionism, nomological skepticism, critical theorism, grounded theorism, postmodernism), but they all share a common epistemological (i.e., philosophical) position. The different schools known by unique labels can be confusing to outsiders. The following text explains some of the most commonly encountered terms in qualitative research. Figure 10.1 helps illustrate relationships between quantitative and qualitative research and within schools of qualitative research.

Interpretivism.   Interpretivism is basically synonymous with constructivism. Proponents of this view claim that explanations of human behavior are structured differently from explanations of the behavior of physical objects (Collingwood, 1994; Weber, 1962). They claim that actions are the result of reasons (or intentions), not of causes. Consequently, they argue that it is very difficult to appreciate what is happening in an event or to explain why it happened simply by observing only the outer aspects of the event. To make sense of the event, they argue that it is necessary to pay attention to the context of the environment and to see what people are expressing when engaged in the action (*verstehan*). This is because people bring to a situation a history that may bear on events. Interpretivists battle with the conflict of wanting to be objective about subjective events.

Interpretivists subscribe to the ideas of phenomenology, but they vary among themselves as to how strongly they hold to the idea that human actions result from reasons and not from causes. Critical theorists totally deny that there can be any explanation of human behavior in terms of laws. In contrast, nomological skeptics accept that there can be causal laws governing human behavior, but they do not believe these laws will ever be found in the same way as those in the physical sciences (Salmon, 1992).

Symbolic Interactionism.   Researchers who work from a social inter-actionism perspective subscribe to the ideas of interpretivism, but they go one step further. They argue that it is not sufficient to imagine someone else's point of view (Blumer, 1986; Charon, 1998). Rather, they say, it is necessary to see the action of the event (i.e., observation) and to be able to faithfully represent these observations. Observations accord a dimension of reality to the experiences of those they study. To represent what they observe, these researchers rely on ob-serving dialogue between people. Language and its use are taken to symbolize the perceptions and experiences of those they want to study. The methodology used by symbolic interactionists to study dialogue and interaction is derived from ethnography (borrowed from anthropology). Symbolic interactionism has itself given rise to another methodological position, known as *grounded theory*.

Grounded Theorism.   Advocates of grounded theorism generally argue that research should initially proceed without being guided by theories or hy-potheses (Glaser & Strauss 1967; Strauss & Corbin, 1999). Theories and hypothe-ses constrain the investigator's inspection of the data and also constrain which aspects of the data are taken as evidence for or against the hypothesis. The inves-tigator approaches the situation and collects data either through observation of the situation or through interviewing of the people under study. The data are then examined for interesting features or trends; in other words, the direction the researcher takes in the study is guided by the data rather than by any overriding theory or hypothesis about what one should be looking for in the data. Grounded theorists, therefore, approach data *inductively*. They steep themselves in the data, hoping to discover interesting trends. When they find something interesting, they consult the literature in an attempt to reconcile their observations with existing theories. If the data cannot be accounted in this way, the researchers might then propose a new theory or hypothesis on the basis of what the data show. In this way, the new theory is firmly "grounded" in the data. An investigator working from the specific to the general (i.e., works from the data back to a theory), is known as an inductive approach (Robertson, 1999).

Critical Theorists.   The term *critical theory* refers to questions about ideology (Horkheimer, 1995; Tallack, 1995). It originated in Germany during the 1930s. Critical theorists are concerned with power, culture, and ideology. Re-searchers working within this realm are concerned with asking questions about the relative power relationships between people and ideology. They are largely interested in how some groups of people are able to hold and maintain power over others. Critical theorists are also interested in how power is represented in a social culture and how it dominates and oppresses weaker members of society. They study the structure of language and how it is used to marginalize, dominate, and oppress people. Common themes within critical theory research involve looking at behavior such as sexist language, racist language, and language that oppresses or trivializes people and their problems. The common policy changes in language to produce "politically correct" labels in referring to disabled people touches on this particular issue. For example, the term *people with aphasia* is preferred over *aphasic people*, and *specific learning disabilities* is preferred over *mentally retarded*. People embracing a critical theorist's point of view would also advocate empowerment (i.e., empowering people toward the emancipation of themselves; Brown, Bayer, & Brown, 1992; Charlton, 1998; Fenton, 1989; Holdsworth, 1991).

Modernism and Postmodernism. Modernism is an ideological conceptualization of truth in terms of objective truth derived by means of logical scientific argument and explanation. The evolution of modernist ideas on truth and reason can be traced to Galileo in the 16th and 17th centuries. The idea is that there is a lawful relationship between events (e.g., in economics, in culture, in society) waiting to be discovered by scientific methods of observation, measurement, and explanation. Modernists have faith that science will deliver the answers to solve problems afflicting humankind.

In contrast, postmodernism challenges traditional conventions of how truth is defined. The postmodernist is skeptical about science and its promise of answers and solutions. This view holds that many methods are possible in the search for truth and suggest that advocates of a single method are concealing sinister motives such as political interests and power over society. Researchers working from a postmodernist perspective are prepared to accept multivarious perspectives in determining reality and truth based on people's experiences. A postmodernist doubts all previous approaches and argues that there can be no universal theory or approach that can deliver authoritative knowledge (Denzin & Lincoln, 1998).

Postpositivism. A *postpositivist* researcher is a qualitative researcher who incorporates research methods from both quantitative and qualitative research approaches.

Other Meanings of Qualitative Analysis

Qualitative analysis sometimes refers to analyzing data qualitatively even though the data are collected from a controlled study (e.g., using a survey questionnaire). It is important to distinguish between the uses of the term *qualitative*. For example, a researcher or clinician might be interested in examining the quality of a patient's errors and therefore provide a qualitative description of these responses. However, this interest in the quality of a patient's responses is not qualitative research in the same sense as, say, analyzing a patient's perception of his performance and what meaning the patient accords to this experience.

Multivarious Methods of Qualitative Research

A doctoral student in a research methods course was struck by how many "long, complicated words" appeared on the subject of qualitative research. This impression is partly created by the fact that various concepts expressed in qualitative research are subject to the influences of moderate to extreme schools of thought in qualitative research. As suggested by Punch (1998), qualitative research is really an umbrella term for a wide range of data collection and observation methods. Denzin and Lincoln (1998) summarized qualitative research as

> multimethod in focus, involving an interpretive, naturalistic approach to its subject matter. This means that qualitative researchers study things in their natural settings, attempting to make sense of, or interpret, phenomena in terms of the meanings people bring to them. (p. 3)

The nature of what was observed by anthropological researchers led them to use methods of observation and analysis that captured those situations rather than, say, using the methods of laboratory experiments. The methods used by anthropologists are sometimes referred to as *ethnographic* methods and have been adopted in other fields, such as social work (Riessman, 1993), education (LeCompte, Preissle, & Tesch, 1993; S. Wilson, 1977), nursing (Street, 1992), and linguistics (Gumperz & Hymes, 1986). Among these fields, sociology is one that draws largely on qualitative research methods. Its various methods of inquiry include interview, autobiographical account, case study, ethnography, personal experience, interactional, historical, participant observation, and introspection (Denzin & Lincoln, 1998). Only two methods are described here, to give the reader a flavor of the qualitative research procedures.

Ethnography.   One feature of ethnography is the investigator's suspension of his or her normal understanding of events (Werner & Schoepfle, 1987). Every situation is approached as though it were being seen for the first time (i.e., anthropologically strange). The investigators explore social phenomena and prefer to work with unstructured data (i.e., data that has not been coded into a closed set of categories). Ethnographers are also required to make an assumption that the group of people being studied share a cultural norm or meaning, and this norm underlies the behavior of individuals or an individual in the group. The task of the ethnographers is to discover what this shared cultural meaning is and how it affects the behavior of individuals. Ethnographers approach their research by observing individuals systematically. In this respect, ethnography is similar to naturalistic observation. Ethnographers, however, also engage in analyses that involve explicit interpretation of the meanings and functions of human actions, usually through the analysis of verbal descriptions and explanations. Sometimes, it can be useful to adopt this approach before planning an investigative study in an attempt to delineate what might be important factors influencing a novel situation.

Participant Observation.   Participant observation is a methodological research approach in which an observer has several possible positions from which to make observations (Jorgensen, 1989; Vidich, 1955; Whyte, 1993):

- *Being a complete observer*—The observer is not visible to those being observed and is quite detached from the situation (e.g., observing a child via audiovisual camera or behind a two-way mirror).
- *Being a complete participant*—The observer observes from within the group by immersing himself or herself totally in the culture as well as concealing his or her identity as a researcher (e.g., an undercover police officer investigating drug trafficking, a clinician posing as a client's mother in a speech and language therapy reception waiting area).

An observer can also use a combination of being a complete observer and being a complete participant.

Several issues are related to participant observation. For example, what happens when

- the researcher's cover is blown?
- informed consent is required?
- the researcher interacts with the individuals he or she wants to study?
- the researcher becomes overly familiar with those he or she studies?

Naturalistic Observation and Qualitative Research

There are situations in which researchers or clinicians engage in procedure called *naturalistic observation*. Although the main procedure is to collect observations in an uncontrolled situation, these researchers are not necessarily engaged in qualitative research. They observe the behavior of a participant in a natural setting (e.g., observing child play with his peers, where a linguist might be collecting speech samples from native speakers). One of the main advantages of naturalistic observations is that it allows the investigator to observe how individuals function in their natural environment. No controls are used in this type of research. The investigator usually has a structured checklist of events or behavior he or she plans to observe and record when they occur. It is possible to simply observe with no preconceived ideas about what one might see (i.e., describe), but often these investigators have a theory or a hypothesis to guide their selection of which events or behaviors they should target in their observations. In their analysis, they usually tally up the number of occurrences of these events (i.e., frequency).

Speech and language therapy students are often trained to observe children in a nursery (a natural setting). Usually, the purpose of this exercise is to teach students to develop structured observation skills. The task can be approached in different ways. In a descriptive approach, the students are instructed to observe and make accurate notes of events that happened, how the children responded, what they did or did not do with the teacher, and so on—the goal being to teach students to describe events objectively. A hypothesis-driven approach requires the students to first make up a list of behaviors described by developmental experts or theorists for children in that age group. Because the children are described as typical, the students will predict that they will observe many of these behaviors in these children (i.e., learn to formulate predictions). The students then observe the children and focus their observations on the target list of behaviors (e.g., ability to build a three-block tower, ability to ask questions, ability to play alone). Finally, they will verify whether the developmental theorists are correct and discuss reasons why they might not have observed certain events.

Why is Qualitative Research is Considered Unscientific?

First, Induction is a problem. There is a question about whether qualitative research represents *scientific* research (i.e., can these methods produce scientific knowledge?). Although there are several schools of qualitative researchers, they all share the practice of interpretivism/constructivism and a relaxed attitude toward objectivism. This affects how data are interpreted and, ultimately, what constitutes truth or reality. Several criticisms have been launched at inductive research. Typically, these comments refer to difficulties in seeing what has contributed to the complexity of the patterns observed in the amassed data. The eye may detect some trends, but one cannot assume or expect to observe complex interactions among the data. Also, the data are usually collected under uncontrolled conditions. It is therefore difficult to know which factors in the environment contributed to or were responsible for producing the patterns observed in the data. This not only makes it difficult to develop a causal account of the observed relationships, but it also makes it difficult to replicate the observed events. If we cannot replicate research, then we have no basis for distinguishing between real and imagined results from a study.

Another reason qualitative research is considered unscientific is that there is a problem with subjectivity in defining truth. A major defining principle of science is objectivity (Chalmers, 1999; Longino, 1998). Objectivity is one of the few benchmarks by which individuals can define reality or factual knowledge that can be distinguished from knowledge that is anchored in other mental states. For example, insisting on objectivity allows us to exclude knowledge resulting out of dreams, hallucinations, wishful thinking, and other private experiences. Knowledge that can be experienced or verified by others (i.e., public experience) allows us verify reality.

Third, there is a problem with a lack of causal explanation. John Mill's idea of seeking explanatory laws of human behavior has been modulated over the years, though there is still an expectation that human behavior can be subject to logical explanations. Davidson (1980) took issue with the claim made by interpretivists that there cannot be a causal connection between reason and actions. He argued that reasons are causes of actions and that there are causal laws connecting reasons and actions. As Davidson saw it, the question is not Is there a causal relationship between reasons and actions? but rather How can we describe and represent descriptions of reasons in terms we can use to construct a law? Furthermore, Davidson thought we might be misguided if we assume that a law of human behavior might be similar in form to a law in the physical sciences. The form of the laws of human behavior, he suggested is waiting to be discovered.

FURTHER READING

Breakwell et al. (2000) Chapter 4 on experiments
Coolican (1996) covers qualitative research in several chapters
Gilhooly (1996) on induction–deduction
Halpern (1996) pp. 121–122, 214–215 on induction–deduction
Malim & Birch (1997) pp. 17–46 various
Mays & Pope (1999) Chapter 1 on differences between Qualitative & Quantitative
Polgar & Thomas (2000) Chapter 8 Simple and brief on qualitative methods
Tesch (1990) on types of qualitative research

GRADUATE READING

Denzin & Lincoln (1998) provide a comprehensive overview of all the different schools in qualitative research and their associated methodologies.
Lambert & Brittan (1992) present a succinct account of the philosophy of the social sciences and evaluate the arguments presented against traditional definitions of science in Chapter 11.
Palys (1997) describes and contrasts qualitative and quantitative approaches to research simply and comprehensively in Chapter 2.
Salmon, M. H. (1992) pp. 404–425 offers a few arguments in defense of why it is appropriate to persist with the view that human behavior may be reducible to fundamental laws.

11

The Scientific Clinician

The best lack all conviction, while the worst are full of passionate intensity . . .
Surely some revelation is at hand.

—W. B. Yeats, 1865–1939

THE SCIENTIST–CLINICIAN MODEL

The major theme emphasized in this book is the application of scientific thinking in speech and language therapy. There has also been a strong emphasis through-out this book on the commonalties that can and should exist between a clinician and a researcher if we are to argue that both come from the same *scientifically based* profession. If the clinician and the researcher were to adopt a common approach to their work, then it follows that they would almost certainly share an understanding of a core set of values and principles governing how one evaluates and determines what constitutes knowledge in the profession. Both the clinician and the researcher are engaged in problem solving (i.e., they are both required to engage in reasoning and rational argument).

The rules that guide valid thinking in one context (e.g., research) cannot be different from the rules that guide valid thinking in other contexts (e.g., clinical work, everyday living). Scientific thinking is just one instance of valid thinking, and valid thinking is relevant in all sectors of life. This point was made very clearly by Giere (1997), as he attempted to describe the qualities of scientific reasoning that render it a generic skill, transportable and applicable to a variety of problem-solving situations. Clinicians and researchers depend on being able to reason scientifically to become informed consumers of published research, but clinicians alone are expected by the public and their patients to be critically informed of the scientific merit of new interventions and therapy tools they offer to their patients. Both clinicians and researchers, however, being members of the public, are themselves consumers of intervention and a host of available products, and like their patients, they would not want to become victims of ignorance.

A speech and language therapist is identified with many roles:

- A clinician—who prescribes and administers remedies for a disorder, who educates, who counsels, and who is a referral service.
- An administrator—who manages a department or hospital.
- A lecturer—who teaches and facilitates learning
- A researcher—who investigates specific problems

It is very common to view these roles as serving separate functions (i.e., they have different objectives in what they do). It is important not to confuse different roles and their associated goals with the objectives of good reasoning and practice. For example, the roles and goals of the researcher and the clinician can be enunciated in these terms:

- The clinician values public service above all else, whereas the researcher values discovering new knowledge.
- The clinician values knowledge that can be applied, whereas the researcher values knowledge for its own sake.
- The clinician in the pursuit of public service is bound by policies and regulations governing practice, whereas the researcher depends on academic freedom to foster a climate for innovation (Stricker & Trierweiler, 1995).

Despite these inherent differences between the work goals of researchers and clinicians, if there is a scientist (i.e., a critical thinker) behind these roles, the differences between these roles are minimal. To be a scientist means, in essence, to think critically (or validly) and naturally, the way one conducts research or therapy will follow from this. This type of thinking or reasoning is considered to require considerable practice as it is a learned skill (Giere, 1997). Cohen (1988) proposed seven markers of scientific thinking:

1. Be skeptical.
2. Consider the source of the information.

3. Ask if there is a control group.
4. Look for errors to distinguish between whether two associated events are causally related or are simply correlated.
5. Distinguish between observation and inference.
6. If money is an incentive, then ensure that a particular product or idea is not oversimplified to help it sell.
7. Remember that an example is not proof for what is claimed.

Thinking scientifically means you possess a set of values that define the way you view the world around you. How a person expresses scientific thinking can vary according to his or her occupation, but the core set of values defining scientific thinking remain unaltered (see Fig. 11.1). Hence, the distinction between being a scientific clinician (or a clinical scientist) and a scientific researcher is minimal, as shown in Table 11.1.

The scientist–clinician model attempts to give expression to the fact that being a clinician does not preclude thinking and adopting an approach to clinical problem solving according to scientific principles. A clinician is confronted with a new situation every time a new patient walks through the door. No two patients are alike, even when they present with the same disorder. The scientist and the

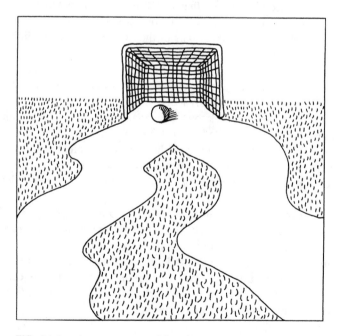

FIG. 11.1.   A common goal for clinicians, researchers, and administrators in a scientific profession.

TABLE 11.1
How Clinicians and Researchers Compare in Their Objectives

Similarities	*Differences*
They both define what they want to measure in evaluation of the patient or the participant.	The researcher has greater opportunity to exercise more control over a situation than the clinician.
They seek objectivity in their observations.	The researcher and clinician differ in the question they wish to investigate.
They seek valid and reliable measurements.	The researcher is more than likely than the clinician to engage in testing theoretical hypotheses.
They formulate and test hypotheses.	
They seek to write and commuicate in unambiguous terms.	
They seek to understand the research literature as a guide to their work.	
They test theories.	
They aim to solve problems affecting people.	

clinician are both required to solve a puzzle when dealing with a novel or complex situation. There may or may not be factual and reliable information on how to treat the disorder observed in the patient. The theories on the subject may or may not be tested. And even if there were adequate theories, and tried-and-tested treatments, these may not apply or work with a particular patient as there might be individual differences between patients that influence the outcome of therapy.

The clinician, as a clinical scientist, is well placed to investigate the patient's problem and should ideally be equipped with the knowledge and skills to do so. Furthermore, an assessment can determine whether the patient's problem can be accounted by a current theory, can determine whether the patient is responding to therapy as described in the literature, and can measure change in the patient's performance. The clinician also has the responsibility to communicate new findings through professional and scientific journals and conferences so that this knowledge is shared among the research and clinical communities to further advance knowledge in the profession for the patient's benefit.

HOW SCIENTIFIC PRACTICE IS REALIZED

Observation.　It is important to define precisely, in unambiguous terms, what you are going to observe before you start (i.e., operationally define terms). If you can define what you are observing in a patient, another clinician will be more likely to be able to accurately identify and observe the same phenomenon in the patient. Observations that can be made public can serve as scientific observations.

It is also important to specify the conditions and the duration of the observation period. Stipulating the conditions under which a phenomenon is observed in

FIG. 11.2.   Systematic observation and accurate measurement.

a patient increases the likelihood of being able to replicate or reproduce the same phenomenon later.

A behavioral checklist (i.e., a list of the behaviors you are going to observe) and a grid can help you record every occurrence of the target behaviors (see Fig. 11.2). Reliable and accurate observations depend on being highly methodical in one's approach to observations. If what you have to record is complex, then consider using a tape recorder or a video recorder to record what you are observing so that you can later check your observations. Accurate observations depend on reliable recording of observations. It is important to determine whether you need an independent observer. To minimize the effect of observer bias as well as improve reliability of recordings, an independent observer can be helpful. In clinical work you can opt for another observer if what you are observing is complex and obscure, particularly if working on a legal case.

Assessment.   All tests adopt some particular position (i.e., theoretical or non-theoretically motivated). It is important to understand the background to the development of the assessment. Some tests are products of a particular theoretical framework, and it is assumed when one administers the test that the patient's results will be interpreted accordingly. Other assessments might not have a particular theoretical orientation, and it is also important to know this.

A test is usually administered to test a hypothesis about the patient's condition. There are basically two main approaches to assessment: one approach is for the assessor to reduce the problem-space by administering a test battery that measures a wide variety of disparate functions. General ability assessments exemplified by test batteries that assess a broad-spectrum of functions. Performance in all areas is summarized into a single total score that is then compared to a norm. Comparing performance profiles is another feature of these tests. Another approach is to administer tests that measure some discrete function (e.g., memory) i.e., to have a single-focus. Whichever approach is adopted, hypothesis formulation is evident even if only at a gross level of postulating that a patient has abnormal linguistic and/or cognitive function.

Some examples of assessments or test batteries that measure a broad spectrum of functions include the Wechsler Adult Intelligence Scale, Western Aphasia Battery (Kertesz, 1982), Boston Diagnostic Examination of Aphasia (Goodglass, 1972), Arizona Battery for Communication Disorders in Dementia (Bayles & Tomoeda, 1993), British Vocabulary Scale (Dunn, Dunn, Whetton, & Burley, 1997), various developmental scales such as the Reynell Developmental Language scale (Edwards et al., 1997), and a broad test battery on literacy skills such as The Wide Range Achievement Test (Wilkinson, 1993). Examples of tests that measure discrete functions include tests such as the Boston Naming Test (Kaplan, Goodglass, & Weintraub, 1983), the Pyramids and Palm Trees test of semantics (Howard & Patterson, 1992), Test of Reception of Grammar (Bishop, 1989), Psycholinguistic Assessment of Language Processing in Aphasia (Kay, Lesser, & Coltheart, 1992).

It is important to determine whether the test manual of the test you are using provides reliability and validity indices of the test. A test is a measuring instrument. It is only a test because its developer has undertaken specific procedures to ensure that it performs reliably and provides information about test–retest reliability, intrarates reliability, interrates reliability, and so on. These are necessary to aid in interpreting your results.

You should also be sure to find out whether the test has norms for the population representing your client. Norms can be validly generalized to your patient if your patient shares characteristics (e.g., age, education attainment, socioeconomic class) represented by the normative sample.

It is important to decide how you will interpret a patient's performance when his or her result is just one or two points below the norm. A well-developed test should describe what constitutes a normal level of performance and how much normal variation is allowed in performance before it is considered to reflect abnormal performance. There are different ways tests achieve this, usually reflecting different degrees of sophistication in psychometric development. The following are some examples:

- *Mean and standard deviation.* Let's say the normative sample consists of a group of 20 typical individuals. The group yields an average (mean) score of 84 and a standard deviation (SD) of 4, so the typical person from such a group will score 84. A standard deviation of 4 means that performance can be allowed to vary plus or minus 4 (i.e., 80–88) and still remain within normal limits. So, if a client or patient returns a score of 82, this person will be considered to be functioning normally because this score is still within the normal range, or within normal variation. If a client returns a score that is outside of the deviation range (e.g., 77), the client's performance is poorer than the worst normal person and it is concluded that the client's performance is abnormal.

- *Median and range.* Sometimes, the median is used instead of the mean. Both the mean and median are measures of central tendency, but there are situations when one is preferred over the other. In a normal frequency distribution of scores, either the mean and the median will return the same numerical value in describing the average performance. However, if the distribution of scores is skewed (i.e., it has an outlier, meaning an unusually high or low score or scores relative to the majority in the sample), the mean score will be higher or lower than the true average, whereas the median will remain the same (see Fig. 11.3). The reason for this relates to how these two measures of central tendency are calculated. The calculation of the mean takes into account the value of all the scores, including the extreme scores (i.e., add them all up and divide by the total). The calculation of the median is based on working out the point in the frequency distribution that divides 50% of the scores. When a median is the choice in describing the average performance of the group, then the range is preferred over the standard deviation, to avoid misrepresenting what constitutes a deviation from the average (Howell, 1997; Phillips, 1999).

The mode shown in Fig. 11.3 is the most frequently occurring value in a distribution, and it is also unaffected by extreme or outlying scores.

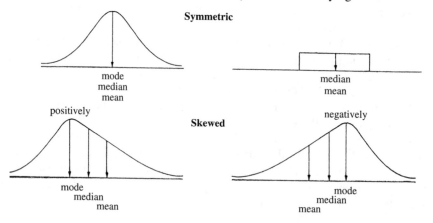

FIG. 11.3.   Effect of extreme scores on the various measures of central tendency.

- *The norm as the lowest value in the range.* Sometimes tests provide a mean value (or a median) and a range of values. Using the earlier test score numbers, this will appear as a mean or median of 84, with a range of 80 to 88. The range describes the lowest and the highest scores achieved by typical individuals.

  Performance in considered abnormal if it falls below the lowest score in the range, in this example 80. The lowest score is sometimes called the *cutoff score* between typical and impaired performance.

- *Standardized z scores.* Tests can also provide z scores rather than raw scores, though few do in speech and language tests. One major reason for this could be due to the large numbers of participants required to develop these measurement scales. In addition, the test developer may have a theoretical orientation that regards psychometric measurement of this kind as being inappropriate to the measurement situation (Lum, 1996).

  z scores are the result of a mathematical procedure that converts raw scores to a new scale. The transformation process of raw scores to z scores has the effect of forcing a set of raw scores into a statistical distribution of scores known as a *normal symmetrical distribution*. This helps test developers overcome the problems of comparing an individual's performance from two different tests that have different numbers of items and different performance characteristics (e.g., comparing math and spelling tests). The group performance on these tests may naturally yield scores bunched up at either the high or low end of the scale (i.e., skewed distributions). When these distributions are mathematically transformed and their scores standardized, it becomes possible to compare scores from different types of distributions representing different types of tasks or skills. For example, we can say that a patient scored 2 standard deviations below the mean in math but he scored 2.5 standard deviations above the mean in spelling.

  z scores, however, usually result in negative values, which are annoying in the interpretation process. To eliminate this problem, it is possible to produce a *standard derived scale*, which basically involves adding a constant (e.g., the value of 5) to every z score value. If we want to increase the scale of the units from 1 unit value per unit to 10 unit values per unit, we can also multiply the derived value by 10. The latter scores are referred to as *scaled scores*, also known as *T*-scores. Fig. 11.4 illustrates the various standardized scores that can be used to describe the same distribution of scores (Anastasi & Urbina, 1997; Phillips, 1999).

Pretest practice items can help train the patient in the procedure of the task before administration of the actual test items. This ensures that none of the test items are wasted because the patient did not understand the task requirements when the test started and therefore produced errors.

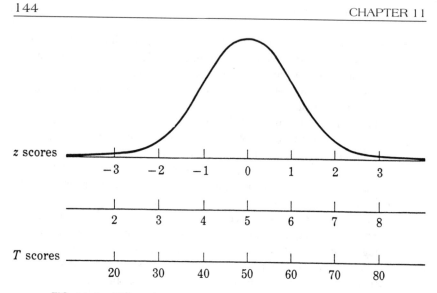

z scores

-3   -2   -1   0   1   2   3

2   3   4   5   6   7   8

T scores

20   30   40   50   60   70   80

FIG. 11.4.   Different ways to represent an individual's test score.

Instructions in the test manual ensure that the conditions under which the test is performed are the same as those under which the test was standardized thereby avoiding invalidating the test. If there were any departures from the specified test conditions, make a note of what you did differently so that in the future you will be able to take these variations into account when interpreting posttherapy test results.

It is important to recognize that informal tests are not tests in any real sense. Informal tests are useful to the extent that they allow a quick sketch of the major problems experienced by a patient. The clinician typically dives into a nearby drawer, a box of toys, or even a handbag to produce items for the patient to name, to point to, to match, and so on (see Fig. 11.5). "Handbag assessments" such as these can be useful to derive some idea of whether the patient's condition will allow him or her to attempt a complete formal assessment procedure. However, handbag assessments or informal tests have unknown value as measurement procedures. Often they involve too few items and cannot be considered reliable. Furthermore, the items may have inherent (and unknown) biases that influence performance. The tester who exploits this procedure is often looking for a quick test of what he or she thinks is wrong with the client and makes it almost impossible to replicate the assessment procedure to determine whether improvement has occurred. This could produce a bias in interpretation of what might be wrong with the patient.

Communication.   After assessment or treatment, it is common to be asked to give an account of the patient. In clinical practice, we do this for professional colleagues, patient families, the care team, and so on. Speaking to such a

FIG. 11.5. Informal tests, interesting for the clinician but a nightmare for the psychometrician.

range of audiences means we are required to vary and shift between different levels of description of patients. This is a skill, and it requires instruction and practice to master clear communication. Offering students the notion of speaking "plain English" is not helpful, and students are rarely offered the opportunity to learn how to communicate to other about a patient's difficulties. Initially, students tend to find it easier to speak as they have read (i.e., they speak about a patient's problem in a register that conforms to the style of language that is quite formal and more suitable for academic communication than for speaking to laypeople). After a few years of employment, the register changes, as they gain more experience in speaking frequently to a variety of non-speech and language therapy audiences. Details of a patient's disorder and its theoretical justification become implicit or appear lost in professional communication because it is perceived as irrelevant and undemanded by the context. This may often appear true, and it is fine except when such communication comes to reflect the loss of ability to think beyond generalities about the patient. Thinking about a patient's problems takes time, and casual speech may lull one into thinking superficially about a patient's problems. Issues of clear communication and its relationship with accountability are implicated here. One way of combating limited opportunities to engage in highly focused analytical activity would be to hold periodic journal review meetings.

Making Up Your Own Test.   If there are no suitable tests to meet your requirements and you must produce your own test, then at the very least, try to obtain norms from a normal sample of 6 to 10 individuals whose characteristics match those of your patients. This is a start and could eventually lead to the development of a better form of this test by you or someone else.

A simple way to develop your own screening test is shown here. Strictly speaking, the procedures described do not satisfy the standards used to define good tests, so in this sense, the product is not a test in traditional terms (Anastasi & Urbina, 1997; Cronbach, 1990). However, a screening test based on these procedures is preferable to one simply produced on the spot in situ in the clinic (i.e., informal tests):

- Determine how many test items you will include. After you decide on a number, double the number of items for your normative study because you will be throwing away quite a few items by the end of the exercise. One student found after she had tested 100 items on a sample of 20 typical subjects that she was left with 45 suitable test items.
- Ensure that practice items have been built into the test.
- Check whether you have controlled for various factors in your items (e.g., word class, frequency, length, imageability, familiarity, concreteness). Focus on the ones that are most important or relevant to what you're testing.
- Determine whether you need distracter items (foils) to go with each test item. The more distracter items you have, the more confident you can be of your patient's correct responses. For example, a test question that provides the target plus two alternatives (the correct answer and one distracter) offers the testee a 50% chance of getting the right answer just by guessing. If the number of alternatives were increased to four, then the testee has only a 25% chance of guessing the correct answer. A limit between two and five alternatives per target item is enough for any visual-selection task.
- Test the wording of your instructions with participants.
- Develop a set of questions or a screening test that allows you to verify that your typical subjects are indeed typical.
- Visit drop-in centers and schools to locate typical participants as well as caregivers, parents, and so on. If you are developing a test for a child, for example, use a normative sample with children, not adults, as your participants. If you find after testing the first 6 to 10 participants that there is a lot of individual variation in performance, you need to increase the sample size, say by another 10 participants. This will hopefully give you better resolution in terms of finding a level that represents how the majority of typical participants perform on this task. Spouses can be a good source of control subjects for adult tests because they are fairly likely to share the same social and educational backgrounds as their partners in Britain.

- Set a cutoff point for the items. A commonly accepted cutoff point for typical performance is 90% to 95% accuracy. So after you have administered the test to each of the typical participants, tally the results. Ask how many people had Item 1 correct, How many had Item 2 correct, and so on. Discard any item that fails to meet the cutoff limit of 90%. The remaining items (after adjusting for various factors, such as class and psycholinguistic variables) should be the items in the screening test.
- Keep a record of the patient's responses and summarize the results.

Memories are fallible, so do not rely on them. Record error responses as well as correct responses because error patterns in addition to the overall test score can be informative.

Example

Several therapists in ABZ community center decided to start a new therapy group for a dozen or so patients. They decided that they would evaluate the benefit of therapy or evaluate the patients' progress following the 12 weeks of therapy. They selected as their pre and post measures a popular screening test. However, this screening test was not so much a test as a set of tasks developed by another group of therapists who thought an existing test battery was too long to be useful in a busy neurological department. They made up a set of screening tasks by selecting a very small pool of items from the existing standardized test battery. This screening test was used routinely to screen patients, and any that showed difficulty on these tasks were not administered the proper form of the test (i.e., the standardized battery). However, the ABZ therapists were either unaware or did not think the development of the test was particularly relevant to their objective. They administered this screening test to all the patients in the group and repeated the results at the end of the 12 weeks. Some patients showed improved scores, others showed no change, and others actually showed worse scores. The results were, not surprisingly, difficult to interpret.

(Informally created tests, even if the items are taken from an existing test battery, have no status as tests. Such tests offer no information about what is normal variation of performance on these tests, test–retest reliability, interrater agreement, and so on. Although the therapists' motives were well intentioned, the exercise was doomed before the first test was administered to the first patient in the group. Much time and effort were wasted in collecting what amounted to meaningless results.)

Avoiding Shortcuts.   It is very tempting to take shortcuts in a busy day when there are many patients booked for clinical sessions. Often a clinician thinks administering 20 items of a 60-item test will yield the same results as administering the whole 60-item test. But we often do not know if this is assumption is true. If the equivalence of a 20-item test to a 60-item test were known, the test designer would incorporate this information in the test manual. Test designers go to great lengths to make tests reliable (i.e., produce consistent results with the same patient when tested soon after on the same test). To achieve this, they ensure that the tests are not so short that it might be possible for patients to guess the right answers or that the effects of fatigue on performance would be missed. It is important to finish testing a patient on a test, even if the patient appears to have no problems in the area tested. It is just as important to know what a patient is able to do as to know what he or she finds difficult.

Avoiding Confusing Testing and Therapy.   Sometimes an assessor feels torn between performing an assessment and ensuring that the patient experiences success. This happens particularly when a patient appears to be struggling or produces many errors in assessment. The clinician then feels a need to provide supportive feedback and even corrective feedback to help the patient achieve success. Often these ad hoc procedures interfere with the validation of the test. There are times, though, when (as part of the assessment) the assessor is interested in establishing which type of corrective procedures work for a patient (e.g., cuing with a sound, cuing with a related word meaning). Strictly speaking, these procedures need to be incorporated into the development of the test to avoid invalidating the test results (as in the Boston Naming Test; Kaplan et al., 1983). The success of assessment in terms of the clinician being able to obtain information and the patient not being totally demoralized by the situation often depends on skilled handling of the situation.

Many patients can accept that they will not be receiving feedback during assessment if it is explained to them that this is an assessment and the conditions require that the clinician give the test without informing the patients of specific aspects of performance during the assessment. Often an explanation, such as the following, helps:

> Mr. Jones, I am going to ask you to name some pictures. There are quite a few pictures, and you will find some easy and others harder to name. I would like you to name all the pictures as best you can. Don't worry if you make a mistake. Everything you say, including your mistakes, tell me about your speech problem. I won't say whether your answers are right or wrong during the test. But when the test is over, we can talk about how you did. Okay? Shall we begin?

If the patient's condition is so severe that no responses or utterances are available, then in one sense, there is probably no point in administering the test as you will learn too little to justify the exercise. A patient could easily become totally demoralized if the assessor persisted in administering a test when the patient is completely unable to respond.

Often, though, there is a temptation to preempt what the patient's abilities might be and terminate testing in the belief that the patient is unable to perform. This can lead to erroneous conclusions. Often novice clinicians and researchers stop administering a test after the first few items because the patient's responses are all incorrect. Terminating the test prematurely results in a serious loss about the types of errors the patient produces. It is important to try to administer the whole test even if failure is evident, since it serves as a basis for comparison later when the patient improves and is able to complete the test, possibly successfully.

Sometimes, clinicians and students engage in what is loosely termed "diagnostic intervention," meaning that the patient or the problem is evaluated in the course of treatment. This approach seems to be favored in situations in which for various reasons formal tests are not attempted and the clinician attempts to assess the client in the course of providing therapy (i.e., as though gauging the client's response to therapy is taken as being part of the assessment process). There is some merit in this view of having therapy serve as a test of the validity of theories. However, a rapid iterative cycle of testing and therapy means that what is considered testing has all the methodological weaknesses of informal tests. Therapy in this context becomes difficult to measure because it is constantly changing in response to the patient rather than the other way around, and there is a tendency to foster therapy activity designed to fit with the client's problems. Given what we know about the importance of defining a problem, measurement issues, objectivity, and the validity and reliability of assessments, it is difficult to find a rational and scientific basis for this approach to assessment and treatment. A "diagnostic intervention" approach accepts that therapy should change in direct response to impromptu assessments that occur during and in the course of executing intervention procedures. This type of approach can lend itself quite readily to various forms of handbag or informal assessments, which are not really tests. To that extent, one could argue that these may not be valid bases on which to define the patient's problem or to base therapy.

Note that in assessment it is important to obtain evidence to verify a hypothesis about a patient's disorder. The attitude adopted in testing directs one to test the hypothesis, not to "prove" the hypothesis.

Treatment

It is a good idea to use normed diagnostic assessments to inform a diagnosis of a patient's disorder before commencing treatment. Sometimes, clinicians feel that an assessment of the patient will be too "punishing" on the patient, and a decision is made to commence therapy without completing any formal assessment. It is conceivable that a patient's condition might be too severe to permit the patient to attempt formal assessment. However, some attempt at assessment of the patient's abilities, even if it is based simply on structured observation or a pretherapy task developed by the clinician, is preferable to having no systematic recording of the patient's behavior. There is no basis for evaluation without some form of a pretherapy assessment baseline.

It is a good idea to repeat the same normed diagnostic assessments at the end of therapy in exactly the same way to measure change in the patient's abilities. It is important to keep this constant so that any change in the results can be attributed to the patient rather than to changes in procedure.

Wherever possible, conduct therapy that is guided by scientific research. Doing therapy "on the run" is probably a true reflection of a clinical situation in which there is no time allocated in the day to treatment preparation or planning. Time spent in therapy preparation is sometimes not regarded as a legitimate use of time in a working day, and clinicians can feel guilty about "taking time away from patients." Such feelings of guilt also extend to taking time to go to the library or to spend time reading relevant literature. There needs to be strong advocacy from professional members to secure treatment planning time, particularly in these more constrained times in health care services. Being guided by scientific research in therapy means that a clinician needs to be reasonably well acquainted with efficacy research of various therapies. Some team case conferences on patients seem to be evolving such that the team expects that clinicians will couch their patients' progress reports in terms of what they know about the efficacy of the interventions they are applying to the patients. Such changes serve to highlight the growing value placed on knowledge of the efficacy of interventions offered to patients.

The goals in therapy would be to apply therapy strategies demonstrated to be effective with particular disorders and to evaluate the patient's therapy program to determine whether this therapy has been effective for the particular patient.

It is recognized that sometimes treatment can be exploited for its ability to test theories about specific functions or skills. For example, a hypothesis might state that knowledge of syntax is amodal and the same representations are shared by comprehension and production processes. It would be possible to test this hypothesis by treating the patient's comprehension to see if it results in the predicted spontaneous resolution of syntax problems in production (Byng, 1988). Clinicians should be aware that whenever they treat patients, they are in a situation in which they are either constantly reaffirming or refuting a theory about specific cognitive-linguistic functions.

It is important to keep a clear written record that tracks the patient's performance in each session. Record the patient's performance as you work, rather than leave it to the end of the session because by that time you will have forgotten how many items the patient passed or failed.

Further procedures are required to evaluate therapy in the clinic, and these are presented Chapter 13.

OTHER ROLES OF THE SCIENTIFIC CLINICIAN

In clinical decision making, it is important to

- avoid fallacies,
- remember that associated events need not be causally related,
- remember to find the baseline for a given condition.

Figures 11.6 and 11.7 are examples of session plans that illustrate the application of the principle of operational definition to a therapy session. A well-written clinical session plan has the same characteristics and format of a clearly written research report. All the terms in the plan are defined. The goal of the session is operationally defined (i.e., the goal is written in such a way that it states exactly what the client will do to demonstrate that he or she has mastered the skill or some understanding of what the clinician claims he or she is teaching, facilitating, or encouraging to occur or inhibit).

In this example, the clinician is aiming to elicit /s/ from a dysarthric patient who has a problem devoicing voiced consonants and who also has a paralyzed soft palate. Consequently, this patient does not differentiate speech, voice, and voiceless cognates (i.e., /s/–/z/, /p/–/b/, /t/–/d/) and cannot produce any velars (i.e., /k/, /g/). Assume that a pretherapy baseline has been recorded on the treatment task three times and that Mr. Jones reads 16 /s/ monosyllabic words spontaneously. Assume that a pretherapy baseline has been recorded on control tasks: three times and that Mr. Jones reads 16 /k/ monosyllabic words spontaneously.

Aim: To elicit /s/ correctly in the initial position of 16 monosyllabic words on 8 occasions (50% success rate).

Procedure: The clinician will:

1. Explain the purpose of the task to Mr. Jones.
2. (*Model*) Demonstrate the production of /s/ three times, while stressing that there is "no voice" at the start of the word when /s/ is spoken. Voicing–devoicing is monitored by the patient feeling his larynx vibrate for /z/ and not for /s/.
3. (*Teach strategy*) Instruct Mr. Jones to apply the strategy of lengthening /s/ to establish its voiceless feature before moving to the final syllable. Instruction: "Hold the /s/ longer than you feel is normal before saying the rest of the word, and listen to yourself."
4. (*Model strategy*) Demonstrate the production of a lengthened /s/ monosyllable word three times. Remind Mr. Jones that there is "no voice" at the start of the word when /s/ is spoken. Voicing–devoicing is monitored by the patient feeling his larynx vibrate for /z/ and not for /s/.
5. (*Imitate with strategy*) Instruct Mr. Jones to repeat 10 monosyllabic words with /s/ lengthened after each presentation by clinician. (Use Feedback Hierarchy 1.)
6. (*Spontaneous production*) Instruct Mr. Jones to produce 16 monosyllabic /s/ words. Record it.

FIG. 11.6. A clear session plan.

Aim: Mr. Jones is to produce /s/ correctly in the initial position in single words as well as demonstrate an awareness of the /s/ and /z/ distinction.
Procedure: The clinician will:

1. Demonstrate the production of /s/ while stressing that there is "no voice" at the start of the word when /s/ is spoken. Voicing–devoicing is monitored by the patient feeling his larynx vibrate for /z/ and not for /s/. The patient will be shown the strategy of lengthening /s/.
2. Mr. Jones will apply the strategy to 10 monosyllabic words with /s/ lengthened when imitating each production of /s/ words by the clinician. The clinician will reinforce the patient's responses.
3. Instruct Mr. Jones to produce a list of /s/ words. Record each response.

FIG. 11.7.   An ill-defined session plan.

A clear session plan is one that another clinician could pick up and use to conduct a session with your patient as you intended. It cannot be ambiguous or lack any vital instructions.

Some students and clinicians may think it is too time-consuming, too artificial, too rigorous, or even unnecessary to operationally define their sessions. One of the main advantages of operationally defining sessions and treatment goals is that the student or clinician is required to be very clear about the aim of the session. Being explicit in the use of language tends to focus the mind on exactly what is meant and intended. Quite apart from its scientific merit, it accords well with the present climate of accountability. It also allows a clinical supervisor to evaluate more easily student performance in the clinic. The method lends itself to developing cumulative experiences in treatment based more on factual data about client performance than on subjective impression. The latter is more likely to foster a research attitude that could result in more relevant questions being asked about the client and the condition under consideration.

EVALUATING EVALUATIONS

Many sources of error that affect the interpretation of results of patients in the clinic are similar to those that are considered by researchers. These effects have been studied and are well known by researchers. In the clinic, we find it difficult to reduce measurement error to the same extent as used in a research study, though error never quite disappears completely even in research. It is important, however, to be cognizant of these sources of error so that we remember to interpret observations of the patient after taking these factors into account (i.e., conservatively).

In the event of not being able to completely eliminate sources of error, researchers have evolved various research designs to control or limit their influence. The value of the research and our observations of the client depend on the rigor of the methods and procedures employed. If a study or the procedures we employed were poorly designed for the task, then the findings (be they from research or from the clinic) may indeed be wrong or misleading. Clinicians will not be able to exercise the same degree of control in their procedures, and the best strategy in these situations is to be conservative in one's interpretations of the patient's abilities and of the patient's situation.

Refer to Chapter 13 for further details on how to evaluate a research paper, an efficacy study, and surveys. Checklists are provided that list prompts to help you undertake these evaluation tasks. Researchers attempt to evaluate events in an attempt to discover truthful knowledge. The scientific clinician (like a researcher), however, has the task of evaluating these evaluations before incorporating the findings into his or her work. These are skills that can be developed to a high degree of proficiency through education and practice.

FURTHER READING

Anastasi & Urbina (1997) offer a classic perspective on the subject of test development and very comprehensive coverage of testing methodologies.

Drummond (1996) presents information on the link between the researcher and the clinician.

Phillips (1999) explains statistical concepts very plainly and is helpful even when students have not started to formally study statistics.

12

Efficacy of Interventions

Absolute certainty in the face of no data is always a dangerous sign.
—D. McGuiness

The subject of therapy and what it encompasses is a big issue and goes beyond the scope of this book. To situate the material in this chapter, a scenario common in many clinics is presented:

At 2:00 p.m., Mr. Jones arrives at the outpatients area to see his speech clinician. He has been coming for the past 4 months, seeing his clinician once a week. He waits in the sitting area. The door opens, a patient leaves, and Mr. Jones's clinician greets him. The clinician looks quickly though his file to remind herself of what they did a week ago. She decides it would be a good idea to review some of the work they did last week. This will also help set the stage for what should come next in his program. She asks Mr. Jones how he has been and what he has done since they last met. She goes through last week's work and commends him on his effort. "That's not bad," she says. "You did that quite well. Now, maybe we'll try another exercise. This time, I'll demonstrate the movement. Watch me and then you do the same." The patient follows as best he can. "Not bad," says the clinician. "Can you do 10 of those? No, no maybe make it 5," says the clinician. That's great. Now, let's see . . . maybe we can try something else. Here is a different exercise. I want you to tell me whether what I do is correct or incorrect. This will help you be a bit more as- tute when it comes to watching out for mistakes. Okay, that was really good." At the end of the session, she says, "This was a good session today. We got most of them right, didn't we? Maybe next week, we'll go over this again and try something else."

This clinician has executed a number of therapy exercises, but in essence her approach represents doing therapy on-the-go. This scenario shows that there was no attempt to record accurately the patient's performance. The clinician appeared to be making up tasks in the session rather than targeting specific performance ob- jectives. Any judgment of the patients' performance later will depend on the clini- cian's recall. When a clinician is treating up to 10 patients per day, recall of any patient's performance is bound to be unreliable. If this example were situated in a group therapy situation, this recall difficulty would be compounded many times.

Part of the problem stems from clinicians not taking or being given time to plan therapy or chart a patient's progress or responses to treatment. The reasons for this are partly historical. It is possible that, 20 years ago, in the absence of proven ther- apies or even research on therapy, there was less need to pay close attention to what defined treatment in service delivery. Goals in therapy can easily become lost in the course of time, and events and measures of performance are nonexistent. Ultimately, we must ask whether therapy has made a difference to the patient. To be able to answer this question requires a change in the way therapy is currently approached. Services taking efficacy and accountability issues seriously will need to be designed around the idea of having clinicians see fewer patients in a day, or seeing clinicians as professionals who design therapy programs (with evaluation built-in) for several patients that are delivered by several trained assistants.

THE MULTIPLE MEANINGS OF EFFICACY

The term *efficacy* is heard a great deal in therapy circles. However, it is a term that lends itself quite easily to various meaningful nuances and so can take on a number of forms. The Concise Oxford Dictionary provides a standard definition of the term *efficacy* as being "a thing that will produce the desired effect" (Thompson, 1995). However, there are different kinds of efficacy. Some of them are described here. Although they do not have any particular formal status within the clinical work, it remains true that patients can present as having improved at different points in treatment.

Immediate efficacy refers to a positive change resulting during and/or immedi- ately after a therapeutic manipulation. For example, cuing by a clinician is a very effective therapeutic strategy for eliciting words from a patient during a treatment session. However, its effect may not be maintained after the session, and the patient will still have difficulty saying the wants he words to speak.

Patient-specific efficacy refers to a demonstration via controlled therapy that a patient's improvement has been due to the administration of therapy. However, it is not necessarily known whether the treatment strategy used with this patient is also successful with other patients. This particular meaning of efficacy can also be called *accountability* in the clinic.

Treatment-specific efficacy refers to a demonstration via scientific research that a particular treatment technique is effective in treating a given disorder. It may be thought of as effective without all patients showing benefit. A technique can be regarded as efficacious even if it works for only 90% of the patients treated. The most important thing is that there has been a controlled evaluation that this technique above all others is the most effective technique.

In research, an investigator may choose to study any or all of these instances of efficacy. This person will decide on a research question, select the right study design, and use procedures that allow him or her to evaluate the efficacy of a particular intervention effect and to write and publish the findings.

The average clinician is usually working in an environment that is best suited to evaluating immediate efficacy or patient-specific efficacy. The clinician confronts the issue of efficacy on various levels daily. Most clinicians probably feel that they do not have enough time in their day to engage in evaluating therapy with their patients. This can be true if one were thinking about evaluating specific techniques for particular patient disorders. Treatment-specific efficacy studies require the right patients to be present in the clinic and in sufficient numbers to allow replication of treatment effects across patients. However, a clinician who is prepared to put in a bit of effort to plan therapy will be in a good position to evaluate both immediate efficacy and patient-specific efficacy. The dividends from this exercise could result in outcomes achieved more efficiently and therefore, possibly take up less therapy time overall.

WHY WE NEED EVIDENCE

The speech and language profession's interest in evidence has evolved mainly through concerns about treatment efficacy and accountability in service provision. The emergence of government or profession-driven bodies under the title Clinical Governance in the United Kingdom (Chambers, 1998) and National Outcomes Measurement System (NOMS) in the United States (www.asha.com), further reinforce the view that the public and the clinical professions have accountability listed as a major agenda item. Table 12.1 lists many of various sources dealing with the evaluation of evidence current at the time of writing.

Although the fanfare surrounding accountability is excellent news for all concerned, it has a down side, too. Linking accountability with the justification of health services and the implications for the deployment of its staff tends to focus the minds of people (certainly students and new clinicians) on employment

TABLE 12.1
Sources Dealing with the Evaluation of Scientific Evidence for Interventions

RESOURCES FOR FINDING INFORMATION ABOUT EVIDENCE

INTERNET—Largest computer network in the world
Access: via JANET (Joint Academic Network linking most academic institutions) or via dial-in modem from home (e.g. hotmail, demon etc.).

WORLD-WIDE WEB—This is part of the internet. It provides access to a network of interlinked documents and information services across the internet. All coded information starts with *http:* and it can be accessed with software called *Browsers* (e.g. Netscape, Internet explorer.)
Access: Via on-line services or Janet as above.

ELECTRONIC DATABASES

BATH INFORMATION AND DATA SERVICE (BIDS)
Designed to be used by non-expert searchers and includes other databases eg. Embase, Citation Indexes etc.
Access: http://www.bids.ac.uk

COCHRANE LIBRARY—Evidence base medicine database
Consists of two parts:
(a) The CDSR (Cochrane Database of Systematic Reviews) and
(b) DARE (Database of Abstract of Reviews of Effectiveness)*
(c) The CCTR The Cochrane Trials register*.

Access: http://www.cochrane.co.uk

*CDSR is a structure systematic collection of reviews of controlled trials. Evidence is included or excluded according to explicit criteria. Meta-analyses are also conducted wherever possible which may lead to increasing the statistical power of these studies.

*DARE is database of research reviews of the effectiveness of health care intervention and management of health services. The reviews are appraised by reviewers at the National Health Servise Center for reviews and Disseminatiion at the University of York.

*CCTR is a biography of controlled trials conducted throughout the world-include conference proceedings

MEDLINE—Electronic database produced in the US containing details information about journal papers relating mainly to medical disorders. Available as Cd-Rom or on-line.
Access: Free to users. Libraries subscribe.
Overview of some health related sites:
Healthgate at http://www.healthgate.com/medline/search-medline.shtml
Medscape at http://www.medscape.com/ (provides on-line articles about a wide range of medical specialities, plus a journal club).

EMBASE—Is part of MEDLINE. More updated information on drug research and research in Europe.
Access: Via BMA pages on the Internet. Go to http://www.medline@bma.org.uk

NICE—National Institute for Clinical Excellence.
Access: http://www.nice.org.uk/nice-web/
SIGN—Sign Scotish Intercollegiate Guidelines Network
Access: http://www.show.scot.nhs.uk/sign/home.html

(Continued)

TABLE 12.1
(Continued)

Subject-specific sites on the Internet:
CINAHL—The cumulative Index to Nursing and Allied Health Literature. Comprehensive database of 950 journals in the English language related to nursing and health disciplines.
Access: http://www.healthgate.com/cinah/search-cinahl-pre.shtml
PsychINFO—Includes world-wide literature on psychological aspects of medicine and psychology from 1967 onwards.
Access: http://www.healthgate.com/psycinfo/search-psycinfo-pre.shtml

Other sites on the Internet:
HEALTH ON THE NET—The Health on the Net Foundation has developed a code of conduct for medical and health web sites. Web sites bearing the health on the net logo indicate that they are committed to ensuring that the information on the web site abides by this code of conduct. Basically, this entails making sure the information is provided by either medically-trained or professionally trained people. The logo does not guarentee the quality of the information.
Access: http:www.hon.ch

NHS Centre for Reviews and Dissemination.
Access: http://www.york.ac.uk/inst/crd/welcome.htm

TRIP—a service from Gwent Health Authority that searches across 61 evidence-based sites simultaneously.
Access: http://www.tripdatabase.com/

ASHA—American Speech-Language-Hearing Association, the professional association for USA therapists have a web site that includes a bibliography on Treatment Outcomes. Worth a peek from time. Also see NOMS.
Access: http://www.asha.org/

PAPER-BASED RESOURCES:
STEP—Stroke Therapy Evaluation Programme funded by the Chest, Heart & Stroke Association in Scotland.

Access: Write to STEP,
Academic section of geriatric Medicine,
3rd floor centre block
Glasgow Royal Infirmary Glasgow G4 OSF
United Kingdom

FREE ELECTRONIC JOURNALS

BRITISH MEDICAL JOURNAL
Access: http://www.bmj.com

JAMA (JOURNAL OF THE AMERICAN MEDICAL ASSOCIATION)
Access: http://jama.ama-assn.org/

BANDOLIER
   Bandolier is a print and Internet journal about health care, using evidence-based medicine techniques to provide advice about particular treatments or diseases for healthcare professionals and consumers. The content is 'tertiary' publishing, distilling the information from (secondary)

(Continued)

TABLE 12.1
(Continued)

reviews of (primary) trials and making it comprehensible.
Access: http://www.jr2.ox.ac.uk/Bandolier/

Journal of Evidence-based healthcare
Access: http://www.Harcourt-international.com/journals/ebhc/

Free Medical on-line journals
Access: http://www.freemedicaljournals.com

FIG. 12.1.   An example of where evidence alone is not enough!

issues rather than on science. Science is confronted in an oblique way in this
context. The present excitement about accountability encourages a very restricted
view of the role of evidence, and it underplays a greater relationship between
evidence and the profession.

The need for evidence to justify professional practice is not in question.
However, many clinicians appear unsure about the role of evidence and how it
is linked with the identity of the profession. A profession that views itself as a
scientific profession must see that its quest for evidence assumes more than an
accounting role for its members. Being a scientific profession means having a
commitment to a specific doctrine that encompasses a set of values, standards,

and procedures that assist in determining valid knowledge. It includes holding an attitude that always seeks evidence before accepting new or novel ideas as factual knowledge as well as a readiness to consider competing arguments or hypotheses. The quest for evidence is then viewed as being integral to the responsibilities of members of a scientific profession and sought by clinicians who view themselves as clinical scientists. This is in great contrast to a view of evidence simply serving to stall any threats to employment or reallocation of services. Basically, if speech and language therapy were a scientific profession, we would want evidence for our practices independently of the implications in employment and not because of it. Evidence is important, but evidence alone is not enough. The practice of magic offers evidence, too (see Fig. 12.1). Consequently, it is important to situate evidence in the context of a scientific theory as well as subjecting it to scientific methods of evaluation.

EFFICACY RESEARCH

Efficacy research typically aims to establish whether a particular treatment or intervention is effective in producing a desired outcome in a patient. The intervention may refer to a drug treatment, a particular type of intervention, a counseling course, a behavioral modification programe, a rehabilitation regime, and/or a system of student teaching. The context in which efficacy research occurs varies with the domain of the profession. Physicians might investigate the efficacy of a particular anesthetic in surgery, a clinician might investigate the efficacy of a programe in treating a stutter, a psychologist might want to evaluate the effectiveness of cognitive therapy versus psychoanalysis in the treatment of agoraphobia, and an education professional might evaluate the effectiveness of mainstreaming versus special school education on learning disabled children.

The minimal requirement in efficacy research is the comparison of an intervention with no intervention under controlled conditions. Some studies often compare two or more interventions and may incorporate a placebo condition. The *Concise Oxford Dictionary* defines a placebo as "a medicine given more to please than to benefit the patient" (Thompson, 1995). Ultimately, all efficacy research asks the question, "Does this intervention or treatment produce the desired results in the individual?"

Prospective Versus Retrospective Efficacy Studies

The terms *prospective study* and *retrospective study* are loosely interpreted to mean that some studies predetermine the data needed for the study before it is gathered (i.e., prospective), and other studies capitalize on data that is already in existence (i.e., retrospective). In prospective studies, the clinician plans the study and then collects the data. In retrospective studies, the clinician typically looks back to existing records (e.g., department case records) to find information relevant to the study. In general, prospective investigations are preferred because they allow the clinician to have more control over events influencing the study. A retrospective study that relies on a search of existing records can bias the results when the records are incomplete or have been completed by clinicians who might have different interpretations of what was required. It is also rare that the goals of record keeping accord with the data one needs to answer specific research questions. If, however, the type of data held in the records were collected with the view to answering a research question at a later date, then this type of retrospective data acquisition presents the clinician with fewer problems. It is worth noting that the interpretations of prospective and retrospective study take on different characteristics, depending on the professional discipline (Pak & Adams, 1994; Riegelman & Hirsch, 2000).

Audits of Patient Services Versus Efficacy Research

The word *audit* has many variant terms. Whereas physicians use the term *audit*, nurses tend to use the term *quality assurance*, and managers talk about *total quality management (TQM)*. All these terms have a common goal to improve quality of care in patient management (Smith, 1992). Anyone first introduced to the practice of audits cannot help but notice that these procedures have the appearance of research activity, and yet there is an explicit understanding that audit procedures do not constitute research (see Fig. 12.2). Their differences, however, are rarely articulated, and it is easy to confuse the two activities. The following are the most obvious differences between audits and research:

- Audits do not test hypotheses or predictions.
- Audits are not directed by theory.
- Audits are not subject to the rigorous procedures necessary to control confounding factors.
- Audits are quick, easy-to-administer procedures designed to assess a service, often repeatedly at periodic intervals.
- Audits are useful for giving objective descriptions of the status of events, but they are not suitable to answer questions of a causal nature.

Research is aimed at discovering new knowledge, whereas audits commonly aim to check that a service or person performs according to predetermined standards set by the institution. Audits, in contrast to research, are sometimes thought to define quality of care (R. Smith, 1992).

To demonstrates the distinction between audits and research let's say that it is claimed that recent audits of prescription habits show that many general

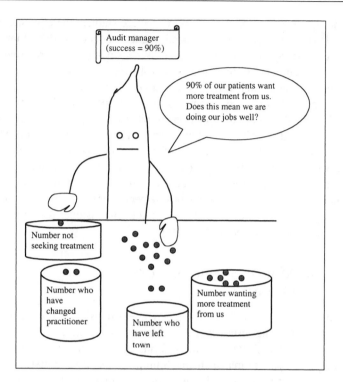

FIG. 12.2.   An audit is not scientific research.

practitioners continue to prescribe antidiuretic drugs in the management of cardiovascular failure, despite the overwhelming research evidence that this is not an effective course of treatment. In this case, the survey (or audit) identified the current state of practice, but research tested and evaluated the effectiveness of this treatment.

Outcome Studies Versus Efficacy Research

Outcome studies share many of the characteristics of audits because they are usually audits of a particular kind. These studies were originally performed in acute services in the United States, to derive formulas for figuring out the cost of treating specific disease conditions (e.g., uncomplicated appendicitis, uncomplicated gall bladder surgery). Outcome studies are usually about determining *cost-effectiveness* rather than the effectiveness of treatment or services. In other words, the question this type of study might ask is, Can the same outcome of care be arrived at with less expenditure of resources? (Malby, 1995).

Outcome studies gave rise to diagnosis-related groups (DRG). Health insurance companies used DRGs to aid financial planning and standardized costs of care. DRGs did not translate to extended care easily (i.e., nursing home care, rehabilitation), and a different system of measurement of these services was required. Two such systems are Functional Independence Measure (FIM; Kidd et al., 1995) and its derivative, Functional Ability Measure (FAM; Tesio & Cantagallo, 1998). Systems such as these are continually being refined to provide better measurements of patients. Information from outcome studies is used to prioritize health services and the amount of time clinicians can devote to caring for certain diagnostic groups (e.g., prioritization of care in elderly patients versus children).

Outcome studies in health care services typically refer to investigations aimed at identifying a set of variables that will predict a patient's outcome, often after a period of treatment. Applied to rehabilitation, the variables might include a patient's demographic details, medical diagnosis, score on an aphasia test, score on a test of functioning on activities of daily living, and measures of patient physical performance. A record of these values might be taken when a patient is admitted to a rehabilitation center or a language unit, and then again just before the patient is discharged.

By using statistical techniques (such as regression analyses), an outcome study can attempt to determine which set of measures or variables best predicts the patient's level of function at the end of rehabilitation or at a determined time. Many assumptions are made in these studies. For example, it is often incorrectly assumed that intervention is a constant in the equation that predicts outcome, or that what is measured by outcome studies is a valid index of the changes in a patient. Outcome studies of speech and language recovery or change can be used to provide gross descriptions and fairly objective measures of change. It is questionable how useful these studies are in predicting a patient's outcome because these studies rely on very gross measures to detect change in a patient's level of function.

Unfortunately, some clinicians have encountered situations in which a patient's poor outcome score has been interpreted to represent a measure of the effectiveness of therapy. This is, of course, faulty reasoning. Outcome studies do not control for the possible influence that intervention (or spontaneous recovery) might have on the patient's outcome, and so they are not studies that can address the issue of the efficacy of an intervention. This form of investigation is open to different interpretations. Clinicians can find themselves caught in silly arguments that go something like this: If the patient's outcome is poor or has not changed, then a view tends to prevail among rehabilitation specialists that the lack of improvement is attributed to treatment being ineffective. However, if improvement is observed in treatment, then this change tends to be attributed to spontaneous recovery. Either way, clinicians are faced a no-win situation for the service providers. Implicit in this argument is the assumption that an intervention cannot make a positive contribution to a patient's outcome. It is, therefore, difficult not to accept that the only way to assess the contribution of an intervention is to take account of the literature on efficacy research as well as evaluate one's own patients in the clinic more systematically.

Anecdotal Reports Versus Efficacy Research

Popular magazines and the media commonly amaze the public with fantastic reports describing "miracle recoveries" and "instant cures" in connection with tragic events. The clinician understands the publicity value of such news items as subserving the media's interest and usually disregards these unauthoritative accounts as false or melodramatic. Anecdotal reports of whether patients respond to treatment typically lack experimental control, and one cannot tell if the changes in the patient are indeed due to therapeutic intervention. One cannot discount the possibility that there might be observer bias operating in the person making the report or that there might be other explanations for the observed outcome in the patient. However, clinicians are used to anecdotal accounts in encounters with fellow clinicians or in professional literature. There is a tendency to regard these sources as credible sources of information, even though the basis for establishing the factual accuracy of this observation is little different from that given by tabloid newspapers or popular magazines.

Although anecdotal accounts typically are retrospective reports about interesting patients, anecdotal reports can also distort perceptions and impact on a health service.

Example

A rehabilitation hospital had earned a reputation for being one of the best rehabilitation centers in the United Kingdom, mainly because when it started it was one of very few new rehabilitation hospitals in the early 1960s. Over the decade, this hospital earned a good reputation as being one of the best hospitals in town. Many people held the belief that patients who went there always made a good recovery because of the excellent care they received. Staff morale was high, and the center was regarded as an enviable place of employment. Everyone who spoke about this center attributed the success of its rehabilitation program to the quality of therapy service, teamwork, and dedication of the staff to patients. Although all this could be true, this explanation was confounded. This rehabilitation center, having its pick of referrals, was able to apply selection criteria that favored the admission of patients whose characteristics were associated with a good recovery (possibly independently of an intervention). Some of these criteria required the patients to be under 60 years of age, show no signs of progressive illness, have no need for acute nursing care, have a concentration span of 30 minutes, have no history of alcoholism or drug abuse, and preferably have no previous incidents of brain damage caused by strokes or head injuries. Patients who did not fit these criteria were not admitted for rehabilitation.

Other facilities have been known to be selective in this and other ways too. Sometimes, hospitals might use a procedure like FIM to selectively decide who should be admitted to rehabilitation. This practice involves a circular argument. The staff say, "Therapy works best on patients carefully chosen for their ability to benefit from therapy," but then patients so well chosen may also be less damaged and therefore have a better prognosis, irrespective of therapy. People wanted so much to believe the work of the center described here was responsible for the success of the patients' rehabilitation that no one considered an alternative explanation for the center's success rate. We shall never know however, whether this hospital was more successful with its patients than others without a properly controlled study.

Why We Need Efficacy Research

Identifying Effective Interventions. How can we know which treatments or interventions are effective in ameliorating a patient's condition without efficacy research? Many people expect pharmaceutical products and various forms of medical treatment to be subject to rigorous clinical trials before being released for use by the public. In contrast, fewer people demand that same standards be met for the methods applied to teaching school children or to a particular therapy given to a speech-disordered child. The need to guard personal safety is a strong motivating factor for deciding which interventions are trialed and tested before administration to the public. What are the standards that guide the allied health professions' acceptance of some treatments and not others? Apart from the obvious issues related to safety and ethical considerations, there are currently no standards imposed by the health professions (e.g., clinical psychology, speech and language therapy, physiotherapy, occupational therapy) that prescriptively state that some forms of treatment are more admissible for professional practice than other. In practice, it is possible for a clinician to claim that wearing pink glasses is a remedial technique for overcoming dyslexia. As long as the clinician can tolerate unwanted attention, the intervention poses no apparent threat to anyone's health, and the patient is happy with the treatment, the intervention in principle can be implemented by the clinician. Efficacy research is really the only basis available for deciding whether wearing pink glasses is effective in aiding reading and whether this is an intervention to be condoned and implemented by one's professional peers. Efficacy research appears to be the only basis for setting standards that professional bodies and clinicians can define and recognize as acceptable interventions.

Knowing How Interventions Work. When an intervention is shown to be successful, people want to know how the intervention actually works to bring about the changes observed in the patient. Very often, this knowledge also forms part of the process that enables theories and hypotheses to be tested and verified.

Being Accountable to the Public. Another factor could, of course, be responsible for the rise in interest shown by clinicians in the efficacy of their treatment methods. Economic recession has created a consciousness of accountability whereby managers are required to justify the resources need to operate their services. Changes in methods of service delivery and calls for working with more efficient methods contribute to creating a demand for information that can be used to justify public expenditure on services. This demand translates into a need for information about interventions and their costs.

Effective and Successful Interventions

A clinician contemplating efficacy research is always going to be confronted with the difficulty of defining what constitutes *effective* and *successful* treatments. Both terms are open to a variety of interpretations. An effective intervention can mean that the problem is completely cured, the severity of the problem, is reduced, or the problem remains static but the patient has learned an alternative but effective way of communicating. The meaning of *therapy* is subject to a variety of interpretations and what it is meant to achieve. This presents something of a challenge in some efficacy research studies as one has to decide how long to apply an intervention before it is deemed effective. For example, does *effective* mean that some improvement must occur instantaneously or after a period of weeks? Does the meaning of *effective* tolerate the fact that patients may fail to maintain the therapeutic benefit?

Defining *success* in therapeutic interventions is another problem in efficacy research. Success is in the eye of the beholder. What can we take *successful treatment* to mean? A clinician might think that just because a client has improved his ability to read an additional 15% of words correctly, treatment has been successful. However, the client's wife may regard this as no improvement because the client is still unable to hold a conversation. The clinician might also think that treatment has not been successful because the client is unable to return to work. A clinical intervention might produce a statistically significant improvement in the patient's performance as measured by tests. However, this change may not be reflected in everyday function and can assume different meanings for the family and other significant caregivers. Such problems have plagued researchers, too. For example, Morris (1997) treated two adult patients, JS and JAC, for an auditory discrimination deficit with auditory tasks such as minimal pairs, phonological tasks, and lipreading. Morris reported success on the basis that these patients showed improvement on tests of minimal-pair discrimination and/or repetition tests, though their overall comprehension as measured by a synonym-judgment task did not change. Later, Maneta, Marshall, and Lindsay (1999) reported a study of another patient with auditory comprehension problems, PK. These investigators defined success of therapy based on an improvement in the patient's communication (not necessarily comprehension), and they claimed success when it was demonstrated that PK's spouse had learned to modify her own communication strategies with her husband. In neither study were the patients' overall comprehension (however defined by each study) improved, though in each study the researchers were able to claim success in therapy on the basis of different criteria they adopted in their studies.

Despite the similarity of the terms *effective* and *success*, they are in fact, not synonyms. This is made clear in situations in which clinicians commonly report a treatment as showing immediate efficacy in that it produces a change in the patient's performance levels instantly when the patient is in the clinic, but the effect is not maintained after the patient leaves the clinic. Clearly, clinicians seek more enduring treatment effects before declaring success.

Maintenance, Generalization, and Lapse

If therapy or an intervention is to be regarded as successful, then it is important to show that its effects are enduring long after the intervention is completed. If the patient demonstrates a lapse in performance and returns to preintervention levels of performance, then it would be difficult to claim that the intervention was successful, even though it was effective for a time.

Generalization is very important in therapy, too. When the effect of an intervention generalizes to noncontrol items or to control environments or contexts, two outcomes are possible. A researcher could become dismayed because if the nontreated items were the only control task and generalization effects were apparent, then the researcher has no way of telling whether therapy was effective because improvement on both the treated and nontreated tasks could have been affected by spontaneous recovery or similar factors. In contrast, a clinician should be delighted about generalization effects to nontreated items because it means the clinician need only treat some items—and not every item in the client's repertoire—for improvement to result. If an intervention has generalized to these other contexts or items, the clinician can feel relieved in knowing that there will be no need to treat every instance of the target behaviors (e.g., teaching every word in the English vocabulary, teaching how to walk on every conceivable floor surface).

USING GROUPS VERSUS INDIVIDUALS IN EFFICACY RESEARCH

Groups, Single-Case Designs, and Case Reports

The choice of design depends on the nature of the population studied and the question the clinician is asking. A traditional view asserts that randomized controlled trial (RCT) studies are desirable. Such a view originates from studies of typical people where the range of interparticipant variability is low and from nonhuman investigations (e.g., agriculture, microbiology). The assumptions in

RCT studies are that the participants are relatively homogeneous or, that failing to be true, that it is possible to obtain large numbers of participants (more than 100) to override the effects of individual variability in the group. Patients, as a sample, are almost always heterogeneous (i.e., they differ from each other enormously even when they have the same principle diagnosis). For example, they may differ in severity, the pattern of presentation, and the variety of co-occurring impairments with impact on the primary diagnosis. Often it is also not possible to gather large numbers of patients, particularly for a condition that is rare or unusual. Note however, as shown in Fig. 12.3, that homogeneity does not mean that individuals are identical. They only need to be similar in ways that are important in the study.

Group studies have traditionally been the preferred approach to research because investigators believe that results from such studies result in better generalization of findings to individuals whom they have not directly studied. This is achieved on the basis of statistical probability or inference. However, valid statistical inferences about populations are achieved only by *random* sampling from those populations, a condition rarely satisfied in most studies of patients or any specialized group of individuals. In most intervention studies, researchers tend to select patients simply because they happen to be in treatment at the time of the study rather than through some process of random selection. Studies that do not involve random sampling rely on logical rather than statistical inferences when evaluating the generalization of effects to other individuals. The clinician or researcher basically ends up saying that the results of this study apply to individuals who have attributes or qualities like the participants studied.

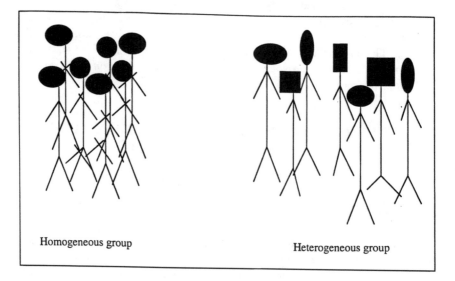

Homogeneous group

Heterogeneous group

FIG. 12.3. Homogeneity versus heterogeneity.

Consequently, the argument that only group studies permit generalization is overestimated (Edgington, 1987).

Case-Series Design

Case-series design is an emerging design feature in an increasing number of research studies. Instead of presenting just one patient case, a researcher can present data from several (single-case) patients. Case-series studies retain all the advantages of single-case studies, while also allowing the researcher to address important research issues such as replicability, individual differences, and how differences may or may not significantly contribute to different results observed in patients (i.e., it offers some insight into within-patient variability). However, comparing single patients in a case series has methodological problems, too. When the level of granularity of the data is so detailed, it is spoken of in terms of one having very rich data on each patient. Depending on the tests administered to the patients, it can sometimes be quite difficult to discriminate between results that represent the patients' true performance and results that capture something else about the patients (e.g., previous knowledge, test anxiety) or random variation. Using tests for which there is information about the performance characteristics of the test (i.e., psychometrically developed tests) help minimize the problem of discriminating between true performance or error. However, most research, by the nature of the study, requires experimental tasks to be developed, and information about the performance of these tasks is usually limited to only providing norms. When there is variability among the patients' scores and comparisons are made between three or four patients, interpreting the patients' results can be challenging.

Research presenting a case series is research that can also be added to over time by other researchers. This is possible because the patients are described in great detail. This approach to research is particularly important in studying rare disorders.

Significantly, case-series design provides an argument framework such that a few patients can be compared with each other to detect the presence or absence of dissociations. *Dissociations* are a form of evidence that is based on the researcher demonstrating that two performance skills can appear independently in a patient. For example, the pattern of performance "PHD shows an impairment in naming objects presented to him, but he can define the objects if he is given their names", tells us that the patient has two independent modalities (auditory and visual) for accessing knowledge about objects. The importance of this information is that it provides evidence for there being separate information processing routes into the semantic system. This example is an instantiation of a *single dissociation*. One could argue that the reason for this patient failing in one task and not the other task might be related to the tasks not being comparable. Perhaps one task is actually easier than the other. This is why single dissociations are useful but are not as strong a form of evidence as *double dissociations*.

Suppose the researcher comes across another patient, Dr. O, but this new patient shows a pattern that is the opposite of PH's. This patient finds it easier to name objects presented to him, but he cannot define the object when he is given its name. Taking the data provided by the two patients, PH and DO, we can say that there is evidence of a double dissociation and that their failure in one and not the other task cannot be attributed to the tasks being incomparable. Both of these patients can also be observed via a reference to PATSy, an online clinical and research database (Lum et al., 2001).

Fractionation is a process by which researchers may successively deduce the identity of the components and or processes contributing to typical performance on

TABLE 12.2
Advantages and Disadvantages of Case-reports, Single-case Studies and Group Studies

Advantages	*Disadvantages*
Case report/case study:	
• Can challenge an existing theory.	• Lacks the principled controls needed to be able to attribute the patient's response to the treatment described by the investigator.
• May offer the only report of a very rare condition.	
• Can suggest how to design a suitable study.	• Terms are rarely defined and so replication of the findings in another patient can be very difficult to show.
• May invoke new hypotheses that can subsequently be tested.	
Single-case treatment studies:	
• Useful for objectively evaluating treatment in the clinic	• Difficult to assess the interaction of the patient's attributes (e.g., personality, motivation, education level) with the treatment.
• Overcome the problem of insufficient numbers, particularly if patients have an unusual condition.	
• Allow researchers to study an individual objectively and to consider idiosyncratic variables without sacrificing rigor.	• Difficult to generalize to other cases.
	• Difficult to replicate these studies because patients rarely have the same problems.
• Allow one to assess the contributions of each treatment component by systematically adding or eliminating specific components that facilitate change.	• With a marked degree of variability in the patient's performance, it can be difficult to assess whether significant change has occurred.
• Can assess the effect of different treatments in the same individual.	• In some designs where the participant is his or her own control, the inability to unlearn a treatment effect can jeopardize the study.
• Useful in overcoming problems presented by small heterogeneous populations.	• Not easy to find independent behaviors/skills that can serve as control conditions.
• Cost-effective and allow for small-scale testing before a larger group study is undertaken	• Difficult to constrain because the study is led by the patient's condition and the rules for deciding how long to gather data, when to implement treatment and what should be the criteria for evaluating change depend on the patient.

(Continued)

TABLE 12.2
(Continued)

Group treatment studies:	
• Traditionally allow for results to be generalized to other cases.	• Can be problems in collecting a sufficient number of patients to form a homogeneous group.
• Large sample sizes allow the use of certain statistical tests and analyses that can facilitate understanding the relationship between different factors.	• Have administration problems and are expensive.
	• Averaging results in a heterogeneous Group of patients can obscure the individual patient's response to the treatment.
	• If the average performance in a group does not represent the individual patient in the group due to heterogeneity of the group, then it is difficult to identify the characteristics of the patient who would respond to a specific type of intervention.
	• Statistically significant results in group-designs do not necessarily translate to clinical significant results (i.e., the change detected statistically may not be sufficiently large to produce a clinically meaningful result in the patient and vice versa). This outcome can occur when a treatment is effective for only some patients but not for all the patients in the group.
	• Comparisons between groups of patients rely on the variability between the groups being larger than the variability within the group of participants. When variability is great within the groups, this often produces a nonsignificant result or a weak or unstable effect, meaning sometimes the result will be significant, depending on the composition of the groups.

a task or of a skill. For examples, Warrington (1982) reported the fractionation of arithmetic skills, and Nickels, Howard, and Best (1997) described an example in articulation. The theoretical significance of dissociations and fractionations is more fully explained in Shallice (1988) and similar neuropsychology literature.

Meta-Analyses

Meta-analysis can be defined as the analysis of all analyses. Individual research studies evaluate whether a particular treatment is effective. To have confidence in this study's findings, it is important to replicate the study. After some time, several studies of similar kinds exist, some showing the same results and others not. One way of evaluating the overall finding of these studies is to simply read them all and write a qualitative literature review. See Law (1997) for an example of such review on intervention of language-impaired children. Qualitative reviews have the problem of subjective interpretation of the reviewer. A more objective approach is to conduct a meta-analysis. The meta-analysis researcher gathers all the available studies and then combines and recalculates the statistical results of these studies (usually group studies' means and standard deviations) by using specific statistical procedures. This also achieves the effect of increasing the sample size, which in turn has the benefit of improving the power (i.e., capacity to detect) of statistical tests in detecting whether there is a true effect of treatment (Wood, 2000). For an example of meta-analyses, see Sommers, Logsdon and Wright (1992), who reviewed treatment research related to articulation and phonological disorders.

In practice, straight replication of a study is less common than for different researchers to investigate the same treatment effect but with some minor variation (e.g., the type of participants selected, the type of words used in therapy, how frequently items are presented, how patients' responses are cued). However, successful meta-analysis depends on researchers using similar tests, participants, and so on to ensure that similar studies are being grouped together. Although varying the different variables in new research assists with identifying which variables are salient or critical in influencing treatment, such variability in studies poses other problems in meta-analyses.

CHANGING BEHAVIOR IN THE CLINIC

During the 1970s, learning theory dominated thinking in teaching, in clinical psychology, and in the therapy professions. This was expressed as behavior-modification programs in schools and in psychology clinics (e.g., reducing the rate of self-afflicted injury among learning-disabled individuals, modifying intrusive classroom behavior) and as behaviorism (e.g., applying behaviorist principles to changing stuttering or to articulation therapy). A notable feature of learning theory is that it has been possible to evolve a methodology for changing behavior that is congruent with a theory of human behavior. This methodology embraces the principles of learning such as shaping, reinforcement, punishment, and extinction. To see these principles applied in speech therapy, the clinician executes therapy in the following sequence[*]:

1. Operationally define the target behavior for the therapy session, stating what the clinician is required to do to elicit the desired response from the

---

[*]This example is based on teaching a cleft-palate child to articulate anterior sounds (e.g., /t/, /d/, /s/) with a newly acquired prosthesis.

child, how often it is to be produced, how it will be reinforced, and how it will be measured. *(Operationally defined goals)*

2. Present the target speech sound. *(Modeling)*
3. Praise the child for his attempts to produce the correct response. *(Positive reinforcement)*
4. Later, reinforce only the target sound and ignore any productions that are less than correct. *(Selective reinforcement)*
5. Count success when the child produces the target sound reliably. Then reinforce the child when the target sound is also produced in different words or to different people. *(Stimulus generalization)*
6. Change the reinforcement schedule such that the child is praised only for every other correct production rather than every production.
7. A month later, check to see whether the child has maintained the newly acquired target sound. *(Maintenance)*

There are variations on this process in terms of the choice of reinforcers, what is reinforced (or punished), whether reward or penalty (punishment) is used, and how and when it is applied. Irrespective of the type of disorder or theoretical orientation held by a clinician, a great deal of didactic (i.e., one-on-one) *skill-based* therapy involves staging tasks through graduated steps from easy to levels more demanding levels of function. The goal is to shape the patient's behavior until the desired performance is attained. Therapy strategies reflecting a particular theoretical position might be adopted, but the fundamental aspects in the delivery of therapy appear to be similar.

Depending where in the world one is taking a course in speech and language therapy, few clinicians recognize the features of "structured" therapy as belonging to behavior therapy. Although behaviorism has moved aside to allow for more cognitive accounts of human behavior, the application of learning principles still prevails in therapy practice (even if unrecognized as such by clinicians). Therapy practice appears to incorporate a combination of cognitive theories and behaviorism. In this case, the behavior is explained by cognitive theory, and behaviorist principles are used to modify the patient's behavior in successive steps toward a target behavior. The contribution of each depends on the nature of the case. Disorders involving voice, neuromuscular speech, and hearing disorders tend not to draw on cognitive accounts for therapy and rely instead on more mechanistic neurological accounts of those behaviors.

EVALUATING THERAPY WITH A PATIENT

Many factors, impinge on the decision about what behavior to target in therapy, including the patient's preferences, the nature of the problems, the theoretical orientation of the clinician, and the number of therapy sessions allowed by health insurance. This section is not intended to be prescriptive about therapy. This section describes some factors a clinician should consider when conducting therapy to optimize the conditions for evaluating the effectiveness of the therapy undertaken with a single patient. These are the main events involved in evaluating therapy with a single patient:

- Specify as fully as possible the nature of the patient's problems.
- Decide on the time frame of the evaluation (i.e., change within a session, following several sessions, following several weeks of sessions).
- Select the behaviors to be changed.
- Decide which will be control and treatment behaviors or tasks.
- Decide on the form, schedule for reinforcement, and type of feedback.
- Decide on the format of the therapy task.
- Decide on the content of the therapy task items.
- Decide on the staging in therapy (also known as approximating the desired outcome or target).
- Decide on the strategy for changing behavior.
- Decide which tasks (or tests) will be used to measure pre- and posttherapy performance.
- Decide on the length of the pretherapy baseline phase.
- Decide on the number of measurements (i.e., data points).
- Decide whether to use probes or continuous measurement.
- Define time intervals for reassessment and maintenance.
- State predictions about generalization effects.
- Develop therapy tasks.
- Document decisions made in a patient's therapy plan and the patient's response to these.

A detailed description of each of these events follows.

Specifying the Nature of the Patient's Problems

A full specification of the patient's problems does not mean simply a diagnosis of whether the patient has dysarthria, aphasia, dysphonia, or a stutter, or whether a child has a phonological problem or language delay. It is recognized, however, that how far a case is specified is dependent on the theoretical orientation (or its absence) and the objectives of the clinician. Different kinds of assessments guided by these perspectives have an impact on how much time is required for assessment and therapy. Clinicians using a test battery approach in assessment will employ the same standard test battery across a variety of patients, and the idiosyncratic nature of a patient's speech and language problems have little importance. Other forms of assessment entail more detailed specification of the patient's problems, depending on the theoretical framework of the assessment. Irrespective of the clinician's own theoretical orientation, therapy should be systematically applied because it would be difficult to evaluate treatment if it were administered on an ad hoc basis.

In the clinical services, there is tension between scheduling in many patients and being able to plan and evaluate therapy for these patients. With the advent of new constraints operating on health services, it is not unusual for clinicians to speak of offering their clients "treatment contracts" or a fixed number of treatment sessions, limited by that particular health service organization or health insurance company. Rather than question or challenge the status quo, clinicians may find it easier to go with the flow and adopt the position that one should not spend too much time assessing patients. Unless a patient were too sick or disabled to tolerate testing, it is inconceivable to think of therapy being administered without a proper assessment of the patient's problems.

Guilt seems to feature in this situation, too. Personal communication with clinicians has indicated that sometimes a clinician feels that assessment is more for the clinician's benefit than for the patient's. This view then invokes a sense of guilt in the clinician, and assessments are viewed as events to be done quickly and put aside. In other cases, the clinician may feel that the team would not understand why her assessments require more than a week to complete. Assessing "rough and ready," even if the clinician is highly experienced, is no substitute for a detailed, rigorous assessment of the patient's condition that allows more target-specific therapy. As stated earlier, diagnostic intervention is sometimes invoked as a substitute for pretherapy assessment. Of course, as with other things in life, a balance must be found.

It does seem unethical, however, that a clinician should think of proceeding with therapy before having defined the patient's problem. One could speculate that patients, like clinicians, might want to know that a full diagnosis has been made before therapy begins. In other words, most people would want a dentist, a psychologist, a plumber, a doctor, an optician, and so on to know the details of the problem before prescribing a remedy or a therapy program. This point must be felt even more strongly whenever money is transparently involved in therapy services or where legal and ethical responsibilities to the patient are concerned.

The concern about spending time in assessing the patient is not uncommon among clinicians. The irony is that unless a patient's problems are well defined, evaluation of the benefits of therapy with that client will be difficult. It may be that a bit more time spent in assessment and in therapy planning might result in less time spent in therapy because one will be able to target therapy more specifically at the source of the patient's problem. The message here is don't be afraid to assess the patient, but do explain your plans and the rationale for what you do in therapy to the patient.

The other matter related to specifying the patient's problem is the formulation of hypotheses (see Chapter 6). The hypothesis is not whether the patient has a problem or not; the hypothesis is usually a hunch about what is responsible for the patient's problem.

Deciding on the Time Frame for the Evaluation

Evaluation of therapy can be undertaken over different time intervals. The length of the interval depends on what skills or functions the clinician is interested in changing in the patient as well as the approach to treatment. For example, if the clinician were interested in evaluating the effect of counseling the patient about his attitudes toward his disability, then it might be appropriate to allow several weeks to pass before reevaluating the patient. In contrast, if the clinician is interested in finding out how effective a particular cuing strategy is in assisting a client produce the names of object pictures in naming, then the patient could be evaluated and reevaluated within one therapy session. However, if the clinician were interested in finding out whether this cuing strategy leads to longer-term benefits, then a reevaluation would be required after some weeks or months.

Selecting the Behaviors to Be Changed

Where you start and what you choose to work on in therapy should be guided by a theory of normal and abnormal behavior and/or processes. Without theory-guiding assessment and therapy, it is easy to feel lost when confronted with a patient who presents with multiple disorders. Therapy also assumes an ad hoc approach of one day working on this and another day working on that in the hope that some good will result.

Deciding on Control and Treatment Behaviors and Tasks

In treatment research, the following rule (adapted from the principle of statistical regression) applies to provide optimal conditions for evaluating therapy: Check that the control and treatment behaviors have the potential for change (i.e., not at floor [approximately 30% and below] or ceiling [approximately 80% and above] levels of performance). The reason for not choosing to work on behaviors that are at floor level is that there may be more than one problem contributing to the patient's poor performance (e.g., a dysarthria and a phonological output problem affecting naming). A therapy technique might be very effective for treating the phonological output problem but have no effect on the patient's naming performance because the dysarthria persists. Floor-level performance can also mean that the mechanism responsible for normal function might be almost totally obliterated or has failed to develop, and this may be a situation that cannot be modified.

Clinicians can find themselves having to attempt remediation of skills, that are at floor levels. This is understandable, but the points raised previously should alert the clinicians to the fact that it could be difficult to evaluate the effect of therapy on performance and it is likely that no change will be observed. Similar ideas apply to attempts to change social skills or behavior. Further consideration of the latter is provided by Barlow and Hersen (1984), for those wishing to measure communication and pragmatic skills in naturalistic settings.

Here are a few examples of target and control cognitive-based skills:

TABLE 12.3
Examples of Target Skills and Possible Control Conditions

Target Behavior	Suggested Controls
Auditory processes (e.g. discrimination, word recognition, sentence comprehension).	Reading or writing words and/or nonwords.
Concept formation or comprehension.	Reading or writing words and/or nonwords.
Naming.	Nonword repetition, reading or writing nonwords, auditory discrimination, sentence comprehension.

Another point relates to the distance between the control and treatment behaviors. The closer these are, the more likely it will be that treatment on the target behavior will generalize to the control behavior. So, be sure to choose a control task that is functionally as dissimilar as possible from the treatment behavior (e.g., naming with writing nonwords) and that has the potential to improve.

Depending on the design of the evaluation, it may be necessary to split the therapy task items into a treatment set and a no-treatment set. In this case, a no-treatment set becomes a control task against which to evaluate the effectiveness of therapy. It is important to recognize when two conditions interact to confound treatment (e.g., trying to improve comprehension of prepositions when the patient has grave short-term memory problems, attempting to improve writing when the patient has persistent semantic problems) (see Table 12.3).

Deciding on the Format of the Therapy Tasks

At this stage it is important to decide the task format—whether the choice of therapy items will be pictures, sentence completion exercise, word-picture matching, and so on. For example, there are a multitude of ways to treat a problem in auditory phonemic discrimination. Some of these approaches include minimal-pair discrimination, selection of a written word from an array that matches a spoken word, matching of a spoken word to a target among an array of pictures, and spoken rhyming judgments. The factors to consider include the patient's condition (e.g., does he have visual problems? can she read yet?) and the nature of what is to be treated.

Deciding on the Content of the Therapy Task Items

The first consideration here is the personal relevance of the items to the patient's interests. It follows that selecting items relevant to the patient might influence motivation levels. The opposite may also be true—selecting items not familiar to the patient might be more successful in capturing the patient's interest. This has to be discussed with the patient. The information needs also to be considered in conjunction with other factors, such as whether the items represent various psycholinguistic variables (e.g., frequency and imageability).

Deciding on the Staging in Therapy

Deciding on the staging, also known as approximating the target, applies to situations in which it is necessary to proceed in incremental steps toward the target behavior. It may be the case that the patient has too much difficulty working at the level of the target behavior. For example, if the target of therapy is comprehension of passive-voice sentences, then the first stage might be to work on teaching the patient to identify the subject, verb, and object (SVO) elements in an active declarative sentence. This step might require the patient to identify the SVO elements denoted by different colors in a passive sentence. Success at this stage can be followed by a third stage, in which the patient is required to identify the elements (no longer distinguished by color), followed by matching a passive sentence with its corresponding picture.

Deciding on the Strategy for Changing Behavior

The theory of therapy varies according to the basis of the disorder being treated. If there were a theory that stated, "Hammer away at what's wrong and it will improve," then all the clinician would need to do is drill practice and encourage the patient to practice and practice until everything returns to function again. This approach might tend to be adopted with treatment of voice or dysarthria therapy. Often, in therapy, it is necessary to think of strategies that the patient can use to help himself or herself. This creative idea is the strategy, something new that the clinician teaches the patient to used to help overcome obstacles hindering access to function. One example of this could be a self-cuing device (Best, Howard, Bruce, & Gatehouse, 1997).

The form that reinforcement assumes depends on patient factors (e.g., age and sex of the patient, what the patient finds rewarding or punishing). In adults, verbal praise might be sufficient. In children, both verbal praise and a token reward (e.g., stickers) might be important. Little thought seems to be given to the schedule of reinforcement in speech therapy courses these days, but it is widely known in the learning literature that different schedules of reinforcement have different effects on how efficient learning occurs. Feedback can appear in several forms, too. Feedback can tell the patient whether his or her response to an item is correct without telling him or her how to improve on the last action. Corrective feedback incorporates information about how to repair an incorrect response, usually incorporating another attempt at the same item. The clinician should decide which type of feedback and reinforcers will be used and whether there will be a hierarchy of feedback information given to the patient.

Deciding Which Tasks to Use to Measure Performance

It is possible to evaluate a patient on commercially available standardized tests or tasks designed in a clinic to measure and treat patients. There are some considerations to keep in mind here. Some commercially standardized tests may be too broad and assess too many functions with too few items. If these were used to evaluate therapy pre and post, then it is highly likely that improvement in a specific skill by the patient might not be detected by these tests. It is therefore important to select tests that consist of enough items and that are representative of the behavior or skill being treated. Tasks devised in a clinic can be used. Usually, after removing the items the patient has passed, the remainder of the task is split into two halves, consisting of items the patient has failed. A pretherapy measure is taken (and may be repeated several times to assess the stability of performance). One half of the items are treated and the other half are held back as a control task and are not treated. At the end of therapy, both halves are readministered to the patient. If therapy has item-specific effects, then only the treated items will show improvement. Sometimes, generalization occurs and the untreated tasks may improve as well as the treated tasks. Different possibilities exist regarding control tasks or conditions.

It is also important to ensure that the tests used as pretests are the same tests used as posttests; this means including the same items. The only time you can depart from this is if a test comes with a parallel version, and it has been shown that either version measures the same knowledge or skill in an individual (e.g., Wide Range Achievement Test; Wilkinson, 1993). The test conditions present in the administration of the pretest should be the same as those in the posttest.

One of the problems with many tests and with clinic-produced tasks is that we have no knowledge of the range of variability expected from the test or task arising just by chance (i.e. test–retest reliability) or arising from the nature of the items selected in producing the test. It can be difficult to establish how much change in test scores is tolerated before we can claim that the observed change is due to improvement and not to chance variation. Consequently, one of the most important phases in evaluating therapy is the pretherapy baseline period.

Deciding on the Length of the Baseline Phase

There is no hard-and-fast rule about the length of a pretherapy baseline period, though its main purpose is to establish whether the behavior one wants to change is changing spontaneously anyway (e.g., in recovery from brain trauma). With children, maturation effects have to be considered. The other type of spontaneous change we tend to forget is deterioration of behavior from disorders such as dementia and various other progressive diseases. It is necessary to have an overview of how the target behavior fluctuates before we can assess what impact intervention has on a patient.

What is being measured and the context in which the behavior occurs also influence the length of a pretherapy baseline period. Some interventions might focus on behavior in natural settings (e.g., classroom, home). Other interventions might focus on a patient's ability to name object pictures or to discriminate between minimal pairs. When behavior is measured in natural settings, it may be appropriate to baseline the target behavior by observing it in six 15-minute blocks per daily session for 2 weeks before introducing the intervention phase. However, if the target behavior is the ability to name object pictures, then it might be more appropriate to take a minimum of two, or preferably three, pretherapy baseline measures on the same task items (spread over 3 weeks) before introducing the intervention phase. Limiting the number of pretherapy assessments will also help minimize reactivity (i.e., familiarity with the test items). In the case of severely speech-impaired patients, it will keep to a minimum the difficulty the patient has in experiencing repeated testing.

Deciding on the Number of Data Measurements

Deciding on the number of data measurements is partly related to the determination of the length of the baseline period in the context of behavioral therapy (e.g., changing spitting behavior, changing the loudness of speech in social skills training, improving eye-contact time, improving on-task work time, improving duration of nonbreathy voice production, measuring the number of questions during a day). There can be many data points (e.g., 10 to 20) in the pretherapy baseline phase, particularly if the measures are taken daily. Each data point reflects the total number of times the target behavior occurred during, say, 15-minute observation sessions on that day (Barlow & Hersen, 1984; O'Leary & Wilson, 1987).

It may not, however, be very practical to administer a 100-word picture-naming test more than once per day with speech-impaired patients and even less so for every day of the week. In the latter example, there might only be two or three data points, though the general understanding is that the more pretherapy baseline points, the better.

It is also likely that there might be more data points in the pretherapy baseline phase than in subsequent phases. The purpose of the pretherapy baseline phase is to establish the natural rate of occurrence of the behavior before introducing therapy. Subsequent baselines serve to evaluate the effect of intervention on the individual's performance when intervention is withdrawn or has ceased. Figure 12.4 illustrates the baseline and intervention phases in evaluation of therapy in social skills training for a learning disabled child who is disruptive in a speech therapy group by spitting. The baseline involves recording the number of times the child spits his during five daily 15-minute periods. During the baseline, an assistant records the child's spitting behavior while the clinician is interacting with the children in the group. During the intervention phases, the clinician selectively ignores the child; she attends to the child when she is engaging with the group and ignores her when she is spitting. The results show that the child's spitting increase during the baseline phases, when the intervention strategy is not applied. This suggests that the intervention is effectively minimizing spitting by the child.

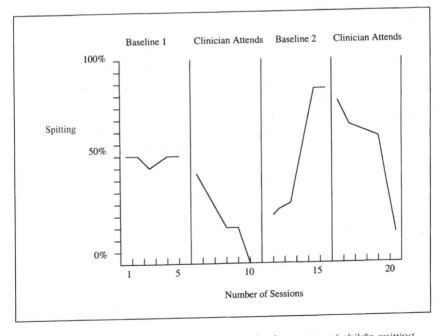

FIG. 12.4.   Effect of clinician's attention on the frequency of child's spitting.

Deciding Whether to Use Probes or Continuous Measurement

The ongoing evaluation of behaviors can be checked periodically with probes. A probe is a brief test procedure that evaluates the performance of the target behavior, often across successive sessions. The probe could assess the treated behavior (e.g., oral naming) or it could assess an untreated behavior where generalization is expected (e.g., written naming). Probing helps keep reactivity to a minimum.

Continuous measurement of target behaviors is most often applicable to evaluating behaviors when the behavior is easily observable and when measurement procedures have minimal impact on what is being measured.

Defining Time Intervals for Reassessment and Maintenance

It is important to plan ahead of time when the target behavior will be reevaluated (e.g., commonly in the sixth week after the commencement of therapy) and when the posttherapy phase will occur. These decisions are important, to allow time for a speech therapy evaluation when deciding a patient's discharge or review plan, when these are discussed at case or team meetings.

Stating Predictions About Generalization Effects

Some therapies can have generalizing effects. It is important to consider this and plan therapy with this in mind. For example, if a patient has problems coordinating voice–voicelessness in producing plosives, fricatives, and affricates, then it is while gradually introducing voice likely that the strategy of lengthening the voiceless fricative (used to treat fricatives) will generalize to affricates but not to plosives. This is because affricates and fricatives are continuants and are unlike plosives which are stops. In this case, plosives can be used as a control condition, fricatives as the treatment condition, and affricates as the untreated, but generalization-expected, condition. If this hypothesis is true, then the predictions will be borne out, and it will not be necessary for the clinician to treat the affricates at all. These predictions were informed by a knowledge of distinctive features of various consonants.

Developing Therapy Tasks

A theory-driven approach to therapy, which incorporates a methodical evaluation of therapy, is relatively new in speech and language therapy. It is becoming the basis of what defines good practice in therapy. Few off-the-shelf therapy-programmed approaches are available. Consequently, most clinics double as "production houses" for therapy tasks. There are some considerations here. It is important to be careful that a patient does not fail an item for reasons other than his or her disorder.

If a clinician uses pictures, then it is important to have people with similar social–demographic background to the patients check that the pictures or the text used is unambiguous. A patient who fails an item should not fail because a picture of snow looks like rain. A picture should be an item that any individual of similar age, education, and socioeconomic status would have no difficulty identifying. This is difficult to verify in a clinic, but it can be a factor that decides whether one buys a therapy resource. So naming agreement for each picture is desirable if you are purchasing therapy resources consisting of picture material. This tells whether a group of typical individuals with the same attributes as the client is able to name or do whatever the task calls for.

Documenting Decisions in a Therapy Plan and Getting the Patient's Response

When a therapy program is planned (i.e., designed to target specific functions for treatment whilst leaving other functions as controls to gauge the effect of therapy), then a more objective to assessment of the patient's progress is possible. This has to be preferred to impressionistic judgements that result in a clinician claiming the patient is "doing well today". A therapy plan is an account of what was done to and for a patient, and this is also part of the accounting process. Notations for each of the different areas described previously should be held on record. At this early stage in therapy research and knowledge, there is ample opportunity for clinicians to make valid contributions to knowledge about therapy (even if it fails) by writing this up as a report or a paper to disseminate knowledge about treating a given disorder. This is the only way cumulative scientific knowledge can build up about what works or does not work in therapy.

DESIGNS FOR EVALUATING THERAPY IN THE CLINIC

The designs presented here have their origin in single-case research methodology. The most famous single-case study reported in the literature is probably Pavlov's dog (Pavlov, 1927). Subsequent use of single-case methodology was popular in the education context during the 1970s, when behaviorism was favoured as an approach to modifying classroom behavior (Barlow & Hersen, 1984; Kazdin, 1978). Educational psychologists required a methodology for assessing the effectiveness of their training or behavioral-modification programs on individual students. These designs also provided a methodology for evaluating the effectiveness of behavior (Wilson, 1987; Wilson & O'Leary, 1980). In time, single-case designs were also recognized by psychologists as being a useful approach to studying individuals undergoing remediation in the context of rehabilitation (Coltheart, 1989; Wilson, 1987). Remember that not all single-case design studies evaluate efficacy. For example, in cognitive neuropsychology and aphasiology, single-case studies can be used as a paradigm to test predictions made by current theories of speech and language (Bub & Bub, 1988; Caramazza & McCloskey, 1988). The idea here being that an individual who has acquired brain-damage (e.g., following a stroke) is an instance of a 'natural experiment'. Researchers may test hypotheses about normal brain function in say, language processing, by observing how brain damage (loss of function) interferes with language processing.

The single-case designs described here are those that are suitable for evaluating the effects of intervention with single patients. It may be helpful to show two of the most common designs used in clinic currently; a consideration of these will make it easier to understand the value of other designs that follow. Keep in mind that this chapter is simply about designs for evaluating therapy. The actual content of therapy and what informs therapy (i.e., the theory of therapy) is a separate issue and is not within the scope of this text, though the reader can refer to Byng, (1995), and Byng & Black (1995).

Common designs that cannot evaluate the contribution of therapy are shown in Fig. 12.5.

The problem with the AB and BA designs is that we do not have a basis for comparison to know whether there has been change in the patient's performance before and after therapy. With the ABA design we can assess whether change has occurred, but we will not know if the observed change is due to therapy or due to recovery (or to maturation or extraneous factors, such as placebo effects, the Hawthorne effect, or extraneous events co-occurring simultaneously). An example of this design in popular use is in the context of outcome studies with patients measured on either the FIM or FAM in rehabilitation centers (Dittmar & Gresham, 1997).

Considerations in Single-Case Designs

Test-Based Versus Structured Observations in Single-Case Evaluation.   In all single-case designs, conventional notation typically uses A for assessment and B for intervention. However, there are several variations on what A and B may represent. For example, A usually represents the baseline, and A1 may represent a placebo condition or a second baseline condition (Kratochwill & Levin, 1992). It is important to note that A, in the speech and language therapy literature, can have two possible interpretations, depending on the nature of the intervention under investigation. When assessment is in the form of a test administration (e.g., from a test battery or a clinic-based task), A is a usually a total test score, shown pretest (pretherapy baseline), and B is still

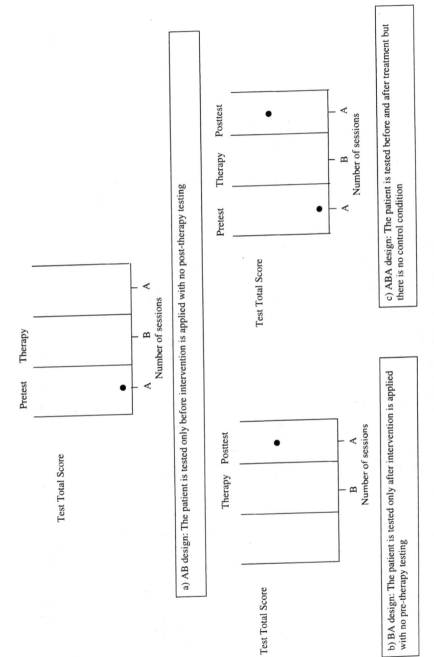

a) AB design: The patient is tested only before intervention is applied with no post-therapy testing

b) BA design: The patient is tested only after intervention is applied with no pre-therapy testing

c) ABA design: The patient is tested before and after treatment but there is no control condition

FIG 12.5. Common designs that cannot evaluate the contribution of therapy.

185

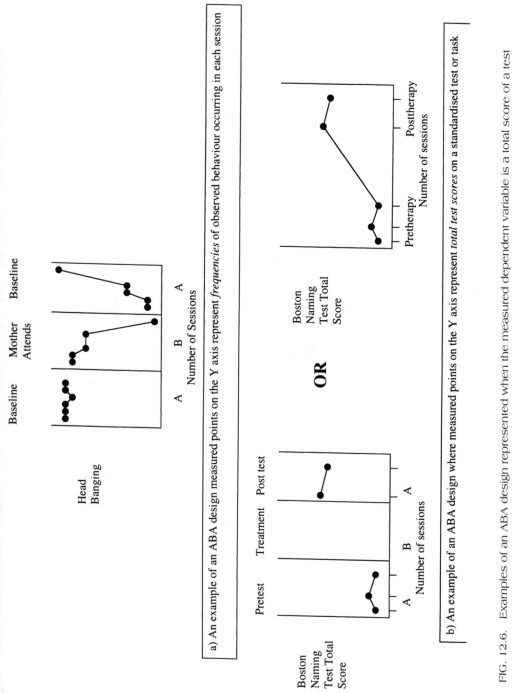

a) An example of an ABA design measured points on the Y axis represent *frequencies* of observed behaviour occurring in each session

b) An example of an ABA design where measured points on the Y axis represent *total test scores* on a standardised test or task

FIG. 12.6.   Examples of an ABA design represented when the measured dependent variable is a total score of a test or a set of observations.

intervention, but the posttest or second-baseline is usually shown as A1 and maintenance as A2. The example in Fig. 12.6(b) shows data points representing the total score of the patient's success on a set of treated and untreated task items.

In Fig. 12.6(a), the phase A represents an observation phase and not a test. In this situation, each data point represents the total number of times a target behavior (i.e., talkouts) was observed (e.g., in five 15-minute observation periods in each session during a week).

A baseline is a period before the commencement of therapy when the patient's performance on therapy is evaluated several times (on tests or clinic-produced tasks) or counted in several sessions (in behavioral observations) before the introduction of the intervention. The purpose of a baseline is to establish whether the patient's function is stable before therapy begins. If spontaneous change is evident, then this has implications for whether one commences therapy and/or which design one chooses to evaluate the patient. Unless stated otherwise, the following evaluation designs represent therapy situations where tests or clinic-based tasks are used to evaluate the patient's performance. Any of these designs can be adapted to reflect evaluations based on behavioral observations. To read more about designs that use behavioral assessment, consult Barlow and Hersen (1984), Kratochwill and Levin (1992), and Richards, Taylor, Ramasamy, and Richards (1999).

Reversal Design. The reversal design, also called the withdrawal design or the ABAB design, is suitable for measuring the effect of an intervention as long as the intervention represents an aid or some form of support that, if withdrawn, produces a decrement in performance (e.g., visual feedback affects on arm movement, the clinician's cues affect a patient's naming of pictures). A withdrawal design is not suitable if the intervention is going to teach the patient a new behavior or skill that cannot be unlearned (e.g., cognitive skill). In Fig. 12.7, the data points are total percentage counts of the target behavior occurring (i.e., correct production of /t/) rather than total test scores. The control conditions are the phases when intervention is absent.

The following phases are present in Fig. 12.7:

A = Pretherapy baseline data are collected until a stable baseline is achieved.
B = Intervention is implemented until performance stabilizes.
A = Intervention is withdrawn.
B = Intervention is reinstated when performance shifts (i.e., drops) to a new
   level.

To conclude that the intervention has had an effect, the target behavior must be seen to change directly in response to the introduction or withdrawal of the intervention. If the intervention is introduced before the patient's performance is

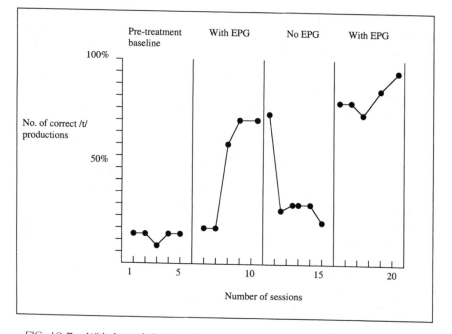

FIG. 12.7. Withdrawal design showing intervention and withdrawal phases in therapy evaluation.

stable, it will be difficult to separate the observed "improvement" from spontaneous recovery, normal maturation, or random variation.

The ethical problem of using a no-treatment condition may be an issue in this design, and this is not a suitable design when a learned behavior or skill cannot be unlearned.

Multiple-Baseline Design. A multiple-baseline design is a special case of single-case design in which different variables are measured in parallel (i.e., simultaneously). The intervention or treatment is not withdrawn in this design; rather, data are gathered across several behaviors, tasks, or sets of items to which the intervention is applied. Other variations exist for this design (e.g., measuring target behavior in different settings, such as the classroom, home, and clinic. This design can be used with both behavioral training and in changing cognitive skills. In Fig. 12.8, a pool of object picture items that a client finds difficult to name is divided to form three comparable sets of words for naming. The data points in the pretreatment phase represent results from either a standardized naming test or total test scores of a naming task. In this example, the data points during the treatment phases represent results from a probe task (i.e., a much-shortened task given to check on progress made at the end of each treatment

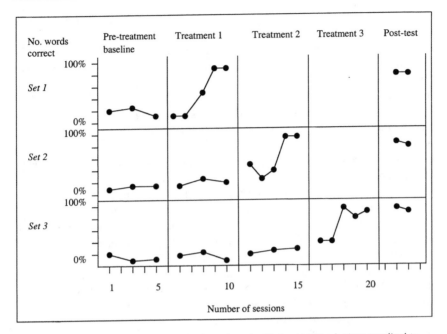

FIG. 12.8. Multiple-baseline design showing intervention being applied to different sets of words at different times.

session). Finally, the data points in the posttest represent scores taken from the same test or task that was used in the pretest phase. The control condition in this design is the phases when intervention is not applied to the other sets of words.

In Fig. 12.8, the following phases are present:

A = Gather baseline data on, Sets 1 to 3 naming items until the baseline is stable.

B(1) = Apply the intervention to Set 1 naming items only. Baselines for Sets 2 and 3 items should remain stable during the intervention of Set 1 items. When Set 1 items plateau at the ceiling, start the next therapy phase on Set 2 naming items (B2).

B(2) = Apply intervention to Set 2 items only. Performance on Set 3 items should remain unchanged. Allow Set 2 items to stabilize at the ceiling.

B(3) = Apply intervention to Set 3 items only.

Finally, retest all the items immediately at the end of the last treatment session and again in about 6 weeks (or longer) to assess maintenance of performance. It is also important to keep the method of intervention the same for each set of words; otherwise, it will be difficult to argue that changes in performance were a direct result of the specific type of treatment used. Intervention is effective if it can be shown that performance on each category of items changed only when intervention was introduced and if any change caused by the intervention on one set of items is later replicated across other sets of items. Results like this provide a convincing demonstration that intervention is directly responsible for a change.

There are many variants of the multiple-baseline design. For example, a clinician might want to stagger the introduction of therapy in naming, reading, and writing. Alternatively, a clinician might want to evaluate the effect of therapy in different contexts (e.g., speaking to the clinician, speaking on the phone, speaking to a group of visitors).

Ideally, the treated behaviors (or items) need to be independent (or different); otherwise, the intervention will affect (or generalize to) the untreated behaviors. Although generalization might be a desirable treatment outcome, it will violate any test of the efficacy of the intervention. A further consideration arises when different skills are compared across conditions—for examples, if the conditions being compared were treatment in reading, writing, and naming. In this situation, the clinician or researcher would be required to assume that these skills are comparable and that no further spontaneous recovery is likely for any of these functions. These assumptions may not be correct in the case of adult patients recovering from brain injury, where different functions are known to recover at different rates (Basso, 1989; Farmer, 1996; Kertesz, 1984; Meier, Strauman, & Thompson, 1995) or with children who develop these skills at different times.

Counterbalanced Design.   A counterbalanced design overcomes the ethical problem of treatment withdrawal and the no-treatment condition, and it allows the effects of therapy to be tested. Like the withdrawal and multiple-baseline designs, the counterbalanced (or crossover) design requires that pretest (baseline) measures be taken to establish the stability of the patient's performance before intervention begins. In the crossover design, measurement is taken on at least two tasks, functions, or behaviors, with the view to first treating one function and then treating the next function (see Fig. 12.9). In several respects, the counterbalanced design is really like the multiple-baseline design, except that it is limited to two dependent variables and the posttesting of the first treated function is conducted during the same phase as the second function is being treated.

The following phases are present in Fig. 12.9:

A   = Gather baseline data on both types of sentences until stable.

B(1) = Apply the intervention to prepositions only. Continue to maintain the comparatives baseline.

B(2) = Apply the intervention to comparatives only. Then reassess both sentences at the end of the therapy in the posttest phase.

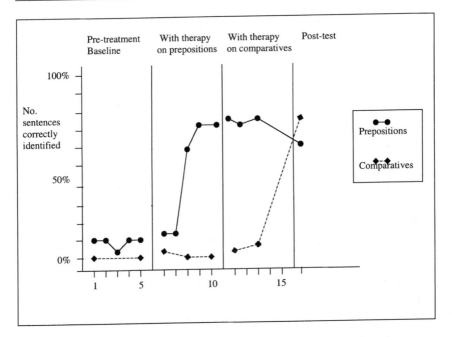

FIG. 12.9.   Counterbalanced design in a sentence comprehension
treatment evaluation.

One issue with this design is that it is difficult to know how much treatment of the first condition, B(1), has contributed to the effects observed in the treatment of the second condition B(2), particularly because there has been no intervening no-treatment phase between the two conditions. As for multiple-baseline designs, certain assumptions must be made about how spontaneous recovery and maturation naturally occur, and how these might interact with treatment is difficult to establish. The latter depends very much on what is being remedied and how distant these skills or functions are from each other.

A Final Consideration.   There are many more variations on the basic single-case design (see the sources listed at the end of this chapter when planning research). The ones described so far are simple designs to implement and can be adapted to various normally occurring clinical situations. There is, however, one major aspect not touched on by the designs describe here: the placebo treatment. Although the previously described designs are experimental designs and allow for controlled comparison between treated and untreated conditions, it can still always be argued that there is nothing intrinsically special about the intervention and that the treatment effects really represent other effects (e.g., observer and subject expectancy effects). In research, it can be argued that it is important to build in a control condition, where a benign activity (e.g., play, conversation) is conducted as though it were an intervention and then study the client's response to it. This control condition will allow the researcher to assess whether a placebo effect is present as well as its magnitude.

Single-Case Evaluation in Research

If you were planning an efficacy study with a single-case or case-series design, it would be important to consider a number of improvements in the methodological rigor of therapy evaluations.

Observer Expectancy.   A research clinician holds certain beliefs about the therapy administered to a patient. For example, if two different treatment approaches representing different theoretical orientations were being evaluated, it would be very difficult to expect one clinician to be equally committed to both therapy approaches. However hard the clinician tries, it will be difficult to completely avoid communicating this personal bias in some way in the course of a therapy program. Personal biases can unconsciously influence the way therapy is delivered, even when there are very clear instructions for what should be done. The clinician can never be blind to therapy approaches.

Table 12.4 shows potential for biases to operate in particular therapy evaluation situations. If at all possible, in research, it would be desirable if the assessor were not made aware of the aims of the research or of the phases when the patient is being assessed. Patients themselves, however, often give hints chatting with the assessor about what they have been doing in the treatment sessions. It can be difficult to keep a patient blind to the aims and whether the patient is engaged in the treatment and no-treatment phases of the evaluation. However, whenever possible, the more the assessor is blind about the aims of the research, the more likely he or she will be to be able to argue that the results reflect the true effects of therapy and not the biases (unconscious or otherwise) of the assessor.

Computer-Based Therapy.   Although it may be impractical due to time constraints in clinical practice to evaluate treatment with some of the sug-

TABLE 12.4
Sources of Subjective Biases in Efficacy Research

Sources	Bias in Therapy Delivery	Bias in Assessment
Computer delivered.	None.	None.
Therapist and assessor are different people.	Very possible.	Less likely if assessor is "blind".
Therapist and assessor are one and the same person.	Very possible.	Observer expectancy effects and participant expectancy effects.

gestions given here, these should not be difficult procedures to arrange in efficacy research. Having given consideration to blind assessors and observer expectancy effects, it is worth mentioning the role of the computer in efficacy research.

Some clinicians may find the idea of computer-delivered therapy irksome or unnatural and may not want to advocate strongly for this mode of treatment delivery. Other clinicians have argued strongly in favor of computer-based treatments, usually to reduce the economic effort of supporting conventional treatments. The issue of whether computer-based treatments are desirable is separate from whether computers serve a valuable role as a research tool in efficacy research. Therapy consists of many components (Byng & Black, 1995), such as the treatment task itself, the interaction of the therapist with the client, and the milieu of activity and events surrounding someone receiving treatment. In researching the efficacy of treatment, a researcher may be interested to learn how the specific characteristics of a treatment task affects the outcome rather than study the effects such as the therapist's personality and experience, the interaction between the client and the therapist, patient education, counseling, and other related events on patient performance. Some clinicians might feel that these aspects are very important contributions to the therapeutic process. The factors constitute the basis for different research questions. The main point to be remembered is that if the question being asked is "Does Treatment Task X improve the patient's performance?" then use of a computer to deliver therapy may improve the methodological rigor of the research. It would also allow questions to be answered more accurately, about issues such as amount of therapy, types of errors, timing of therapy. It follows that if the results of such a study were positive and if our assumptions are right about the value of the clinician, the other components of therapy might enhance but not degrade the outcome of these results. If the research question is "Does speech therapy (as compared to volunteers) improve the patient's performance?" then a computer will be appropriate. It is possible to address questions about the various components of treatment separately in research. In general, given what is known about observer expectancy effects, computers (like tape recorders or camcorders) are useful research tools in bringing objectivity into the evaluation (e.g., Crerar, Ellis, & Dean, 1996; Deloche, Dordain, & Kremis, 1993).

Statistical Analyses of Single-Case Designs.   Statistical analysis is used to decide whether the results one has obtained fall within or outside the range of results that could have been obtained just by chance. These analyses are also useful in detecting whether small but significant effects are present or whether interactions between several variables are present. Many texts provide look-up statistical tables to help users select the right statistical test for their particular data sets. It is tempting to rely on visual inspection of data from single-case designs to decide whether improvement has occurred. Depending on the design and the type of data chosen, there is some evidence that visual analysis is not reliable in deciding whether improvement has really occurred or whether the improvement is statistically significant (Matyas & Greenwood, 1990). Although the small data sets of single-case designs can constrain the range of statistical analyses available, it is important to be aware of the problem of relying soley on visual inspection.

PROBLEMS ENCOUNTERED IN EVALUATING THERAPY IN THE CLINIC

The following problems encountered in evaluating therapy in the clinic are well known to many clinicians:

- *I don't have time.* This is the most common response clinicians give in re-action to the suggestion that "good practice" in therapy means evaluating the effectiveness of therapy provided to a patient. It is difficult to separate this from issues like I do not like change, I can't be bothered, It's too hard, I don't like being so constrained and so on. But most clinicians do want more positive affirming experiences which show that the therapy they do with patients is really effective. It is an important part of job satisfaction.
- *I don't think I know how to do it.* If this is a problem for you, find out who in your locality is doing experimental therapy research and approach this person for support. There are also an increasing number of professional development courses and advisors who show clinicians how to evaluate therapy in the clinic. Find a colleague who might be as interested in evalu-ating therapy as you and work collaboratively. One will only learn by practice, and you will get things wrong at the start but soon improve.
- *I will never do any therapy.* This expression (usually spoken by final-year students) suggests a belief that too much time will be spent in evaluating the patient at the cost of providing therapy to the patient. This is a rather shortsighted view and negates the fact that a clinician's role is to attempt to provide effective therapies rather than activities that make the clinician feel that he or she is doing something useful.
- *I have cold feet.* After planning therapy and having started, sometimes one gets cold feet, particularly when the therapy shows no signs of working after a few sessions. The temptation to abandon therapy and find some-thing else is very strong at these times. This is difficult when one is con-scious that the patient or an insurer is paying for the sessions. There may be good reasons to change therapy, but before doing so, one should think about why the therapy might not be working. Sometimes there are clear reasons, and the therapy may be worthwhile changing. In other cases, one should persevere and see if some improvement becomes evident.

Whatever happens, you should have a very principled basis for changing or for continuing therapy.

- *My patients are not ready.* It is important to remember that not all patients are suitable candidates for therapy evaluations (or for therapy itself). These patients may have poor arousal, may be severely depressed, may feel sick, may have very short attention spans, may lack motivation, may be poor attendees, or may have major social–emotional upheaval in their personal lives. All these factors can interfere with the patient's learning or cause the patient to be too erratic to allow therapy to be evaluated. In these patients, therapy may not be a primary concern for the patient until other problems have been resolved.

- *No one will be doing this except me.* Leaders are often alone in their views until others catch up. Catching up can take several years, and that may be too long for some people. A systematic approach to evaluating therapy with a patient enables clinicians to work in a more principled way, to know what progress they have made, and it allows clinicians to be accountable (e.g., are things more possible than present methods allow, is there any choice to do otherwise?). Ultimately, a moral issue emerges since it will become increasingly difficult to claim ignorance in light of knowledge being available about how one might be more responsible in judging the effectiveness of therapy with a patient.

- *I can't find a suitable control task.* Most times, you will be able to find a control task, unless the patient has very little impairment. If it is not possible to find another impaired behavior to serve as a control, then use the "split-task" method, where you treat for half the items but not the other half.

- *My patient cannot cope with too many treatment items.* Sometimes a patient's condition means the patient has a low tolerance for how many items can be used in a therapy session. For example, a dysarthic patient with emphysema might cope with speaking 5 but not 20 words. Pretests, reassessments, and posttests might have to be based on 10 items to accommodate the patient's condition. There is little one can do to alter this, and working with 10 items is about as low as one can go before measurement for change becomes meaningless or unreliable. In other situations (e.g., with aphasia patients), a low level of performance would suggest that the patient is at the floor level of performance and the value of therapy could be questionable.

- *Doing therapy this way may not improve the patient's real-life communication skills.* There is little evidence available to support the generalization of any clinic-based therapy task. This does not mean, however, that these tasks are ineffective in improving communication outside the clinic. More research evidence is required here. There is, however, no reason therapy tasks cannot be tasks that represent real-life events. This will depend on the disorder and the theoretical orientation of the clinician. In principle, the clinician can choose to work and evaluate therapy with real-life tasks or with clinic-based tasks.

- *I don't see how the evaluation methods described for test items will work with functional therapy.* The principles of evaluation are specific to any particular type of therapy. These are generic principles that can be applied to benign events (e.g., evaluating washing soap powder) to highly specific treatments. Working on so-called functional tasks does not mean you do not have to have a control condition that consists of an untreated set of behaviors, a set of communicative acts, communication in a different environment, and so on compared to a treated condition (i.e., another behavior, task).

- *It feels unnatural to work under such restrictions.* Applying a methodology in evaluating therapy is a new practice that becomes familiar quite quickly. Clinicians who work this way usually report that they feel confident about where they are going with the patient and, more importantly,

TABLE 12.5
Some Possible Outcomes in Therapy Evaluation

| *Observed Target* | *Measurement on Target* | |
	Improvement	*No Improvement*

Improvement	(a)
	Desired outcome
		(d)
		Task is not sensitive
		OR
		
		Task is not a valid measure of the
		   behavior/function to be changed
		OR
		
		Change is limited to
		   item-specific effects
		OR
		
		Change is restricted by
		   ceiling and floor effects
		OR
		
		Observer is not observing
		   the right behavior

No improvement	(b)
	Task is possibly
	   measuring something
	   different
	
	(c)
	Observer is not
	   observing the right
	   behavior
		(e)
		Therapy is ineffective

they have a principled basis for their decisions about how therapy is executed and for determining reviews and discharge from therapy.

- *I don't know when to stop.* Therapy goals do not change simply because one is evaluating therapy. Planning a therapy evaluation does, however, require a clinician and the patient to decide at the start of therapy what is going to determine success in therapy. Success may be improvement on a particular task or the ability to communicate effectively outside the clinic. It may take one or several evaluations (depending on the range of difficulties and the patient's aspirations) before a patient's therapy program is completed. For example, the first evaluation might focus on improving phonemic knowledge, the second evaluation might focus on improving semantic knowledge, the third evaluation might focus on sentence generation and so on.
- *I don't know how to tell if the patient has improved.* Currently, the most common method for determining improvement is to rely on visual inspection of the patient's results. Different outcomes are possible in therapy evaluations, as shown in Table 12.5.

Situations such as (a) and (e) in Table 12.5 do not present difficulties in interpretation of the results, but it is not uncommon to encounter the situations shown in (b) through (d) in treatment evaluation. Furthermore, some therapy effects remain highly specific to the items worked on in therapy and do not generalize to other, untreated, items (i.e., item-specific effects), whereas some therapies show generalizing effects to untreated items but effects are still poorly understood.

FURTHER READING

Byng & Coltheart (1986) give a description and argue in favor of single-case design in evaluating the effectiveness of therapy.

Coltheart (1989) offer a description of how single-case methodology could be applied in a clinic.

Franklin (1997) provides an easy-to-read source on single-case methodology. The definition of multiple-baseline design in this article is unconventional.

Seron (1997) offers a useful overview of how single-case methodology is applied in the context of cognitive–neuropsychological research, which typifies much of aphasia research.

Wilson (1987) provides one of the few articles dealing with the subject of research designs in the rehabilitation context. This is useful source for the researching-clinician.

GRADUATE READING

Barlow & Hersen (1984) provide one of the original texts (precognitive neuropsychology) dealing with single-case design and related issues. Covers mainly behavior change in the classroom or educational settings, and has a chapter on statistical analyses for analyzing serial data points.

Cooper (1998) offers a clear overview of research methodology.

Kratochwill & Levin (1992) provide a fairly recent reference on the topic of single-case design in both education and other contexts.

O'Leary & Wilson (1987) provide a source for studies on changing behavior.

Richards, Taylor, Ramsamy, & Richards (1999) offer an up-to date reference on single-case design, with sections on statistical analysis. Chapter 13 Covers data analysis of single-case designs.

White, Rusch, Kazdin, & Hartman (1989) cover meta-analyses in single-case studies, with regard to behavioral measures.

Willmes (1995) covers data analysis issues relevant to single-case design in cognitive–neuropsychological or aphasia studies.

Wood (2000) offers a comprehensive overview of meta-analysis.

13

A Clinician's Guide:
Evaluating the Evaluations

Discovery consists of seeing what everybody has seen and thinking what nobody has thought.

—Albert Szent-Gyorgyi, 1893–1986

This chapter is divided into five major parts, each addressing a particular area that commonly requires critical appraisal and/or some knowledge of research methods:

- Part 1 presents a list of prompt questions that the clinician should consider when evaluating or reviewing a publication. It is oriented toward reviewing efficacy research papers.
- Part 2 presents a list of prompt questions for the reader to consider when evaluating or when planning to design a simple survey questionnaire.
- Part 3 presents a checklist to assist the reader with the evaluation of different approaches in individual assessment.
- Part 4 presents a checklist of prompt question to assist with evaluating a test.
- Part 5 deals with evaluating therapy. Although therapy designs are described, the main purpose of this section is to provide a set of pointers to assist with evaluating a report of an intervention study.

Many publications provide considerably more detail on these topics. The main purpose of this chapter is to make available a quick reference to all the issues normally considered in performing evaluations and planning evaluations.

PART 1: GETTING THE MOST OUT
OF READING RESEARCH

As a consumer of research, a clinician requires the knowledge and skills to be able to read a study from a journal article and evaluate it for its scientific merit. No study is perfect, but some errors have graver consequences than others. The clinician has to evaluate a study in light of its methodological errors and weigh them against the claims being made by the investigators. Errors that seriously compromise the truth of the claims (i.e., internal validity) made by the investigators suggest that the study might have little to offer other than a passing curiosity value. Hopefully, such an article will also provide a reason for someone else to improve on the study in a subsequent replication.

Table 13.1 is a checklist that will help you review a research paper. The questions serve as prompts to help you assess whether the researchers have executed a study to the best of their ability, allowing you as the clinician, a consumer of research, to decide whether the findings of the study are well founded.

TABLE 13.1
A Guide to Reviewing a Published Study

Statement of the proposed research

- Can you identify the aims, hypotheses and/or predictions in the study?

- Is this a theory or hypothesis-led study, a descriptive study, or a "data trolling" exercise? (Some studies have no identifiable hypotheses or predictions, and this is acceptable in descriptive studies or exploratory (pilot) studies that are working in unknown territory. Other studies exemplify unscientific research practice by simply gathering lots of data in the hope that something interesting will show up; the term data-trolling refers to this type of research. If conclusions are made on this basis, then the line of reasoning is usually inductive).

- Are the aims, hypotheses, and predictions clearly articulated in such a way that there is no ambiguity about what is being investigated?

- Are the behaviors or events being measured operationally defined? Is there ambiguity in what is being measured, how it is measured, by whom, and when?

Design of the study

The design of the study is evaluated by the following questions to determine whether the comparisons made by the researcher are valid.

- What type of study is it e.g., observational, experimental, longitudinal, group design, single-case, case-series?

- Is the design of the study adequately described e.g., the conditions and the procedures?

(Continued)

TABLE 13.1
(Continued)

- Is the design of the study able to answer the research question?
- Are there any sources of confounding effects that are not controlled by the design?

Sources of error

There are two sources of error; reliability and validity. Reliability consists of two types of error; constant and random error.

- Are there any sources of error that are constant rather than randomly present? (e.g., instrument error is likely to be a constant error while errors committed by humans are more likely to be source of random error. Constant and random error have implications for how the data is collected and or analyzed. When error is constant, it is possible to partial out its effects statistically. However, random error often requires sampling as a way of attempting to distribute its effects across different groups of participants or different conditions).
- Do the readings from the tests/instruments or ratings from observers become inaccurate due to fatigue or changes occurring over time? E.g., instruments may work best after a warm up period was this allowed for in the study. Another example is when an assessor marks essays more severely on the first day than on the third day of marking, so essays on top of the pile may fare worse than those at the bottom, despite being qualitatively the same.
- Is observer error including memory failure/recall bias, expectancy effects, Halo effect (prejudice) and Rosenthal effects likely?
- Are participant biases operating such as Hawthorne and placebo effects present?
- Are questionnaire/survey participant effects such as social desirability, prestige effect and acquiescence effects operating?

Internal validity

This refers to whether anything has happened in a study to make it difficult to conclude that X caused Y?

- Are the tests valid measures of what they purport to measure?
- Could any unplanned event, independent of the study, that happened during the study be responsible for the observed change or the outcome of the study (e.g., outbreak of influenza during the study affecting one group and not another)? [*history*]
- Could changes such as developmental changes, increasing fatigue, increasing boredom, degeneration and spontaneous recovery be responsible for the observed change or the outcome of the study? [*maturation*]
- Could taking the first test influence the scores of a second test? (For example, students are known to achieve better scores when they take the same or an alternate form of the test the second time). [*practice effects*]
- Have any of the groups been selected on the basis of extreme scores (e.g. selecting only severely impaired patients for a remediation study)? (If patients' scores cluster at the bottom of the scale, then there is only one way to go, up the scale (or the patients may be too impaired to have any capacity to change). In a similar way, patients whose scores cluster at the top of the scale will have little scope to show significant improvement. They can only change downwards. It is important that the patients have the potential to change either up or down the full range of possible scores). [*statistical regression*]

(Continued)

TABLE 13.1
(Continued)

- Are selection biases operating such that the groups being compared are already different, even before the intervention in introduced? (For example, if treatment and no-treatment group are compared, but the treatment individuals were selected by the clinician and the no-treatment individuals were asked to volunteer. Query the difference in motivation levels). [*sampling error*]

- Has sampling bias been introduced by unmotivated participants dropping out of the study, or patients dying during the study or items being discarded from a test? Are the remaining participants/items representative of the population of interest? [*participant attrition*]

- Are the tests/instruments designed to measure what they are used for in the study? (If the researchers were interested in measuring short-term memory, it would be invalid to conclude this from a test of sentence comprehension.)

Appropriateness of analyses

- Are the statistical analyses appropriate for the design and for the number of participants/items in the group?

- Have the prerequisite conditions of the selected analyses been met by the data?

- Are there any correlations? (If the correlations are reported, look at the scatter plot or list of individual scores for outliers i.e., an extreme high or low score by an atypical performer, as this will inflate or deflate the correlation index, suggesting the variables are less related than they really are. Correlations performed on scores that have a limited range of scores [e.g., 0, 1, 2] tend to yield a low correlation index due to a range of restriction problems and so is difficult to interpret. Ensure that the correlation index is between 0 and 1.)

- Have the prerequisite conditions of the selected analysis been met by the data? (Small participant samples (fewer than 30 participants) are inclined not to produce normal distributions, in which case nonparametric analyses would be preferred to parametric analyses. A quick, rough check can compare the mean and the median. Their values would be the same in a normal distribution though there is always still the problem of distributions having different degrees of flatness [kurtosis] which affects the normality of the distribution, too.)

- Are the groups being compared similar in the aspects that matter? (If their standard deviations are different, maybe even reported as being statistically different, then the groups are either different in their characteristics or there is an outlier among the participants in one of the groups.)

- Are the calculations correct? (If percentages are given, do they add up to 100%? Make sure the totals add up. If the hypothesis simply states that there will be no difference (null hypothesis), then a two-tailed test is appropriate. If, however, it states, that Group A will be better than Group B, the researchers have a directional hypothesis and can apply a one-tailed test with an alpha value of .10 instead of .05. The implication is that if the researchers know something about the nature of what they are testing, it not necessary to have a conservative probability value such as .05).

- Do graphs misrepresent information correctly? (If graphs are given, check for a misapplication of graphing techniques [Runyon, Coleman, & Pittenger, 1999]. The vertical axis must start from zero frequency, and not with a higher value because this has the effect of exaggerating differences along the axis. To minimize bias, the graph should ideally be between .7 and .8 of the length of the horizontal axis.)

(Continued)

TABLE 13.1
(Continued)

Conclusions

- Have the results been interpreted with reference to the aims and the hypotheses of the study?
- Do the findings support the investigator's predictions?

External validity

This form of validity refers to whether one can generalize the findings of this study to people and conditions not actually included in the study.

- Are the implications of the findings articulated in the study?
- Are there any reasons why these findings cannot be generalized to other patients or other contexts from the population of interest?

PART 2: EVALUATING SURVEYS

In this section a brief protocol is presented as a rudimentary guide for clinicians who want to design and/or evaluate a survey. Of all research procedures used by clinical researchers, surveys are among the most commonly employed methods of clinical investigations, particularly if audits are included.

You need to determine whether you or your team have the necessary skills and resources to conduct a survey. If gaps appear, then these are areas in which you will require support and/or expertize from elsewhere (e.g., an in-house research unit, a local university, a known expert). Anyone evaluating an investigation that has used survey methodology will find it necessary to read this section. The main stages in designing a survey as shown in Fig. 13.1.

Many good resources are dedicated to the topic of questionnaire and survey design (Coolican, 1999c; Dijkstra & van der Zouwen, 1982; Fife-Schaw, 1995; Moser & Kalton, 1993; Oppenheim, 1992; Schuman & Kalton, 1985). This chapter provides a basic consideration of all the major and common points covered by most references of surveys. Refer the sources listed previously for further information, particularly information about procedures for atypical or special survey situations.

Designing a survey begins with having a clear definition of the problem and the issue to be addressed, as well as an understanding of the population to be surveyed. If these are not obvious, then a small pilot survey usually helps identify the salient issues as well as any practical problems one might encounter. Practical problems may include difficulties in executing the survey and problems in responding to the survey. The characteristics of a survey sample need to be representative (i.e., reflect the characteristics of the population to which you want to generalize your conclusions to individuals, contexts and so on that you have not studied yourself).

Surveys can be in the form of questionnaires, telephone surveys, or face-to-face interviews. The data collected from surveys will need to be put in a form that is ready for analysis. Surveys that use open-ended questions are usually

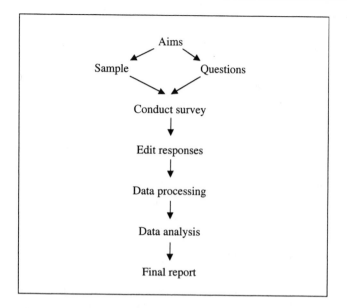

FIG. 13.1. Stages in survey design.

edited into a format that is suitable for analysis. Data analysis may consist of statistical analysis and/or simple frequency counts that describe the data. Any analysis represents an attempt to answer the objectives of the survey. Ultimately, all this information is collated into a report.

The following are some suggestions to keep in mind when laying out the questionnaire:

- Use introductions to explain the purpose of the questionnaire or the interview.
- Make sure the questionnaire is clear and well presented.
- Begin with easy questions, move on to intermediate and difficult questions, and then move back to easy questions (when motivation might be falling). It is more motivating to end a questionnaire with demographic questions than to start with them.
- Keep the style consistent to make reading easy.
- Space out questions for easy reading.
- In interviews, set all the interviewer's questions in italics.

Planning and Evaluating a Survey

The questions in Table 13.2 serve as prompts to help in designing or evaluating a survey. Is this survey being used as a test (i.e., individuals will be classified depending on their answers to the survey)? If yes, then it is necessary that the survey instrument be the product of psychometric procedures, such as item analysis, which involve particular statistical procedures.

TABLE 13.2

Questions to Aid in Designing or Evaluating a Survey

Question	Yes/No

- Has a literature search been undertaken to establish what is known about the issues addressed?

- Has a written statement been prepared, detailing the aims of the survey and how the results will be used?

- Has the written statement been discussed with all relevant parties (head of department, patient general practitioner ethics committee) (*Design stage only*)

- Has it been made obvious who is responsible for the survey and how the results will be disseminated? (*Design stage only*)

- Has it been determined that a survey (postal survey) is the most optimal approach to securing the desired outcome compared to interviews, observation, and so on? (*Design stage only*)

- Is the size of the sample large enough to provide valid answers?

- Is the size of the sample adequate to ensure reliable results? Consultation with a statistician will be appropriate at this time (*Design stage only*)

- Circumstances might limit how many characteristics of the population can be represented in the intended sample (e.g., age distribution, incidence of disease in the region). Has it been considered how this might be handled and what impact this might have on the final report?

- Have the questions been designed in a way that will elicit the information needed?

- Do you have or require experience, training, or support to address these areas: (*Design stage only*)

  —Designing an appropriate question-and-answer format?

  —Dealing with ambiguous questions?

  —Knowledge about item scaling (e.g., yes/no vs. very sad to very happy)?

  —Eliminating bias in the questionnaire?

  —Validity and reliability of the survey?

- Have the costs of the survey been worked out (i.e., costs in time, administration, computing, data analysis) in relationship to existing resources?

- Is it evident which statistical analysis will be suitable?

- Is a plan in place that will assist with enhancing return rates for postal surveys (e.g., stamped reply envelope, publicity, second questionnaire for non responders, reminder letter, contact names, phone numbers)?

Evaluating Survey Questions

Most surveys aim to describe what people think. In all surveys, it is very important to consider the questions in the survey (see Table 13.3). Consequently, studies employing survey methodology should present a copy of the questionnaire in
the final report.

The following are some common traps to avoid in surveys:

- *Catch-all questions.* These questions produce ambiguous answers (e.g.,
  "Can you tell me about Sean's birth history, your reactions to his problems, and the changes you've seen?").
- *Don't-know problem.* A don't-know option in a questionnaire creates a
  problem because it becomes difficult to discern between those who truly
  do not know and those who are indifferent to the issue. To minimize this
  problem, try, "asking questions such as," "Have you heard of X treatment?" (If not go to the next question) "Have you had time to think about
  it?" "Do you think it matters whether the treatment is available or not?"
  and "Do you think the treatment should be provided?"
- *Agreement bias.* This is also known as an "acquiescence response." The
  individual either responds yes or no to every question simply because it is
  too much effort to think about the right answer. The way to deal with this
  is to have some questions to which yes is the right answers and some questions to which no is the right answer.

TABLE 13.3
Checklist for Evaluating Survey Questions

Survey Question Characteristics	*Yes/No*
• Questions use words, phrases, and a style that is familiar.	
• Questions use simple and direct sentences to help comprehension.	
• Questions avoid too much detail and are specific.	
• Questions do not result in ambiguous answers.	
• Questions are short (fewer than 20 words each).	
• Questions are not biased and leading.	
• Questions do not make presumptions.	
• Questions that rely on recall of past events more than a week ago do not allow accurate recall and are avoided.	
• Questions tap only issues that the respondent understands.	
• Questions are very precise.	

- *Social desirability.* In interviews, this is known as the *prestige effect*, where the respondent "puts on his or her best face" for the interviewer. In questionnaires, social desirability effect means the respondent answers questions in a way that is likely to satisfy the investigator. The respondent is aiming to create a good impression. Postal questionnaires tend to produce higher satisfaction levels with services than do face-to-face interviews with a neutral interviewer.
- *Biased questions.* There are a number of types of biased questions, such as the follow presumptuous questions (e.g., "How often do you talk about Sean's problem in front of him?").
  —*Emotional questions.* Emotional questions use terminology such as "snatched out of his hands" instead of "took it from his hands," and "pushy" instead of "assertive."
  —*Leading questions.* Leading questions (e.g., "Would you say you were in favor of special schools for disabled children?") tend to elicit more agreement responses than do more neutral questions (e.g., "Do you favor special schools as the best option for disabled children?").
  —*Hypothetical questions.* Hypothetical questions tend to produce unreliable responses because at the time individuals could have different reasons for responding differently from the way they have. For example, to the question *"Would you prefer to receive treatment at home?"* a respondent might say yes out of frustration. But yes could mean "I would feel better in my own place than being here" or "I would receive individual attention in treatment then" or "I need a change."
  —Questions with *familiar words.* Some phrases are too vague (e.g., *how often? how much? how long?*). A preferred alternative is a more specific form (e.g., *"How many words have you heard Sean say?"*)
  —*Ambiguous questions.* These are questions that could elicit both an agree and a disagree response (e.g., "Do you think clinicians should not stop discharging patients early just to satisfy consumer demands?").
- *Length of questionnaire.* Interview surveys are ideally kept to a maximum of 45 minutes. Survey questionnaires should take less than 15 minutes to minimize feelings of boredom, inconvenience, and loss of concentration by the respondent.
- *Form of questions.* The forms of questions are very important. There are two main forms:
  —*Closed questions.* Closed questions provide the respondent with several choices from which to select an answer. In interviews, the interviewer asks an open question but then selects a closed answer based on what the respondent has said. The options for a closed question should be exhaustive and exclusive to minimize problems of having no box to tick or find that several answers are possible. These question are useful in measuring attitude or opinion.

—*Open questions.* These allow the respondent to choose how to respond. In an interview, all that the respondent says in recorded for later coding and analysis. Open questions are a useful way of learning the scope and salient aspects of the issue that is under investigation.

—Closed questions are much easier to analyze than open questions. However, it is useful to use open question in a pilot survey when the relevant issues are still unclear or unknown.

PART 3: EVALUATING ASSESSMENT TECHNIQUES

All evaluation of change involves some form of measurement. Many assessment techniques are used to determine the nature of the patient's problem and measure the severity of the problem. Some of these techniques are more common in some areas than in other. For example, role-playing and self-report questionnaires tend to be reported in connection with stuttering therapy work, whereas instrumental analyses are usually associated with articulation therapy. Biofeedback training is common in physiotherapy, and paper–pencil tests are common in the assessment of speech disorders. Different assessment techniques have inherently different advantages and disadvantages that can strengthen or weaken an efficacy study. A brief review of some of these assessment techniques and their various methodological considerations are highlighted here.

Assessment can occur via many different methods. Each of these has its own inherent methodological shortcomings. Often a balance has to be struck between the choice of an assessment method and what one wishes to measure. Table 13.4 presents the advantages, and disadvantages of various forms of assessment. Solution's are proposed for the different problems wherever possible.

PART 4: EVALUATING TESTS

The term *test* is often used too casually in clinical contexts to mean any set of items that appear relevant to a skill or type of knowledge we want wish to evaluate in a patient. A clear distinction between informal tests and standardized tests is important to avoid fostering an attitude that regards informal test as being in some way an equivalent but more efficient way of achieving what standardized tests measure.

Sometimes, students loosely describe the distinction between informal assessment and standardized assessments in terms of the former being *subjective tests* and the later being *objective tests*. Strictly speaking, this cannot be true because both forms of assessment, particularly if they are paper–pencil tests, rely on the

TABLE 13.4

Advantages and Disadvantages of Different Forms of Assessment

Advantages	Disadvantages	Suggested Solution
Assessment interview • Self report is often highly predictive of critical future behavior.	• Unreliable, subject to distortion especially if participant is asked to recall past events.	• Minimize unreliability problem by using structured interview.
Self-recording • Used to monitor change or maintenance of behaviors. — Allows self-control where this is an integral part of therapy — Useful where naturalistic observations are not feasible — Permits assessment of infrequent but important behaviors — Provides a method to assess the frequency of thoughts, anxieties, etc.	• Variable reliability • Factors affecting self-recording include reactivity (i.e., the use of the technique interferes with the behavior itself) and the patient's knowledge that his/her recording would be checked.	• Develop a procedure where self-recording can occur but the patient is unable to review the data that has been collected. • All the patient time to become accustomed to self-recording to derive a stable baseline before introducing any intervention.
Observation in vivo • Refers to observing the frequency of observable behaviors. It serves to verify the existence of an impression or subjective sense about an individual's behavior (i.e., lends obectivity to an evaluation about an individual)	• Observer Bias (i.e., the patient is influenced by his/her expectations of the outcome, Rosenthal, 1966); For example, when observers are told to expect certain events to occur, they report the events even though unbiased measures indicate that the events did not occur. • Feedback effects on observational data. Investigators' responses to reports by observers may influence observers' reports (O'Leary & Wilson, 1987). • Reactivity of observation refers to the potential effect of an observer's presence on the behavior being observed.	• Observer bias is minimize or not found if the observer is asked to record the presence or absence of behavior in small time units. • Investigators must not give feedback to observers that might bias the data collection. • Lengthen the observation periods with observer present.

(Continued)

209

TABLE 13.4
(Continued)

Advantages	Disadvantages	Suggested Solution
Self-report/inventories • Useful to estimate the severity of the problem (e.g., stuttering in different contexts or to predict which situations the patient will have difficulty). • Used to assess where testing is not possible.	• Patient distortion (i.e., the patient can easily misrepresent the problem). • Answers to self-report questionnaires do not provide a clear idea of the problem to be treated because they often do not specify the problem to be treated.	• Might be useful to build in questions that assess for social desirability tendencies as an indirect check on the accuracy of the patient's answers. This could be difficult to achieve if the inventory has not been subject to psychometric item analysis.
Role-playing • Patient re-enacts various interpersonal encounters; useful to help the clinician find out how a patient feels about a situation and/or what he or she might do.	• Validity is a problem as it depends on the patient's ability to assume roles.	• No clear solution other than minimize error by allowing the patient to have a lot of practice in role-playing before undertaking an assessment via role-playing.
Formal tests • Provide a structured format for assessment that also delineates the function of specific skills. • Excellent if various psychometric indices and norms are provided as these assist in the interpretation of results.	• Psychometric indices may be absent. • Some tests take too long to administer and are not suitable for frequent administrations to measure change.	
Instrumental measuring tools • If measurements are reliable, these tools are useful for providing objective measures of various functions (e.g. kinematics aspects of speech, respiration, spectral analyses).	• Many instrumental measures of discrete functions do not correlate with global performance (e.g., acoustic analysis of spoken speech).	• No obvious solution.

tester to interpret the findings. Humans introduce subjectivity, and observer error is always a possibility when interpreting test results. This is particularly evident in some published tests that have ambiguously defined measurement criteria such that the assessor is able to bring personal values into the assessment. Objectivity is achieved when the format of assessment leaves little opportunity for an assessor or for variability in the environment to influence the findings of the assessment. There are very clear criteria for what constitutes a good test. Table 13.5 list is for the clinician to consult whenever purchase of a new test is considered. It is important that a resource sold as a "test" is really a test and not something a creative individual whipped up one afternoon.

TABLE 13.5
Checklist for Evaluating a Test

The test manual fully describes

• the rationale of the test.

• the construct that is being measured and how it is conceptualized by the test developers (e.g., the construct may be short-term memory, naming ability, metaphorical knowledge, syntactic comprehension).

• how the test was developed, the procedures culminating in the selection of the items, how the items were evaluated (i.e., test construction).

• the relationship of this test to similar tests (an instance of construct validity).

• the qualifications required of an assessor to allow correct administration and understanding of the test

• whether assessor, training is required (i.e., implications for interrates and intrarates reliability)?

• the norms and some measure of the lowest and highest score obtained by control participants.

• the characteristics of the participants, used for the purpose of deriving norms or controls (e.g., age, socioeconomic class, years of education, gender). The control group should represent the type of people with whom the clinician will want to compare the patient's performance on this test. If controls are normalized how is *normal* defined?

• instructions to the testee for each part of the test and details such as time limits and how to respond to the test item.

• instructions to the tester on how to mark score sheets, convert scores, and deliver practice items for each section, and how to deal with no response answers, error responses, etc.

• how the test results are to be interpreted and their meaning.

• the stability of the test (test–retest reliability). This tells whether the items are sufficiently well designed such that the same individual will respond to the same items in the same way after a short period of time (e.g., 1 day). If individuals vary too much between test and retest, then it could be that the items themselves are too readily interpreted in different ways by the testee and hence are not good test items because they are measuring something other than what is intended.

• interrater and intrarater reliability correlation indices.

PART 5: EVALUATING EFFICACY STUDIES

This part lists areas that might be considered by a reviewer of efficacy research and is largely an adaptation of Campbell and Stanley's (1963) work. This work is to some extent represented in a more recently published text by Polgar and Thomas (2000).

An example of a treatment study is provided here to demonstrate the different designs and the contribution they make to controlling confounding effects. Let's say that a clinician is interested in finding out whether therapy improves patients' communication. The clinician may approach this research question in several ways, using either quasi-experimental or experimental designs in the form of either group or single-case studies—or both. Campbell and Stanley (1963) reviewed a number of research designs used to evaluate the effectiveness of interventions. Although they described these designs in the context of classroom behavior, the focus is on group methodology, with many of the designs being applicable to the evaluating the efficacy of an intervention.

To minimize confusing group and single-case design issues, these are presented separately, even though there is a great deal in common in the designs employed by both approaches. What follows is a description of selected group research designs. The first part of each description presents methodological considerations for evaluating interventions in a group study. These are described in the context of evaluating research that speech and language therapists might read about, even though clinical research tends not to be able to use some of the more elaborate designs for evaluation. The second part of this section presents the equivalent design wherever applicable to the single-case evaluation.

Designs for Group Studies

Quasi-Experimental Designs

Figures 13.2, 13.3 and 13.4 are quasi-experimental designs because they do not have a control group by which to compare a treated group of patients and determine the effects of treatment. The absence of a control group means these particular designs have very little to say about the effects of treatment. Figure 13.2 presents a one-shot group design.

One-Shot Group Design.   The design in Fig. 13.2 translates to the clinician seeing a group of patients, administering a course of therapy, and then administering a post-test to measure the outcome of therapy. In this design, it is not possible to conclude that therapy had any effect on the patient(s) as measured by the posttest because we have no knowledge of the patients' performance before the commencement of therapy (i.e., there is no pre-therapy baseline information to allow this comparison to be made).

Group --------------------Therapy ----------Post-test *(BA design)*

FIG. 13.2.   One-shot-case study.

One Group Pretest/Posttest Design.   Figure 13.3 shows a design in which the clinician administers the patients a pretest, administers a course of therapy, and then reassesses the patients on the same test or a parallel version of it to see if the patients' performance has changed as a result of therapy.

Group --------------Pre-test---------Therapy ------Post-test *(ABA design)*

FIG. 13.3.   One group pretest/posttest design.

With this design would be erroneous to conclude that any change or improvement in the patients' scores was due to therapy because we do not know if the patients were changing anyway, quite independently of the therapy process. For example, we know that patients can show developmental maturation, spontaneous recovery, or other events co-occurring during the course of the study. Any measured improvement could be attributed to those effects and not to any intervention.

Static Group Design.   The last of the quasi experimental designs is depicted in Fig. 13.4, the static group design. The clinician may decide to compare the performance of two groups of patients (those who have been treated with therapy with another group who have received no treatment (or a different therapy).

Group 1----------Pre-test----------Therapy-- --------------Post-test *(ABA design)*

Group 2---Post-test (control)

FIG. 13.4.   Static group design.

With this design it might be tempting to conclude that any measured difference (e.g., better scores) in the treated group is due to the effects of therapy. The problem is that the patients in the two groups might have differed in some systematic way (unknown to the clinician) quite independently of the effects of therapy. For example, the parents of the treated patients were possibly more motivated than the parents of the untreated patients. Highly motivated parents might be more prepared to transport their children to therapy or show greater interest in therapy. Randomization of the patients to each group is absent, and so any inherent biases are unlikely to be distributed between the two groups. Note, however, that randomization helps but does not guarantee that there are no biases present in the groups.

Experimental Designs

An experimental study is a study in which a clinician controls for all known confounding effects while allowing the intervention freedom to vary. This section describes, variation on the ABA design with a control group.

Pretest/Posttest Control Group Design.   Figure 13.5 shows a design that allows the clinician to compare two groups of patients who are randomly assigned to either a treatment or a nontreatment group. Random assignment is a procedure that increases the likelihood of the two samples being composed of similar patients. One of the most common failings of studies using this design is to have patients on a waiting list or patients who find it too far to come to therapy serve as the control group. There may be other factors that distinguish between these patients and those in therapy that could cause the samples to be different. Regardless of what group the patients are assigned to, each patient is assessed on a test before treatment begins and again after treatment has occurred.

This design controls for the confounding effects of maturation. So if Group 1 does improve, then the clinician may validly conclude that these patients benefited from therapy, but not necessarily therapy. It is possible that the patients could benefit simply from the attention they receive (Hawthorne effect or placebo effect), especially if the no-treatment control group were not required to engaged in a control session where it could receive the same amount of contact and attention from the clinician as Group 1.

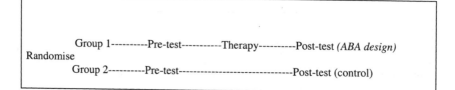

FIG. 13.5.   Pretest/posttest control group design.

If the treating clinician were also the assessor for the posttreatment tasks, then he or she could introduce observer expectancy effects, or biases (e.g., halo effects, treatment preferences). The posttreatment assessor needs to be independent of the clinician and have no knowledge of who received therapy (i.e., blind assessor). Double-blind studies are not easily achieved in therapy studies because the clinician is required to be unaware that the patient is receiving treatment. It is also difficult to conceal the type of therapy administered to a patient from the clinician giving the treatment. In some clinical situations, it may be difficult to carry out a study where the patients are not receiving therapy. There may be difficult ethical issues to negotiate.

Posttest-Only Control Group Design.   Another design, the posttest-only control group design, is similar to the static-group design except that this design requires that the patients be randomly assigned to the two groups. It is a useful design in the event that it is not possible to obtain a baseline before therapy begins. The clinician randomly assigns speech-impaired patients to each group, provides therapy to one group and not the other, and then compares the groups performance on posttests (see Fig. 13.6).

Although the patients in this design have been randomly assigned to the groups, there remains the possibility that they might not have started out with the same levels of ability. In other words, differences in their posttreatment results could be due to preexisting differences between the groups rather than to the effects of treatment.

Counterbalanced, or Crossover, Group Design.   Counterbalanced, or cross-over, designs provide the experimental and control group of patients with the same conditions, but the order in which they receive them differs. So, if the clinician wants to compare a treated group and an untreated group (placebo or different treatments), the study may be designed as shown in Fig. 13.7.

This design can help with overcoming the ethical problem of a no-treatment condition. However, without a no-treatment control group, it not possible to know the extent to which maturation interacts with and contributes to the outcome. For example, if the patients in both groups showed improved scores but had higher scores in the first treated phase, we do not know if the elevated

```
         Group 1----------Therapy------------Post-test (BA design)
Randomise
         Group 2-----------------------------Post-test (control)
```

FIG. 13.6. Posttest-only control group design.

Group 1----Pre-test-----Therapy---(reassess)----Placebo-----Post-test *(ABA A)*
Randomise
           Group 2----Pre-test-----Placebo---(reassess)----Therapy-----Post-test(control)

FIG. 13.7.   Counterbalanced, or crossover, group design.

Randomise to all groups:
        Group 1-----Pre-test-----Reassess------Reassess-------------Post-test (control)

        Group 2-----Pre-test-----Therapy--------Reassess-------------Post-test

        Group 3-----Pre-test-----Reassess ------Therapy---------------Post-test

        Group 4-----Pre-test-----Reassess ----- Reassess-------------Therapy

FIG. 13.8.   Multiple-baseline group design.

placebo scores were due to maturation, spontaneous recovery, or placebo effects. We also have no way of identifying the contributions of repeated testing to the posttest results.

Multiple-Baseline Group Design.   Figure 13.8 shows a multiple-baseline design that can be used with separate groups in a group study or with separate conditions on the same group. The basic principle in this design is to stagger the introduction of experimental interventions while maintaining control measures with parallel baselines. The idea is that if an experimental technique has an effect, we will all improved results only when this technique is introduced with no change being observed in other conditions. It is important that all conditions be stable when the intervention is not being applied.

This design assumes that the participants in Groups 1 through 4 are comparable. If this assumption were wrong, then we would not be able to draw valid conclusions about the effect of the intervention. There is a control group (Group 1), but the other groups also serve as control groups at different stages in the study. It is important that these groups all show stable performance at the pretest (baseline) stage (i.e., their scores should not show improvement before the intervention stage).

Types of Control Groups in
Group Treatment Research

Control groups are necessary to exclude alternative explanations for the observed results. The choice of control group depends on the research question.

No-Treatment and Waiting-List Control Groups.   No-treatment control groups and waiting-list control groups are used when the question asked is, "Does treatment produce a larger change than no treatment?" The patients in these control groups must, however, be evaluated in the same way as the treatment group.

These types of groups control for

- Maturation over time
- Spontaneous remission
- Concurrent changes in the patient's life
- Effects of assessment on measured outcome

These control groups can present an ethical issue of withholding treatment. There is also no basis for assuming that the no-treatment and waiting-list control groups are equivalent.

Placebo-Treatment Control Groups.   Placebo-treatment control groups allow one to ask whether the observed improvement after therapy is due to the intervention technique or to patient or participant expectancy effects. *These types of groups control for* effects due to attention (Hawthorne and placebo effects) and to nonspecific influences. There can be an ethical problem with these groups unless the patients are informed of the possibility of there being a placebo condition in the study.

Typical and Dysfunctional Control Groups.   Many research studies use typical participants for comparison with the experimental group. Sometimes, it is more valid to compare the experimental group with a dysfunctional control group. For example, by comparing right-hemisphere-damage patients' test performance in discourse with performance by non-brain-damaged hospital patients or other brain-damaged patients, we will have a more valid basis for concluding whether problems in discourse are specific to right-hemisphere brain damage effects or whether it is simply a reflection of being in the hospital or of possessing brain damage, wherever it is.

Choosing Patients for Research.   It is important that the patients selected as control and treatment participant groups be individuals who show a potential for improvement. These are patients who perform within a score range of between 35% and 65% before treatment starts. If the patients' scores are too low, a variety of deficits may contribute to the low score, and the treatment (even if effective) will not manifest as improved performance because of the suppressing effects of other coexisting deficits.

Control patients should be considered similarly. If individuals with the lowest scores are selected as the controls, then it could be argued that this control group does not allow a fair assessment of treatment effects because no matter what happens, these individuals may have no capacity to improve (e.g., recovery).

Control patients are necessary to exclude alternative explanations for the observed results. The type of control group used depends on the research question to be answered.

Designs for Single-Case or Case-Series Studies

Single-case studies are becoming increasingly common and accepted as conventional designs in clinical research. They usually involve the study of one individual. Sometimes, however, such a study comprises single-case studies of several individuals. This is called a case series. Case series enable an investigator to evaluate replication of effects across similar or different individuals. Many of the designs for single-case studies are the same designs used with studying groups of participants. One main difference is that, in single-case designs, the groups of participants are replaced by groups of task items. The designs previously presented for group studies are presented again here as individuals unfamiliar with research designs can sometimes find it difficult to concpetualize how the same research designs can be applied to both groups of participants and to single-case research.

Quasi-Experimental Designs

As with the quasi-experimental group designs, quasi-experimental designs in single-case studies also lack a control. The control, is however, not referring to a control group but rather to a missing control task or a control condition.

One-Shot Single-Case Design.   The one-shot single-case design involves the clinician seeing a patient for a course of therapy followed by a posttest to measure the outcome of therapy. See Fig. 13.9.

As with its equivalent in group research, with this design it is not possible to conclude that therapy had any effect on the patient as measured by the posttest because we have no knowledge of the patient's pretreatment status. A pretherapy baseline is necessary to resolve this problem.

Single-Case Pretest/Posttest Design.   Figure 13.10 shows the clinician administering a pretest to a patient and then reassessing the patient on the same test or a parallel version of it to see if the patient's performance has changed as a result of therapy.

Although with this design a pretest baseline measure is available on the patient (i.e., we know the patient's pretherapy status), we have the problem of not

---

1 patient --------------------Therapy ----------Post-test *(BA design)*

FIG. 13.9.   One-shot single-case design.

```
1 patient--------------Pre-test-----------Therapy ------Post-test (ABA design)
```

FIG. 13.10. Single-case pretest/posttest design.

```
Items set 1--------Pre-test----------Treatment ----------Post-test

Items set 2--------Pre-test-----------------------------Post-test(control)
```

FIG. 13.11. Single-case pretest/posttest control design.

knowing whether the change (usually improvement) we measure is due to the effects of therapy or to other effects, such as spontaneous recovery, developmental maturation, or participant and observer expectancy effects.

Experimental Designs

A study is an experimental study when there is a control task or a control condition. Unlike group studies, single-case studies are constrained in the extent to which randomization is used. This is partly because the groups are not people but test items. When the groups are people, then we have, in theory, several samples that are potentially drawn from an infinite array of samples of representing the characteristics of the people we are interested in studying in the universe. It is harder to say this about groups of verbs, or groups of nouns, which are from finite classes of items. If we were to distribute a group of verbs into two or more groups, it would be hard to argue convincingly that the verbs were representative of all of a universe of verbs. Consequently, random sampling of such items often does not make sense and groups are more likely to be matched on specific features inherent in verbs (e.g., length, frequency). If we were working with a patient on a particular class of words, then it would be difficult to randomize words to different word lists as one does with randomizing participants to different groups in a group study.

Single-Case Pretest/Posttest Control Design.

The design shown in Fig. 13.11 requires the clinician to divide a set of items on which the patient has failed into two groups. One set of items is treated, and the other (a comparable set) is not treated. Both sets of items are tested before therapy begins (pretest) and after therapy has been given (posttest). It is not always possible to randomly allocate items to each group, particularly when comparability of the groups of items is necessary to the design of the study.

This design controls for the confounding effects of maturation and recovery. Although it is tempting to conclude that any improvement on the treated items is due to therapy, it is conceivable that such improvement might reflect the patient's familiarity with dealing with these items (i.e., practice effect) rather than any treatment effect (e.g., the patient attempts to say the names of the treated items more often than the untreated items).

Observer expectancy effects can also influence the outcome of this study. That is, if the treating clinician were also the assessor for the posttreatment tasks, then he or she could introduce observer expectancy effects or biases (e.g., halo effects, treatment preferences). As with group research, the posttreatment assessor needs to be independent of the clinician and have no knowledge of who received therapy (i.e., blind assessor). As mentioned earlier, double-blind studies are not easily achieved in therapy studies because it is difficult to conceal therapy from the clinician.

Single-Case Counterbalanced, or Crossover, Design. A counterbalanced, or cross-over, design is popular in single-case studies because it avoids the ethical problem of a no-treatment condition or a withdrawal condition (see Fig. 13.12). There are several ways this design can be used. One example involves testing two different kinds of treatment on performance on two matched sets of items or on two matched skills or behaviors.

It is very important that the patient be reassessed after the first treatment phase and before the second treatment phase starts. By comparing the pretest results with the reassessment, it is possible to establish whether Treatment A is better than or comparable to Treatment B. If the two treatments are comparable, there will be little to learn from the second treatment phase. This design will show differences between treatments or between a treatment and a placebo task.

This design can help in overcoming the ethical problem of a no-treatment condition. However, without a no-treatment control group, it not possible to know to what extent maturation interacts and contributes to the outcome (e.g., if improvement is observed for both types of treatment, we will not know if the elevated placebo scores were due to maturation or placebo effects). We also do not have a way of identifying the contributions of repeated testing to the posttest results.

Single-Case Multiple-Baseline Design. Within the context of a single-case study, a multiple-baseline design can use different (but matched) sets of items, different skills (e.g., reading, writing, speaking nonwords), different contexts or environments in which the behavior occurs (e.g., in the clinic vs. at home). By staggering the introduction of treatment while maintaining concurrent

---

Items set 1-----Pre-test-------Therapy A-----(reassess)----- Therapy B --------Post-test

Items set 2-----Pre-test-------Therapy B-----(reassess)----- Therapy A --------Post-test(control)

FIG. 13.12.   Single-case counterbalanced, or cross-over, design.

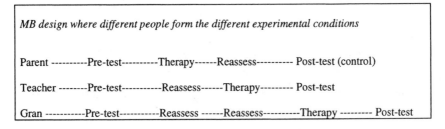

MB design where different skills form the different experimental conditions

Skill 1----------Pre-test----------Therapy-------Reassess----------Post-test (control)

Skill 2----------Pre-test----------Reassess--------Therapy---------Post-test

Skill 3----------Pre-test----------Reassess -------Reassess----------Therapy -------Post-test

FIG. 13.13.   Single-case multiple-baseline design, varying across skills.

MB design where different people form the different experimental conditions

Parent ----------Pre-test----------Therapy------Reassess---------- Post-test (control)

Teacher --------Pre-test-----------Reassess------Therapy--------- Post-test

Gran -----------Pre-test----------Reassess ------Reassess----------Therapy --------- Post-test

FIG. 13.14.   Single-case multiple-baseline design, varying across people.

baseline measures (pretests and reassessment measures), the investigator is able to observe how performance is directly affected by therapy (see Fig. 13.13).

Another example is shown in Fig. 13.14, where the multiple-baseline design study is shown with the client being evaluated on the same behavior (i.e., asking different figures of authority questions).

This design requires the investigator to stage a treatment while monitoring the status of the other conditions. It is important that the pretest phase be stable (i.e., that the levels of performance remain more or less the same on each retest until treatment begins). It is conceivable that therapy effects on one task could generalize to other conditions. The fact that there is more than one condition can help assess whether the improvement in other tasks is due to maturity (recovery) or generalization. This design assumes that the items or contexts in Groups 1 through 3 are comparable. Valid conclusions depend on this assumption being right. Each skill or context serves as a control against extraneous factors such as maturation and recovery in this example.

Types of Control Tasks in Single-Case Treatment Research

It is very important that the tasks selected as control and treatment tasks be tasks on which the patient shows potential for improvement. These are tasks on which the patient achieves a score between 35% and 65% before treatment starts. If the score is too low, a variety of deficits may contribute to the low score and the treatment (even if effective) will not manifest as improved performance due to the suppressing effects of other coexisting deficits (i.e., floor effects).

Control tasks should be considered similarly. It can be very tempting to select the task with the lowest score as the control task; then it can be argued that this control condition is not a fair assessment of treatment effects because no matter what happens, it has no capacity to change (e.g., recovery). Control tasks are necessary to exclude alternative explanations for the observed results. The choice of control task depends on the functions or skills still partly available to the patient as well the similarity of the control task to the treated task.

As with group studies, control tasks in single-case research should provide control for

- Maturation over time
- Spontaneous remission
- Concurrent changes in the patient's life
- Effects of assessment on measured outcomes

Ethical consideration also arises with single-case studies when treatment is withheld or if a placebo condition is introduced.

Single-Case Placebo Control Tasks.   Placebo control tasks in single-case studies allow one to ask whether the observed improvement after therapy is due to the intervention technique or to therapeutic influences generally. However, this can be achieved only if the clinician is naïve to which task is treatment and which constitutes the placebo condition. This design could be difficult to achieve when the clinician is experienced and might be able to distinguish between the two treatments.

If attainable, the placebo condition allows the investigator to control for effects due to attention (i.e., Hawthorne and placebo effects) as well as nonspecific influences acting on patient performance. It is ethically important to inform the patient that there is a placebo condition in the study.

Typical Control Groups and Dysfunctional Control Groups. Although single-case studies are about single individuals, it is common for comparisons to be made with controls who are a group of normal participants. In this case, the same issues concerning different types of control participants mentioned for group studies also apply here.

FURTHER READING

Barlow & Hersen (1984) covers single-case designs for modifying behavior and is one of the first texts published on this topic.

Campbell & Stanley (1963) is still deemed the classic text on the topic on research design.

Coltheart (1989) provides an account of single-case designs for evaluating aphasia therapy.

Oppenheim (1992) is an excellent source on questionnaire design.

GRADUATE READING

Greenhalgh (1997) is a pocket text on critical evaluation of medical research.

Richards, Taylor, Ramasamy, & Richards (1999) offer a recent rendition on single-case designs, with further information about statistical analyses in single-case designs.

Willmes (1990) touches on statistical issues in single-case design.

Willmes (1995) deals with methodological issues in assessment.

14

The Art and Science of Intervention

New opinions are always suspected and usually opposed, without any other reason but because they are not already common.

—John. Locke, 1632–1704

The reader will have hopefully attained a clear sense by now of the depth of meaning of terms such as *research and science*, sufficient to know that research is more than simply knowing about various methodologies or statistics. Furthermore, the reader should be able to appreciate that a commitment to science and scientific practice requires more than a showing of some loose affiliation with the icons of science. Being scientific means thinking scientifically and being able to distinguish between scientific and nonscientific elements in the community at large. Education can inform one about science and all its nuances, but being a scientific researcher or practitioner requires considerable reflection of one's professional and personal values. How one chooses to define the values in one's own life is largely a personal matter and should not be confused with professional knowledge and practice. A profession that has science as the foundation of its knowledge base requires its members to uphold all the principles that go toward fulfilling scientific practice. For members to do otherwise would be unethical.

This final chapter explores several outstanding ideas and issues not commented on in previous chapters.

THE ART OF THERAPY

After having said so much about science and reasoning, it is important to add something here about the "art" of therapy. *Art*, by definition, is creative, intuitive, and based on personal and subjective experiences. As suggested in previous chapters, intuition and personal insights can be a useful basis for generating hypotheses, which are then subject to external validation.

Knowledge as an art form is in nature highly variant, highly individualistic, and determined in a moment of inspiration by the artist. It can offer no basis for explanation, and its truth value cannot be tested or verified. Many people would probably find it hard to imagine that the *Mona Lisa* could exist without Leonardo da Vinci or that the Sistine Chapel might be in existence without Michaelangelo. This is precisely where art and science depart. Great art is ascribed to the great talents of specific individuals. The less replicable the work, the more talented the individual and the greater the public admiration. It would be impossible to think of a great science in terms of great art. Uniqueness would not be tolerated in science. In good science, everyone should be able to reproduce the same effect reported by a researcher or clinician. The value of scientific knowledge depends on it being replicated (i.e., repeated). The latter can be perceived at times as studying what we know to be common sense, but those in the know also know the fallibility of common sense.

When our concern is with the derivation of knowledge, say about disorders or patients, then science provides a principled approach to address these matters. However, therapy is still based on an interaction between at least two or more people. Therapy is an interaction between people that involves a gesture of healing as well as the difficult-to-define qualities of trust, hope, faith, charisma, affect, empathy, and kindness. A therapeutic relationship between the clinician and the patient founded on these qualities possesses an etheral quality and is inaccessible to others. Take, for example, the effect on a patient by a very experienced clinician versus a novice. A clinician with these qualities might be much more successful in instilling confidence in the patient than the novice clinician. The patient might quickly relax with an attitude that everything will be okay because he or she is receiving the best treatment available and with an experienced clinician. This patient might also tolerate a difficult assessment exercise better with an experienced clinician than with an inexperienced, younger clinician. In contrast, a young and inexperienced clinician may have to spend more time trying to win the patient's confidence, particularly when many patients or parents of child clients tend to be older than newly qualified clinicians.

When human qualities appear inexplicable and unique to one person and cannot be easily emulated by anyone else, therapy enters the realm of art. However, what appears inexplicable now may be inexplicable only because no one has bothered yet to define such qualities. Many qualities (e.g., extroversion–introversion, dependency–autonomy, stress) can be defined and measured by psychometrically designed questionnaire instruments.

The patient's perception of the clinician as a healer, the image the clinician projects, and the feelings shared in this situation are largely unknown. There is little research into this aspect of the therapeutic engagement, and the forces that bind clinician and patient will remain to some extent mystical, and maybe this is why this aspect of therapy is often referred to as the art of therapy. The term *art* is intended to capture the humanistic side of therapy, the qualitative perspective, or the holistic side of the therapy situation. No one will deny that there are aspects of human behavior that are difficult to measure. However, it is important to recognize that *art* can also easily become a euphemism or a convenient catchall term for anything we find difficult or feel disinclined to want to define or measure.

HOLISM

Holism is a term often used in connection with therapy. Holism, or *wholism*, is defined as "the theory that certain wholes are to be regarded as greater than the sum of their parts" (Allen, 1992). A related term is *gestalt*, which originated from studies of visual perception in the 1930s. The concept of gestalt has since been imported into counseling (e.g., gestalt therapy) and other humanistic branches of psychology and sociology, and it has been used to describe relationships and social interactions.

Holism is often a major principle in many (but not all) forms of complementary medicine (e.g., reflexology, naturopathy, paranormal medicine, mental therapies; Fulder, 1996). The influence of complementary medicine on conventional health care practice has encouraged traditional clinicians in various clinical fields to regard the patient's disorder in the context of environmental factors that impinge on the patient's life and perspective of the problem. Although it is difficult to evaluate the contribution of factors outside the realm of the disorder, it does engender a better awareness of the external factors associated with various medical and other disorders. So, for example, inquiries into the patient's interests, family, hopes and expectations, likes and dislikes, and so on form the basis of holistic care. From the patient's perspective, there may even be a greater sense of being cared for, which has its own healing qualities (Davies, 1997).

So, injecting a holistic approach in therapy is beneficial for a number of reasons, although it is often difficult to know which sense of holism clinicians are referring to. In medicine, holism means treating the whole person, including mental and social factors rather than just the symptoms of the disease (Allen, 1992). In speech and language therapy, the distinction between disease-based care and holistic care shows up under the terms *impairment-based therapy* versus *functional therapy*. The latter usually tends to be associated with holistic care, though it is equally possible, of course, for those engaged in impairment-based therapy to also have a holistic interest in the patient.

Holism and Functional Communication

Advocates of functional communication are usually referring to communication acts that occur in day-to-day living. This in essence refers to communication activities such as using the telephone, making requests, and reading the newspaper. Another important aspect is that the choice of functional tasks mirror the patient's interest in communication (i.e., personally relevant and implicit in this is the understanding that the patient would continue, for example, after a stroke, to have use of the same vocabulary or activities).

Impairment-based therapy has not been properly defined as such, though it is typically interpreted to refer to therapy that has no transparency with day-to-day living activities. For example, a patient performing a minimal-pair discrimination task in therapy would be thought of as performing an impairment-based therapy. This is because it is directed at the patient's perceptual deficit and is not a task people (expect, perhaps, linguists and speech and language therapists) do in the course of their normal lives. In contrast, functional therapy refers to therapy tasks that appear transparently connected to a patient's life (i.e., activities or words the patient would normally use).

As stated previously, taking a holistic view of the patient does not demand that a clinician work on functional tasks. It may be easier to explain to the patient the purpose of why one is working on certain tasks if the task is recognizable to the patient, but it does not necessarily mean it is intrinsically a better task. Sometimes, the use of the term *functional* is easily confused with the desire for *generalizability* of therapy tasks. Working on a task that has functional relevance does not guarantee that the patient will have functional communication in the sense that the task behaviors will generalize to a real-life situation. For example, what is so functional about a therapy that trains a patient to identify an emergency event from pictures in role playing on the telephone (Hopper & Holland, 1998)? How do we know that the patient will be able to dial for help in an emergency and state the nature of the emergency? Interestingly, some clinicians have argued that these tasks are not good functional tasks because they do not represent events that occur frequently in a person's life. All this suggests that we are not really clear about the purpose of intervention.

How is functional therapy better, and in what ways is it better, than working on a clinical task specifically designed to address specific linguistic skill training? What evidence is there to justify this opinion? Would we feel the same way about therapy if researchers were able to demonstrate that specific linguistic skill training did generalize to spontaneous conversation?

So far, the issue central to the impairment-based versus functional-therapy distinction appears to be based solely on what the therapist perceives to be an ecologically valid task for the patient. The choice of the task may be as much for the clinician's benefit as it is for the patient's. Real-life communication acts are so transparently related to communication in daily life that it must also be enticing to focus on activities that even health insurers understand. After all, the research and evidence supporting the use of other types of therapy tasks are still far from resolved. Nonetheless, the lack of definitive evidence for using tasks targeting specific linguistic skills cannot be interpreted to mean there is any better evidence favoring the use of functional tasks with patients. Ultimately, the effectiveness of any therapy must be decided by scientific research that uses rigorous methods of evaluation. Although these factors can be understood within the context in which they arise, it is difficult to see why such functional therapeutic activity should be any less constrained by scientific rigor than any other area of therapy intervention.

Holism and Rationalizing Away Rigor in Practice

The notions of art, holism, and functional communication appear in various forms in speech and language therapy as described previously. Further scientific definition is necessary for meaningful discussions and debates to take place. In the meantime, however, these unsubstantiated claims can be menacing for those who want to work or teach students to practice within a more rigorous tradition. Holism, although a valid perspective of any patient, sometimes becomes entangled in less worthy views held by some clinicians.

A clinician who adopts a well-considered program of therapy with a patient often finds that the intervention program requires more hours of planning than the health care system permits. A systematic approach to planning and delivering treatment is also necessary if an evaluation of the patient's therapy is to be conducted. Yet, often, complaints tend to be about the lack of time to write reports, to go to team meetings, or to do research. It is less common to hear a clinician bemoan the lack of time for treatment planning or evaluation.

Might shorter tests be created to fit in with limited time schedules because this is easier to achieve than bargaining for more time to allow a rigorous evaluation? Might clinicians not be tempted to find an intervention that fits in with the time allotted to the patient rather than bargain for more time to allow the patient to receive a more suitable form of treatment? Are changes in practice arising as a response to the constraints imposed on practitioners?

Sometimes, a clinician might justify not conducting psychometric assessments by proclaiming "There are many things about a situation we cannot measure!"—appealing directly to holism. The argument offered goes on to say something like, "If we attempt to be too precise in the criteria we adopt in evaluation, then we will fail to see the whole picture—we will lose holism." Then the old story about six blind men and the elephant is usually trotted out to make the point that the whole is greater than the sums of its parts.

One of the problems with this approach to assessment is the lack of explicit criteria in deciding whether the patient's communication performance is normal. This also presents a problem for other clinicians who might want to reassess the patient to determine his or her progress.

The problem is not holism in the sense that one is to consider more than the patient's disorder. The problem is seeing holism as a justification for nonscientific practice. All the evidence in the literature points to the fallibility of impressionist or subjective judgments. So it is difficult to understand what is supporting this confidence in impressionistic qualitative judgments. It is possible to be both holistic (in the sense of regarding the patient in the context of his or her life situation) and scientific (see Chapter 10).

INTERVENTIONS GUIDED BY INTUITION

Sometimes clinicians may feel that there is no choice but to be guided by intuition. When this cannot be avoided, it becomes important that clinicians recognize *when* they are relying on intuition rather than more evidence-informed procedures. It is important that the two are not confused. Intuition poses a problem at several levels.

- *The clinician remains naïve.* The clinician will not know which of the procedures tried was actually effective with the patient. It may be just chance that one of the activities she tried was a task the patient found useful. Patients cannot be relied on to inform the clinician of whether improvement has occurred (Best, Howard, Bruce, & Gatehouse, 1997).
- *The knowledge is private.* Even if a clinician came across a useful technique, it would probably die with him or her. It would not be verified, and no one else would have the benefit of this discovery.
- *Intuition affects the clinician as an observer.* If one's actions are informed by gut sensations, then the judgment is subjective or impressionistic. The clinician will be working in a situation where it will be too easy to seek confirming instances to support his or her beliefs about the patient.
- *Intuition affects clinical education.* A clinician who does what she does but cannot give a scientific explanation for why a technique is used with a patient will be a poor educator of clinical skills and techniques. Students will not understand the methods of techniques used by the clinician. Indeed, many therapy students often remark that success in a clinic is more about quickly learning the pet techniques of the clinician than understanding why a particular technique is used with a patient. Variation in therapy

approaches is not problematic, provided that there is evidence for either approach being of value and both are founded on sound scientific development. Variation is a problem when it simply reflects the personal preferences or biases of clinicians, without recourse to theory or evidence. This is apt to confuse students who will not be able to locate the source and therefore will not be able to understand the basis of this variation.

- *Intuition affects the profession.* When therapy is guided solely by intuition, then it does appear to be an art form and this may well encourage the view that some individuals have personal attributes that make them good clinicians and others do not. The problem is that goodness in this case is in the eye of the beholder because what is good about a clinician is not defined objectively.

- A profession that is unclear about its identity as a scientific discipline is open to its members adopting all sorts of ideas and practices, trying them all out, and keeping the practices they like for use with patients. There will be no principled basis for deciding whether a clinician may use an unknown treatment method with a patient.

SOURCES OF TENSION AND INTERNAL CONFLICT

A patient goes to the physician because he is unwell and seeks a solution to the problem, and hopefully even a cure. It would seem that patients go to clinicians for much the same reason. If this conjecture is true, then speech and language clinicians, like other health care clinicians, are expected to have answers to patients' problems. This situation must place great pressure on clinicians to find the answers to the patients' problems. Typically, the need for a solution is immediate and the availability of tried-and-tested solutions from scientific research is often missing or inaccessible. Consequently, many clinicians find themselves working largely in the dark. They often have to adopt a trial-and-error approach with various intervention strategies in the hope that something will work for the patient. This is common practice. Many of the interventions have face validity, particularly where scientifically motivated criteria are lacking. To the uninitiated, this can be a daunting prospect. New graduates must feel so totally overwhelmed by how much they still do not know, even at the end of their studies.

A particular problem exists when the novice, a new graduate, has no appreciation of where things are in the stage of scientific evolution of knowledge. Without this appreciation, it is easy to believe that there is a great deal to know about a disorder or its remediation, when in fact that information is not as yet available and is awaiting investigation. The fear here is that some novice clinicians could personalize this ignorance as an inadequacy of their own making, when it is an ignorance waiting to be addressed by scientific research. These experiences can also be uncomfortable for clinicians who have many years of working experience.

When a patient expects answers and the clinician knows there is this expectation to be fulfilled, the clinician can fall unwittingly into presenting an image of appearing to know, even when there are no answers. A layperson likely expects a clinician to appear confident and assuring that the treatment offered is the best solution currently available. Consequently, the clinician senses that it is important to the patient that the clinician project and air of confidence when administering therapy. In fact it might even be the case that the effectiveness of one's treatment might depend on the patient's perception of the clinician's confidence in the treatment. We simply do not know. However, one possible outcome under this set of circumstances is that the need for conviction of one's therapy methods can inadvertently over time foster the development and perception of dogma, leading onto arguments by authority and self-fulfilling prophesies.

Conviction and Scientific Skepticism

An attitude in therapy based on conviction or belief is incompatible with a scientific attitude (see Fig. 14.1). Therapy is not a religion where belief forms the

FIG. 14.1.   Clinical conviction meets scientific skepticism.

basis for practice. There does appear to be an inherent difficulty in being both a clinician and a scientist. A scientist is skeptical (not cynical) and readily admits to not knowing very much about anything unless there is evidence and a theory to account for the observed phenomenon. In contrast, it is natural for a clinician to hold a strong sense of conviction that the treatment prescribed is the best form of intervention for the patient, quite independently of whether evidence exists in support of the treatment. A clinician's conviction or belief in the therapy seems almost essential in the administration of therapy. One cannot imagine a clinician offering a patient a therapy while believing it to be an ineffective therapy. Such conviction is often equated with professional confidence and is even admired occasionally by one's peers. It may be a necessary component in successful therapy, particularly because the power of a placebo effect can be quite large.

To call one's therapy into question must be, for some clinicians, quite a threatening experience. This is understandable if the truth value of a therapy is defined solely in terms of personal conviction. What will replace this clinician's conviction? It is easy to understand why some clinicians might be reluctant to engage in dialogue that draws into question the validity of their practices. Therein lies the dilemma of balancing scientific skepticism and therapeutic conviction. Therapy is not a religion where a consensus of opinion is desired from all who are members of that community. Debates and differences of opinion are necessary to scientific progress, and debates characterize the nature of ongoing scientific inquiry in a field. An example is the nature–nurture debate in psychology and sociology. Unless the clinician has worked out the competing values of conviction and skepticism, these will become a problem for the individual and undermine professional development.

Reconciling these two positions—skepticism and conviction—requires a clinician to approach therapy from the standpoint of one who is comfortable knowing that there are few ready answers or solutions but is also confident in knowing how to evaluate an untried procedure or determine the effectiveness of a tested procedure in a novel therapy situation.

Education is important in helping minimize this personal dilemma. A clinician or student who is offered no other view will have no other framework by which to reason about therapy and will be understandably reluctant to abandon conviction as the mainstay of justifying therapy. In recent years, too much has been said about research and not enough emphasis has been given to the science of speech therapy. Basically, if the science (i.e., the reasoning) is right, then the right research has a better chance of happening. There is not much point in equipping the student or clinician with the researcher's tools (e.g., statistics, research designs) when knowledge about scientific reasoning and its application in therapy are poorly understood and rarely integrated into the rest of the course. How many students are required to develop and demonstrate their understanding and application of statistics in the context of clinical training?

Should Therapy be Consumer Led?

Ask a class of soon-to-graduate therapy students, "What makes speech and language therapy different from other caring occupations (e.g., reflexology, iridology, acupuncture, art therapy)?" The response is usually silence, with some students appearing surprised by the question. Ask them, "Why don't speech and language therapists import alternative therapy methods and apply them to the patients seen in a speech therapy clinic?" And again, there is an uneasy silence, one student might venture say, "Because the professional association won't allow it," but not know why. Then, another student might add that a patient should be the one who decides what sort of therapy they have, and speech clinicians are not able to offer these treatments because they are not trained in those techniques. At this point, if the students are asked whether clinicians should receive training in methods expected by patients (e.g., "drawing on the right side of the brain") then the answer is uncertain and confusion is apparent in the student's faces. These soon-to-be-clinician students do not understand the basis of their profession and its methods. These are questions that simply have not occurred to them, and they will become clinicians whose understanding of this aspect of what they are going to do for the rest of their professional lives may or may not change.

The idea of consumer-led therapy is not new. In defense of the nonscience of pragmatics, Smith and Leinonen (1992) proposed that a determination of the effectiveness of a therapy approach can be satisfied by appraising the client's/caregiver's satisfaction with therapy rather than evaluating the therapy method per se. Experienced clinicians are also heard to say that they feel compelled to work on real-life communication behaviors or offer a particular therapy program because that is what the patient's family expects from therapy. This sentiment is also echoed in class experience, when soon-to-graduate students say that as clinicians they would choose to work on tasks that the patient and family find favorable. When asked, though, what their choice might be for the patient if presented with an effective unpleasant therapy program versus an ineffective interesting therapy, they usually start to answer "the interesting one"—and then voices fade as they realize the fuller meaning of their choice.

Consumer-oriented therapy means providing therapy led by the patient's preferences or choice rather than any scientifically motivated theory of treatment. There is some merit in terms of meeting the patient's choices in therapy. However, just as educators doubt that students know best regarding what they need to know to become competent clinicians, similar doubts revolve around whether patients are in a position to judge what might be the best form of therapy for resolving communication problems. Advocates of patient empowerment groups might beg to differ. Patients should, of course, be able to choose whether they want to receive therapy. When having decided to receive therapy, an appropriate program should be used in consultation with the patient, but the final decision must rest with the clinician. Members of the profession may at times know little more than about the process and effects of therapy, but the clinician's concern with efficacy should be paramount in selecting an appropriate form of therapy for the patient. This is the most significant and unique contribution a professional can make to a patient's intervention program.

FINDING A WAY THROUGH THE THERAPY WILDERNESS

A profession that is unclear about its scientific status as a discipline is a bit like someone lost in the wilderness without a compass. In this case, the wilderness is the range of therapies or therapy approaches one could subject a patient to, and the lack of a compass is the lack of a principled set of rules to navigate through the wilderness.

In the current economic climate, monetary constraints in the health system impose restrictions on the delivery of speech therapy. More than ever, the profession must be seen to be a necessary service. If the profession were also unconfident about its place in the health care system, then it would be more vulnerable to adopting practices that accord with those pressures rather than a scientific definition of the profession. One expression of this could be an unconscious temptation to reduce the provision of conventional one-to-one therapy and provide more group therapy and/or an alternative type of service (i.e., counseling). If the scientific identity of the profession were poorly understood, these changes to service would occur without any discussion with reference to their scientific merit and/or whether they represent efficacious methods in the treatment of speech therapy patients.

One particular concern is the blurring of the line between valid and invalid therapy approaches, where the profession adopts as common practice whatever is presented as appearing relevant or as a gap in the service to patients. Cost cutting has affected all other health professions as well as speech and language therapy. Presumably these occupation groups have also had to rationalize their services. It is important, therefore, that the speech and language therapy profession consider carefully whether some of the more recent proposals for changes to service or therapy approaches are not mere temptations to pick up services previously offered by other occupation groups or represent attempts to find a role in some newly structured health service.

PATIENTS' BELIEFS

Much of this text deals with the subject of clinicians' beliefs. What do patients believe? How many of us have had to counsel patients to lower their expectations? It is not uncommon, is it? Perhaps this is because many people who become patients naturally expect or hope to return to normal, and the clinician is expected to deliver

FIG. 14.2.   Patients' beliefs and expectations: Do they match the clinician's?

the goods (see Fig. 14.2). Most professionals forget or perhaps are unaware of the patient's need to believe that someone somewhere can help them out of their dire predicament. The more desperate a patient feels about his or her problem, the more he or she will want to believe help is at hand when it is offered. Patients expect help providers to offer assistance based on principled and proven practice. Patients' beliefs about how therapy works are quite possibly influenced by their experiences in the medical context. They believe that the profession in the evaluation of its therapies applies high standards of proof. They may be surprised to learn of clinicians differing in their beliefs or practices regarding therapy.

Because the speech and language therapy profession implicitly (more explicitly in some places) identifies itself as a practicing scientific community, its member clinicians are obliged to select interventions that have a proven scientific basis. In other words, clinicians, like other scientific researchers, are bound by the conventions of scientific practice.

CONCLUSION

So much of the confusion among clinicians stems from the distinct lack of an education about the process of science and the contributions of its history to current knowledge. Many do not have the vocabulary to describe their perceptions and experiences, and the fluid nature of knowledge must be difficult to assess and interpret. So much of this chaos experienced by clinicians could be made meaningful and harnessed productively if the profession, at large, fostered a better understanding of science as a subject in its own right among its members. This knowledge would equip clinicians with a framework by which to understand the barrage of new information they confront daily. Science in this sense would provide a language to make sense of so much that is largely nonsense. There might be quibbles about what is or is not a science, but in the end many would agree that all good science shares the common values of knowledge being verifiable by the public as well as being the product of rigorous methods. Put simply, if the choice were between embracing a principled method for determining the validity of one's knowledge versus being without such a method, the choice for a scientific profession is clear.

Being a scientific clinician does not mean being an unfeeling clinician. It simply means having a commitment to finding truthful and valid knowledge about what therapy can do for the patient. In a scientific clinical discipline, the commitment will be to delivering an effective intervention that can be scientifically explained. The challenge is to provide the patient with therapy that is beyond belief.

REFERENCES

Allen, R. E. (1992). *Oxford concise dictionary*. Oxford, UK: Oxford University Press.

Anastasi, A., & Urbina, S. (1997). *Psychological testing* (7th ed.). Englewood Cliffs, NJ: Prentice Hall.

Anderson, B. F. (1971). *The psychology experiment: An introduction to the scientific method* (2nd ed.). Belmont, CA: Wadsworth.

Barlow, D. H., & Hersen, M. N. (1984). *Single-case experimental designs* (2nd ed.). Elmsford, NY: Pergamon.

Baron, B., & Sternberg, R. J. (Eds.). (1987). *Teaching thinking skills*. New York: Freeman.

Basso, A. (1989). Spontaneous recovery and language rehabilitation. In X. Seron & G. Deloche (Eds.), *Cognitive approaches in neuropsychological rehabilitation* (pp. 17–34). Hove, UK: Lawrence Erlbaum Associates.

Bayles, K., & Tomoeda, C. (1993). Arizona battery for communication disorders of dementia. Tuscon, AZ: Canyonlands.

Bernard, R. H. (Ed.). (1998). *Handbook of methods in cultural anthropology*. London: AltaMira.

Best, W., Howard, D., Bruce, C., & Gatehouse, C. (1997). Cueing the words: A single case study of treatments for anomia. *Neuropsychological Rehabilitation, 7*, 105–141.

Bird, A. (Ed.). (1998). *Philosophy of science*. London: UCL Press.

Bishop, D. (1989). *TROG: Test of reception of grammar*. Manchester, UK: University of Manchester, Psychology Department.

Blake, R. M., Ducasse, C. J., & Madden, E. H. (1989). *Theories of scientific method: The Renaissance through the nineteenth century*. New York: Gordon & Breach.

237

Blumer, H. (1986). *Symbolic interactionism: Perspective and method.* Berkeley: University of California Press.

Breakwell, G. M., Hammond, S., & Fife-Schaw, C. (Eds.). (2000). *Research methods in psychology* (2nd ed.). London: Sage.

Breakwell, G. M., & Millward, L. (1995). *Basic evaluation methods.* Leicester, UK: British Psychological Society.

Brown, R. I., Bayer, M. B., & Brown, P. M. (Eds.). (1992). *Empowerment and developmental handicaps: Choices and quality of life.* London: Chapman & Hall.

Bub, J., & Bub, D. (1988). On the methodology of single-case studies in cognitive neuropsychology. *Cognitive Neuropsychology, 5,* 562–582.

Bunge, M. (1984). What is pseudoscience? *The Sceptical Inquirer, 9,* 37–46.

Byng, S. (1988). Sentences processing deficits: Theory and therapy. *Cognitive Neuropsychology, 5,* 629–676.

Byng, S. (1995). What is aphasia therapy? In C. Code & D. Muller (Eds.), *The treatment of aphasia* (pp. 3–17). London: Whurr.

Byng, S., & Black, M. (1995). What makes a therapy? Some parameters of therapeutic intervention in aphasia. *European Journal of Communication Disorders, 30,* 303–316.

Byng, S., & Coltheart, M. (1986). Aphasia therapy research: Methodological requirements and illustrative results. In E. Hjelmquist & L.-G. Nilsson (Eds.), *Communication and handicap: Aspects of psychological compensation and technical aids* (pp. 191–213). North-Holland: Elsevier.

Campbell, D. T., & Stanley, J. C. (1963). *Experimental and quasi-experimental designs for research.* New York: Rand McNally College.

Capra, F. (1992) The Tao of Physics: An exploration of the parallels between modern physics and Eastern mysticism (3rd ed.). London: Flamingo.

Caramazza, A. (1986). On drawing inferences about the structure of normal cognitive systems from the analysis of patterns of impaired performance: The case for single-patient studies. *Brain and Cognition, 5,* 41–66.

Caramazza, A., & McCloskey, M. (1988). The case for single-patient studies. *Cognitive Neuropsychology, 5,* 517–528.

Carey, S. S. (1998). *A beginner's guide to the scientific method* (2nd ed.). London: Wadsworth.

Chalmers, A. F. (1994). *What is this thing called science?* (2nd ed.). Milton Keynes, UK: Open University Press.

Chalmers, A. F. (1999). *What is this thing called science?* (3rd ed.). Buckingham, UK: Open University Press.

Chambers, R. (1998). *Clinical effectiveness made easy.* Oxford, UK: Raddiffe Medical Press.

Chapey, R. (Ed.). (1994). *Language intervention strategies in adult aphasia* (3rd ed.). Baltimore: Williams & Wilkins.

Charlton, J. I. (1998). *Nothing about us without us: Disability oppression and empowerment* Berkeley: University of California Press.

Charon, J. M. (1998). *Symbolic interactionism: An introduction, an interpretation, an integration* (6th ed.). London: Prentice Hall.

Clarke, A. E., & Fujimara, J. H. (1992). *The right tools for the right job.* Princeton, NJ: Princeton University Press.

Clements, J. C., & Hand, D. J. (1985). Permutation statistics in single-case design. *Behavioural Psychotherapy, 13,* 288–299.

Cohen, J. (1988). *Statistical power analysis for the behavioral sciences* (2nd ed.). Hillsdale, NJ: Lawrence Erlbaum Associates.

Collingwood, R. G. (1994). *The idea of history* (Rev. ed.). Oxford, UK: Oxford University Press.

Coltheart, M. (1989). Aphasia therapy research: A single-case study approach. In C. Code & D. J. Muller (Eds.), *Aphasia therapy* (2nd ed., pp. 194–202). London: Cole and Whurr.

Coolican, H. (Ed.). (1999). *Research methods and statistics in psychology* (3rd ed.). London, UK: Hodder & Stoughton.

Coon, D. (1998). *Introduction to psychology exploration and application* (8th ed.). Pacific Grove, CA: Brooks/Cole.

Cooper, H. M. (1998). *Synthesising research: A guide for literature reviews.* Beverly Hills, CA: Sage.

Crerar, M. A., Ellis, A. W., & Dean, E. C. (1996). Remediation of sentence processing deficits in aphasia using a computer-based microworld. *Brain and Language, 52*, 229–275.

Crombie, I. K., & Davies, H. T. O. (1996). *Research into health care.* Chichester, UK: Wiley.

Cronbach, L. J. (1990). *Essentials of psychological testing* (5th ed.). New York: HarperCollins.

Crotty, M. (1998). *The foundations of social research.* London: Sage.

Curd, M., & Cover, J. A. (Eds.). (1998). *Philosophy of science.* New York: Norton.

Davidson, D. (1980). *Essays on actions and events.* Oxford, UK: Clarendon.

Davies, C. M. (1997). *Complementary therapies in rehabilitation holistic approaches for prevention and wellness.* Thorofare, NJ: Slack.

Deloche, G., Dordain, M., & Kremis, H. (1993). Rehabilitation of confrontation naming in aphasia: Relations between oral and written modalities. *Aphasiology, 7*, 201–216.

Denzin, N. K., & Lincoln, Y. S. (1998). *The landscape of qualitative research.* London: Sage.

Denzin, N. K., & Lincoln, Y. S. (Eds.). (2000). *The handbook of qualitative research* (2nd ed.). London: Sage.

Dijkstra, W., & van der Zouwen, J. (Eds.). (1982). *Response behaviour in the survey interview.* London: Academic Press.

Dittmar, S. S., & Gresham, G. E. (1997). *Functional assessment and outcome measures for the rehabilitation health professional.* Gaithersburg, MD: Aspen.

Drummond, A. (1996). *Research methods for therapists.* London: Chapman & Hall.

Dunn, L. M., Dunn, L. M., Whetton, C., & Burley, J. (1997). *The British vocabulary scale* (2nd ed.). Windsor, UK: NFER-Nelson.

Edgington, E. (1995). *Randomization tests* (3rd ed.). London: Marcel Dekker.

Edwards, S., Fletcher, P., Garman, M., Hughes, A., Letts, C., & Sinka, I. (1997). *Reynell developmental language* (3rd ed.). Windsor, UK.

Farmer, L. J. (1996). Recovery from aphasia. *Journal of the Mississippi State Medical Association, 37*, 690–693.

Fenton, M. (1989). *Passivity to empowerment: A living skills curriculum for people with disabilities.* London: Royal Association for Disability and Rehabilitation.

Fife-Schaw, C. (1995). Questionnaire design. In M. Breakwell, S. Hammond, & C. Fife-Schaw (Eds.), *Research methods in psychology* (pp. 174–193). London: Sage.

Flew, A. (1997). *Hume's philosophy of belief.* Bristol, UK: Thoemmes Press.

Foster, G., Algozzine, B., & Ysseldyke, J. (1980). Classroom teacher and teacher-in-training susceptibility to stereotypical bias. *Personnel and Guidance Journal, 59*, 27–30.

Franklin, S. (1997). Designing single-case treatment studies for aphasic patients. *Neuropsychological Rehabilitation, 7*, 401–418.

Fulder, S. (1996). *The handbook of alternative and complementary medicine* (3rd ed.). Oxford, UK: Oxford University Press.

Garnham, A., & Oakhill, J. (1994). *Thinking and reasoning.* Oxford, UK: Blackwell.

Giere, R. N. (1997). *Understanding scientific reasoning* (4th ed.). Fort Worth, TX: Holt, Rinehart & Winston.

Gilhooly, K. J. (1996). *Thinking: Directed, undirected and creative* (3rd ed.). London: Academic Press.

Glaser, B. G., & Strauss, A. L. (1967). *The discovery of grounded theory strategies for qualitative research.* Chicago: Aldine.

Goodglass, E., & Kaplan, E. (1983). *The assessment of aphasia and related disorders* (2nd ed.). Philadelphia: Lea & Febiger.

Gower, B. (1997). *Scientific method: A historical and philosophical introduction.* London: Routledge.

Greenhalgh, T. (1997). *How to read a paper.* London: British Medical Journal.

Grinnell, F. (1992). *The scientific attitude* (2nd ed.). New York: Guildford.

Gumperz, J. J., & Hymes, D. (1986). *Directions in sociolinguistics: The ethnography of communication.* Oxford, UK: Blackwell.

Halpern, D. (1996). *Thought and knowledge: An introduction to critical thinking* (3rd ed.). Mahwah, NJ: Lawrence Erlbaum Associates.

Harrington, A. (Ed.). (1997). *The placebo effect.* Cambridge, MA: Harvard University Press.

Holdsworth, L. (1991). *Empowerment social work with physically disabled people.* (Vol. 97). Norwich, UK: Social Work Monographs.

Hopper, T., & Holland, A. (1998). Situation-specific training for adults with aphasia: An example. *Aphasiology, 12,* 933–944.

Horkheimer, M. (1995). *Critical theory: Selected essays.* New York: Continuum.

Howard, D., & Patterson, K. (1992). *Pyramid and palm trees: A test of semantic access from words and pictures.* Bury St. Edmonds, UK: Thames Valley Test Company.

Howell, D. C. (1997). *Statistical methods for psychology* (4th ed.). Belmont, CA: Duxbury.

Hume, D. (1739). [1962]. A Treatise of human nature, Oxford, UK: Clarendon Press.

Johnson, R. H., & Blair, J. A. (1994). *Logical self defense.* London: McGraw-Hill.

Jorgensen, D. L. (1989). *Participant observation: A methodology for human studies* (Vol. 15). London: Sage.

Kaplan, E., Goodglass, H., & Weintraub, S. (1983). *Boston naming test.* Philadelphia: Lea & Febiger.

Kay, J., Lesser, R., & Coltheart, M. (1992). *PALPA: Psycholinguistic assessment of language processing in aphasia.* Hove, UK: Lawrence Erlbaum Associates.

Kazdin, A. E. (1978). Methodological and interpretative problems of single-case experimental designs. *Journal of Consulting and Clinical Psychology, 46,* 629–642.

Kearns, K. P. (1981). *Interobserver reliability procedures in applied aphasia research: A review with suggestions for change.* Paper presented at the Clinical Aphasiology Conference,

Kelly, E. L. (1967). *Assessment of human characteristics.* Belmont, CA: Brooks/Cole.

Kertesz, A. (1982). *Western aphasia battery.* New York: Harcourt Brace Jovanovich.

Kertesz, A. (1984). Recovery from aphasia. In F. C. Rose (Ed.), *Advances in neurology: Progress in aphasiology* (Vol. 42, pp. 23–39). New York: Raven.

Kidd, D., Stewart, G., Bladry, J., Johnson, J., Rossiter, D., Petruckevitch, A., & Thompson, A. J. (1995). The functional independence measure: A comparative validity and reliability study. *Disability and Rehabilitation, 17,* 10–14.

Kidder, L. H., & Fine, M. (1987). Qualitative and quantitative methods:When stories converge. In M. M. Mark & R. L. Shotland (Eds.), *Multiple methods in program evaluation* (pp. 57–75). San Francisco: Jossey-Bass.

Kratochwill, T. R., & Levin, J. R. (Eds.). (1992). *Single-case research design and analysis: New directions for psychology and education.* Hillsdale, NJ: Lawrence Erlbaum Associates.

Kuhn, D., Amsel, E., & O'Loughlin, M. (1988). *The development of scientific thinking.* London: Academic Press.

Kuhn, T. S. (1996). *The structure of scientific revolutions* (3rd ed.). Chicago: University of Chicago Press.

Lambert, K., & Brittan, G. G. (1992). *An introduction to the philosophy of science* (4th ed.). Atascadero, CA: Ridgeview.

Law, J. (1997). Evaluating intervention for language impaired children: A review of the literature. *European Journal of Disorders of Communication, 32,* 1–14.

LeBlanc, J. (1998). *Thinking clearly.* New York: Norton.

LeCompte, M. D., Preissle, J., & Tesch, R. (1993). *Ethnography and qualitative design in educational research* (2nd ed.). San Diego: Academic Press.

Levine, B. S., Wigren, M. M., Chapman D. S., Kerner, J. F., Borgman, R. L., & Rivlin, R. S. (1993). A national survey of attitudes and practices of primary-care physicians relating to nutrition strategies for enhancing the use of clinical nutrition in medical practice. *American Journal of Clinical Nutrition, 57,* 115–9.

Lipton, P. (1998). Inference to the best explanation. In M. Curd & J. A. Cover (Eds.), *Philosophy of science* (pp. 412–425). London: Norton.

Longino, H. E. (1998). Values and objectivity. In M. Curd & J. A. Cover (Eds.), *Philosophy of science* (pp. 170–191). London: Norton.

Losee, J. (1993). *A historical introduction to the philosophy of science* (3rd ed.). Oxford, UK: Oxford University Press.

Lum, C., Cox, R., Kilgour, J., & Morris, J. (2001, January 6). *PATSy: A database of clinical cases for teaching and research* [Online]. Available: www.patsy.ac.uk.

Lum, C. C. (1996). A methodological dilemma. *Brain and language, 55,* 67–70.

Malby, R. (Ed.). (1995). *Clinical audit for nurses and therapists.* London: Scutari.

Malim, T., & Birch, A. (1997). *Research methods and statistics.* Basingstoke, UK: Macmillan.

Maneta, A., Marshall, J., & Lindsay, J. (1999, September). *Direct and indirect therapy for word sound deafness.* Paper presented at the British Aphasiology Society Annual Conference, London.

Matthews, M. R. (1994). *Science teaching.* New York: Routledge.

Matyas, T. A., & Greenwood, K. M. (1990). Visual analysis of single-case time series: Effects of variability, serial dependence, and magnitude of intervention effects. *Journal of Applied Behavior Analysis, 23,* 341–351.

Mays, N., & Pope, C. (Eds.). (1999). *Qualitative research in health care* (2nd ed.). London: BMJ.

Meier, M. J., Strauman, S., & Thompson, W. G. (1995). Individual differences in neuropsychological recovery: An overview. In M. J. Meier, L. Diller, & A. Benton (Eds.), *Neuropsychological rehabilitation.* London: Churchill/Livingstone.

Morris, J. (1997). Remediating auditory processing deficits in adults with aphasia. In S. Chiat, J. Law, & J. Marshall (Eds.), *Language disorders in children and adults* (pp. 42–63). London: Whurr.

Moser, C., & Kalton, G. (1993). *Survey methods in social investigation* (2nd ed.). Aldershot, UK: Dartmouth.

Munson, R. (1976). The way with words, Boston: Houghton Mifflin.

Muir Gray, J. M. (1997). *Evidenced-based healthcare.* Edinburgh, UK: Churchill/Livingstone.

Nickels, L., Howard, D., & Best, W. (1997). Fractionating the articulatory loop: Dissociations and associations in phonological recoding in aphasia. *Brain and Language, 56,* 161–182.

Nickerson, R. S. (1987). Why teach thinking? In B. Baron & R. J. Sternberg (Eds.), *Teaching thinking skills* (pp. 27–37). New York: Freeman.

O'Hear, A. (1989). *An Introduction to the philosophy of science.* Oxford, Clarendon Press.

O'Leary, K. D., & Wilson, G. T. (1987). *Behaviour therapy* (2nd ed.). London: Prentice Hall.

Oppenheim, A. N. (1992). *Questionnaire design, interviewing and attitude measurement* (2nd ed.). London: Pinter.

Pak, C. Y. C., & Adams, P. M. (Eds.). (1994). *Techniques of patient-oriented research.* New York: Raven.

Palys, T. (1997). *Research decisions.* Toronto: Harcourt Brace.

Pannbacker, M., & Middleton, G. H. (1994). *Introduction to clinical research in communication disorders.* San Diego: Singular.

Patterson, K., & Schewell, C. (1987). Speak and spell: Dissociations and word-class effects. In M. Coltheart, R. Job, & G. Sartori (Eds.), *The cognitive neuropsychology of language* (pp. 273–294). Mahwah, NJ: Lawrence Erlbaum Associates.

Pavlov, I. P. (1927). *Conditioned reflexes.* Translated by G. V. Anvep. New York: Dove.

Payton, O. D. (1994). *Research the validation of clinical practice* (3rd ed.). Philadelphia: Davis.

Pearsall, J. (1999). *The Concise Oxford Dictionary* (10th ed.). Oxford (UK): Oxford University Press.

Public Broadcasting Service: People and discoveries [Online]. Available: www.pbs.org.

Phillips, J. L. (1999). *How to think about statistics* (6th ed.). New York: Freeman.

Polgar, S., & Thomas, S. A. (2000). *Introduction to research in the health sciences* (4th ed.). Melbourne: Churchill/Livingstone.

Popper, K. R. (1972). *Conjectures and refutations: The growth of scientific knowledge* (4th ed.). London: Routledge & Kegan Paul.

Punch, K. F. (1998). *Introduction to social research quantitative and qualitative approaches.* London: Sage.

Ramig, L. O., Countryman, S., Thompson, L. L., & Horii, Y. (1995). Comparison of two forms of intensive speech treatment for Parkinson disease. *Journal of Speech and Hearing Research, 38,* 1232–1251.

Rawcliffe, C. (1995). *Medicine and society in later medieval England.* Stroud, Sutton.

Richards, S. (1987). *Philosophy and sociology of science* (2nd ed.). Oxford, UK: Blackwell.

Richards, S. B., Taylor, R. L., Ramasamy, R., & Richards, R. Y. (1999). *Single subject research.* London: Singular.

Richardson, J. T. E. (Ed.). (1996). *Handbook of qualitative research methods for psychology and the social sciences.* Leicester, UK: British Psychological Society.

Riegelman, R. K., & Hirsch, R. P. (2000). *Studying a study and testing a test: How to read the medical literature* (4th ed.). Philadelphia: Lippincott/William & Wilkins.

Riessman, C. K. (Ed.). (1993). *Qualitative studies in social work research.* Newbury Park, CA: Sage.

Roberts, R. M. (1989). *Serendipity.* New York: Wiley.

Robertson, S. I. (1999). *Types of thinking.* London: Routledge.

Robson, J. M. (Ed.). (1996). *A system of logic, ratiocinative and inductive: Being a connected view of the principles of evidence and the methods of scientific investigations.* London: Routledge.

Roethlisberger, F. J., & Dickson, W. J. (1939). *Management and the worker.* Cambridge, MA: Harvard University Press.

Rosehan, D. L. (1973). On being sane in insane places. *Science, 179,* 250–258.

Rosehan, D. L. (1975). The contextual nature of psychiatric diagnosis. *Journal of Abnormal Psychology, 84,* 462–474.

Rosenthal, R. (1966). *Experimenter effects in behavioral research.* New York: Appleton-Century-Crofts.

Runyon, R. P., Coleman, K. A., & Pittenger, D. J. (1999). *Fundamentals of behavioral statistics* (9th ed.). London: McGraw-Hill.

Salmon, M. H. (1992). Philosophy of the social sciences. In M. H. Salmon, J. Earman, C. Glymour, J. G. Lennox, P. Machamer, J. E. McGuire, J. D. Norton, W. C. Salmon, & K. F. Schaffner (Eds.), *Introduction to the philosophy of sciences* (pp. 404–425). Englewood Cliffs, NJ: Prentice Hall.

Schmidt, R. A., & Lee, T. D. (1999). *Motor control and learning: A behavioral emphasis* (3rd ed.). Champaign, IL: Human Kinetics.

Schon, D. A. (1991). *The reflective practitioner: How professionals think in action.* London: Arena.

Schuman, H., & Kalton, G. (1985). Survey methods. In G. E. Lindzey & E. Aronson (Eds.), *Handbook of social psychology* (Vol. 1, pp. 635–697). New York: Random House.

Schwandt, T. A. (1998). Constructivist, interpretivist approaches to inquiry. In N. K. Denzin & Y. S. Lincoln (Eds.), *The landscape of qualitative research* (pp. 221–259). London: Sage.

Seale, C., & Pattison, S. (Eds.). (1994). *Medical knowledge: Doubt and certainty.* Buckingham, UK: Open University Press.

Seron, X. (1997). Effectiveness and specificity in neuropsychological therapies: A cognitive point of view. *Aphasiology, 11,* 105–123.

Shallice, T. (1988). *From neuropsychology to mental structures.* Cambridge, UK: Cambridge University Press.

Shermer, M. (1997). *Why people believe weird things.* New York: Freeman.

Smith, B. R., & Leinonen, E. (1992). *Clinical pragmatics: Unravelling the complexities of communicative failure.* London: Chapman & Hall.

Smith, R. (Ed.). (1992). *Audit in action.* London: BMJ.

Sommers, R. K., Logsdon, B. S., & Wright, J. M. (1992). A review and critical analysis of treatment research related to articulation and phonological disorders. *Journal of Communication Disorders,*

25, 3–22.

Strauss, A. L., & Corbin, J. (1999). *Basics of qualitative research techniques and procedures for developing grounded theory* (2nd ed.). Thousand Oaks, CA: Sage.

Street, A. F. (1992). *Inside nursing: A critical ethnography of clinical nursing practice*. Albany: State University of New York Press.

Stricker, G., & Trierweiler, S. J. (1995). The local clinical scientist. *American Psychologist, 50*, 995–1002.

Tabachnick, B. G., & Fidell, L. S. (1996). *Using multivariate statistics* (3rd ed.). New York: Harper-Collins.

Tallack, D. (Ed.). (1995). *Critical theory: A reader*. London: Harvester Wheatsheaf.

Tesch, R. (1990). *Qualitative research: Analysis types and software tools*. New York: The Falmer Press.

Tesio, L., & Cantagallo, A. (1998). The functional assessment measure (FAM) in closed traumatic brain injury outpatients: A Rasch-based psychometric study. *Journal of Outcome Measure, 2*, 79–96.

Thomas, K. (1971). *Religion and the decline of magic*. London: Penguin.

Thompson, D. (1995). *Concise Oxford dictionary of current English* (9th ed.). London: Oxford University Press.

Tomatis, A. A. (1963). *L'Orielle et le langage*. Paris: Editions de Seuil.

Vidich, A. J. (1955). Participant observation and the collection and interpretation of data. *American Journal of Sociology, 60*, 354–360.

Warrington, E. K. (1982). The fractionation of arithmetical skills: A single case study. *Quarterly Journal of Experimental Psychology, 34*, 31–51.

Weber, M. (1962). *Basic concepts in sociology* (H. P. Secher, Trans.). Secaucus, NJ: Citadel.

Weinsier, R. L., Boker, J. R., Morgan, S. L., Feldman, B. B., Moinuddin, J. P., Mamel, J. J., DiGirolamo, M., Borum, P. R., Read, M. S., & Brooks, C. M. (1988). Cross-sectional study of nutrition knowledge and attitudes of medical students at three points in their medical training at 11 Southeastern medical schools. *American Journal of Clinical Nutrition, 48*, 1–6.

Werner, O., & Schoepfle, G. M. (1987). *Ethnographic analysis and data management*. (Vol. 2). Beverly Hills, CA: Sage.

Weston, A. (1992). *A rulebook for arguments* (2nd ed.). Indianapolis: Hackett.

White, D. M., Rusch, F. R., Kazdin, A. E., & Hartman, D. (1989). Applications of meta-analysis in individual-subject research. *Behavioral Assessment, 11*, 281–296.

Whitfield, P. (1999). *Landmarks in Western science: From prehistory to the atomic age*. London: British Library.

Whyte, W. F. (1993). *Street corner society: The social structure of an Italian slum* (4th ed.). Chicago: University of Chicago Press.

Wilkinson, G. S. (1993). *The Wide Range achievement test*, DE: Wide Range.

Willmes, K. (1990). Statistical methods for a single-case study approach to aphasia therapy research. *Aphasiology, 4*, 415–436.

Willmes, K. (1995). Aphasia therapy research: Some psychometric considerations and statistical methods for the single-case study approach. In C. Code & D. Muller (Eds.), *Treatment of aphasia therapy: From theory to practise* (pp. 286–307). London: Whurr.

Wilson, B. (1987). Single-case experimental designs in neuropsychological rehabilitation. *Journal of Clinical and Experimental Neuropsychology, 9*, 527–544.

Wilson, G. T., & O'Leary, K. D. (1980). *Principles of behavioural therapy*. London: Prentice Hall.

Wilson, S. (1977). The use of ethnographic techniques in educational research. *Review of Educational Research, 47*, 245–265.

Wood, P. (2000). Meta-analysis. In G. M. Breakwell, S. Hammond, & C. Fife-Schaw (Eds.), *Research methods in psychology* (2nd ed., pp. 414–425). London: Sage.

Index